A Basket of Leaves

A Basket of Leaves

99 Books that Capture
the Spirit of Africa

Geoff Wisner

First published by Jacana Media (Pty) Ltd in 2007

10 Orange Street
Sunnyside
Auckland Park 2092
South Africa
+2711 628 3200
www.jacana.co.za

ISBN 978-1-77009-206-8

Set in Sabon 10/13pt
Printed by CTP Book Printers, Cape Town
Job No. 000415

See a complete list of Jacana titles at www.jacana.co.za

*To my parents, Mary Frances Hatfield
and William Wisner*

Contents

Acknowledgements.. xii

Introduction .. 1

Algeria
The Sheltering Sky – Paul Bowles.................................... 7
The Savage Night – Mohammed Dib 10
Algerian White – Assia Djebar 13

Angola
Mayombe – Pepetela .. 15
Another Day of Life – Ryszard Kapuscinski...................... 18

Benin
The Viceroy of Ouidah – Bruce Chatwin............................ 20

Botswana
When Rain Clouds Gather – Bessie Head........................... 23
Whites – Norman Rush .. 26

Burkina Faso
Of Water and the Spirit – Malidoma Patrice Somé.............. 28

Burundi
The True Sources of the Nile – Sarah Stone...................... 31

Cameroon
Mission to Kala – Mongo Beti... 34

Cape Verde
The Fortunate Isles – Basil Davidson 36

Central African Republic
Song from the Forest – Louis Sarno................................. 38

Chad
Komoon! – Heinrich Oberjohann 41

Comoros
Last of the Pirates – Samantha Weinberg 44

Congo (Democratic Republic of the)

The Catastrophist – Ronan Bennett 47
A Bend in the River – V. S. Naipaul 49
Between Tides – V. Y. Mudimbe 52

Congo (Republic of the)

The Fire of Origins – Emmanuel Dongala 55
The Seven Solitudes of Lorsa Lopez – Sony Labou Tansi 58
No Mercy – Redmond O'Hanlon 61

Djibouti

Somebody Else – Charles Nicholl 63

Egypt

Out of Egypt – André Aciman 66
Mountolive – Lawrence Durrell 68
Adrift on the Nile – Naguib Mahfouz 71
In an Antique Land – Amitav Ghosh 73
The Map of Love – Ahdaf Soueif 76

Equatorial Guinea

Tropical Gangsters – Robert Klitgaard 79 ✓

Eritrea

To Asmara – Thomas Keneally 82

Ethiopia

The Emperor – Ryszard Kapuscinski 85
Notes from the Hyena's Belly – Nega Mezlekia 88

Gabon

Travels in West Africa – Mary Kingsley 91

The Gambia

Our Grandmothers' Drums – Mark Hudson 94

Ghana

All God's Children Need Traveling Shoes – Maya Angelou 97
No Sweetness Here – Ama Ata Aidoo 100

Guinea

The Dark Child – Camara Laye 103

Contents

Guinea-Bissau

The Bush Rebels – Barbara Cornwall.....................106

Ivory Coast

The Suns of Independence – Ahmadou Kourouma....................109
In the Shadow of the Sacred Grove – Carol Spindel..................112

Kenya

A Grain of Wheat – Ngũgĩ wa Thiong'o...............................114
A Primate's Memoir – Robert M. Sapolsky............................116

Lesotho

Singing Away the Hunger – Mpho Nthunya...........................119

Liberia

Journey Without Maps – Graham Greene..............................122
Mississippi in Africa – Alan Huffman.....................................125

Libya

The Bleeding of the Stone – Ibrahim Al-Koni128

Madagascar

The Eighth Continent – Peter Tyson131

Malawi

The Chattering Wagtails of Mikuyu Prison – Jack Mapanje.........134

Mali

The Heart of the Ngoni – Harold Courlander
 with Ousmane Sako ..137
Segu – Maryse Condé...140

Mauritania

The Fearful Void – Geoffrey Moorhouse...............................143

Mauritius

Journey to Mauritius – Jacques-Henri Bernardin de Saint-Pierre....146
The Book of Color – Julia Blackburn....................................149

Morocco

The Sand Child – Tahar ben Jelloun151
The Road to Fez – Ruth Knafo Setton....................................153

Mozambique

Voices Made Night – Mia Couto ..156
Dumba Nengue – Lina Magaia ..158

Namibia

The Harmless People – Elizabeth Marshall Thomas161
The Purple Violet of Oshaantu – Neshani Andreas164

Niger

In Sorcery's Shadow – Paul Stoller and Cheryl Olkes166

Nigeria

Things Fall Apart – Chinua Achebe......................................169
The Slave Girl – Buchi Emecheta ..171
The Palm-Wine Drinkard – Amos Tutuola174
Aké – Wole Soyinka...176
Efuru – Flora Nwapa ...179
Jagua Nana – Cyprian Ekwensi...182
Stars of the New Curfew – Ben Okri.....................................184
GraceLand – Chris Abani...187
Waiting for an Angel – Helon Habila...................................189

Rwanda

Gorillas in the Mist – Dian Fossey......................................191
*We Wish to Inform You That Tomorrow We Will Be Killed
with Our Families* – Philip Gourevitch194

São Tomé and Príncipe

'Landscape' – Maria Manuela Margarido198

Senegal

God's Bits of Wood – Sembène Ousmane...........................200
Ambiguous Adventure – Cheikh Hamidou Kane203
So Long a Letter – Mariama Bâ ...205
I Get on the Bus – Reginald McKnight................................207

Seychelles

Beyond the Reefs – William Travis.....................................209

Sierra Leone

The Last Harmattan of Alusine Dunbar – Syl Cheney-Coker212
The Devil That Danced on the Water – Aminatta Forna.............215

Contents

Somalia

First Footsteps in East Africa – Richard Burton......................218
Secrets – Nuruddin Farah................................221

South Africa

Long Walk to Freedom – Nelson Mandela224
July's People – Nadine Gordimer.........................227
Age of Iron – J. M. Coetzee.............................230
Mother to Mother – Sindiwe Magona233
The Heart of Redness – Zakes Mda........................236

Sudan

Season of Migration to the North – Tayeb Salih239
African Calliope – Edward Hoagland.......................241

Swaziland

Sangoma – James Hall..................................244

Tanzania

Paradise – Abdulrazak Gurnah247
The Gunny Sack – M. G. Vassanji.........................250

Togo

The Village of Waiting – George Packer.....................252

Tunisia

The Scorpion – Albert Memmi............................254

Uganda

The Last King of Scotland – Giles Foden....................256
Abyssinian Chronicles – Moses Isegawa....................259

Western Sahara

Smara – Michel Vieuchange262

Zambia

The Eye of the Elephant – Delia and Mark Owens...................265
A Cowrie of Hope – Binwell Sinyangwe.......................268

Zimbabwe

African Laughter – Doris Lessing..........................271
The Stone Virgins – Yvonne Vera..........................274

Suggestions for further reading...........................276

Acknowledgements

I would first like to thank Susan Pedersen and Ken Carstens for providing me with a job where I could learn and write about Africa and do my small part to help protect human rights. I am grateful to the Overseas Development Network (now JustAct) for sending me to Zimbabwe, to Tapuwa Chitombo and Millicent Chieza for giving me a home during my six months there, and to Tracey Gwini and Joseph Tasosa for putting me to work at the Department of Natural Resources. Thanks also to Peter Von Doepp for hosting me in Malawi.

I am grateful to Chris Carduff, David Eberly, Steven Riel, and Randi Schalet for their helpful suggestions on the manuscript, and to Emmanuel Dongala, Sindiwe Magona, and M. G. Vassanji for recommending books. Many thanks to Ann Levison of the *Harvard Post* and to Henry Finder and Mike Vazquez of *Transition*, where small portions of this book first appeared. The staff of the Cambridge Public Library, Widener Library, the Boston Athenaeum, the Brooklyn Library, and the New York Public Library were essential in providing many of the books I needed for this project.

Thanks to my agent, Robert Shepard, for his encouragement and work on my behalf. Special thanks to Gabriella Pearce and the late Peter O'Farrell for providing support when it was needed most. I am grateful to the staff of Jacana Media, including Maggie Davey, Russell Clarke, Russell Martin, Kira Schlesinger, and Serusha Govender, and to freelance editor Bronwyn McLennan for making this intercontinental project run smoothly and pleasantly. Most of all, I want to thank my life partner Jenn Brissett for her love, encouragement, and good counsel.

Introduction

I first went to Africa after working several years for the US office of an anti-apartheid organization. I had met South African exiles and edited a newsletter on southern Africa – but going to the region was another matter. My organization was banned, and the authorities in Pretoria prevented me from travelling to Namibia to help monitor elections there. Then came the chance to go to Zimbabwe on a six-month volunteer program. I would live in Harare and work for the Department of Natural Resources, while the others in my group worked for hospitals, women's organizations, and farming cooperatives.

Before I left, I began keeping a list of everything I read about the country – a list that grew with the volumes I found at the British Council Library in Harare and at the leftist bookstore just down the street from Unity Square, where Dambudzo Marechera, a homeless young writer with a hallucinogenic prose style, used to sit and type. Along with histories and political works, I discovered the ghostly novels of Chenjerai Hove, the melancholy realism of Charles Mungoshi, and the unrelenting African stories of Doris Lessing.

Once I'd returned home, my reading list expanded from Zimbabwe to countries elsewhere in the continent. Eventually, I set out to read at least one book about each country in Africa. Including the newly independent country of Eritrea and the struggling-for-independence Western Sahara, and excluding possessions of foreign powers such as Madeira, the Canary Islands, and Réunion, this came to 54 countries.

In some cases, I found, I had covered countries almost without realizing it. Bruce Chatwin's *The Viceroy of Ouidah* describes nineteenth-century Dahomey, now Benin. Ancient Carthage, the scene of Flaubert's *Salammbô*, is in modern-day Tunisia. Other countries were much more difficult. Once I'd scoured the shelves of the library in Cambridge, Massachusetts, in search of books on Burkina Faso, Djibouti, and Guinea-Bissau, I began to search their electronic database and to put in requests for titles held by other

libraries. Books began coming in from up and down the East Coast.

While filling the blank spaces on the map, I discovered some remarkable books I might otherwise never have seen. *Of Water and the Spirit* (Burkina Faso) and *Sangoma* (Swaziland) are two absorbing accounts of the making of a spirit medium. *Song from the Forest* tells the story of a white American whose fascination for the music of the Pygmies takes him to the Central African Republic, where he eventually marries a Pygmy woman and makes a new home. Thomas Keneally's novel *To Asmara* presents an admiring picture of Eritrea during its struggle to break from Ethiopia.

As my reading list expanded, I was more and more struck by the diversity of the continent as well as the regional patterns in its literature. The savannahs of Kenya were nothing like the jungles of the Congo region. The easy-going multiracial society of the Seychelles islands had nothing in common with the explosive tensions of Rwanda and Burundi. The melancholy of Zimbabwean writers like Charles Mungoshi and South Africans like Mongane Serote was unlike the exuberance of Nigerians like Cyprian Ekwensi and Amos Tutuola, or the spare, cruel Moroccan tales of writers like Tahar ben Jelloun and the expatriate Paul Bowles.

A Basket of Leaves is intended to bring out as much of this diversity as possible, but although it includes many different kinds of books, there are a few guidelines I've tried to follow in making my selections. The books in this collection are chosen mainly for their literary value, by which I mean that they are the best-written and most interesting works I could find. They include novels, memoirs, travel books, and collections of essays – some published as long ago as the nineteenth or even eighteenth century and some very recently. Technical, journalistic, or straight historical works (however good) have been excluded, although interested readers can find some of these under "Suggestions for Further Reading." Though I have tried to include only books that are reasonably accessible, I haven't limited myself to those in print. Books go out of print so quickly today that this would eliminate too much important work, and the Internet makes it easier than ever before to track down out-of-print titles.

Each country gets at least one book, but no author gets more than one book per country. (Ryszard Kapuscinski, however, can be found under both Angola and Ethiopia.) For countries where I could include more than one book, I've tried to provide contrasting points

of view: an African and a non-African, a nineteenth-century explorer and a modern traveller. I have relied on maps to locate authors such as Michel Vieuchange in what is today Western Sahara or Mary Kingsley in Gabon, though the boundaries of those countries had not been drawn when their books were written. In one case – Charles Nicholl's *Somebody Else* – the description of a country (Djibouti) was so much sharper and more revealing than anything else I could find that I included the book even though it is not primarily about that country.

The authors included in this book include Africans, Caribbeans, Americans, and Europeans. Some of the African writers are white (J. M. Coetzee, Nadine Gordimer), some of the American writers are black (Maya Angelou, Reginald McKnight), and one of the Caribbean writers is of East Indian descent and lives in England (V. S. Naipaul). The books were originally written in English, French, German, Portuguese, Polish, and Arabic. Twenty-eight of them are written or co-authored by women – an under-representation that reflects social conditions in Africa and elsewhere.

No selection system is perfect, and mine can be criticised on various grounds. Some of these books, for instance, contain passages that are startlingly racist. Without apologizing for the views of the authors, I haven't included any who didn't also have something valuable and original to say. Racism has been a devastatingly powerful force in shaping Africa, and there may be something to be learned from its different varieties. In Sir Richard Burton's case, for instance, it's worth noting that he delighted in being outrageous, that he had harsh comments to make about nearly every ethnic group he encountered, and yet he spent years learning the languages and cultures of the people he wrote about with such apparent contempt, and risked his life in order to journey among them.

Why organize this collection by country, some might ask, especially when so many of Africa's boundaries were drawn by colonialists in the nineteenth century? Because for better or worse, these are the political entities modern Africans must work with, and are using to create new national identities. Because even the smallest, such as Swaziland, contain distinctive cultures that could be overlooked in a regional overview. And because I hope this book will provide a starting point for those who plan a trip to, say, Togo or The Gambia, and would like to learn more before they go.

If the titles in this collection were chosen purely on literary quality, there would be more books from South Africa and Nigeria, while certain other countries might be squeezed out entirely. There would be more books by Chinua Achebe, Wole Soyinka, Nuruddin Farah, and J. M. Coetzee – but at the expense of many other interesting and lesser-known voices. Still, I am haunted by the awareness that there may be many other books that deserve inclusion but are unknown to me. How many excellent writers may we still be ignorant of, especially those who write in one of the hundreds of indigenous African languages, not to mention French, Portuguese, or Arabic?

Finally, why ninety-nine books? Perhaps because one hundred is too round a number, seeming to imply that one hundred books is all you need to understand Africa, or that it's even possible to compile a complete list of the best of what has been written about the continent. Ninety-nine is an open-ended number. At the least, it leaves room for a favourite book of your own.

I hope this book will give you some sense of the rich literature on Africa, or a starting point to learn more about a country you plan to visit, but most of all I hope it will lead you to read some of the extraordinary books I've discovered on my literary journey around the continent.

Algeria

The Sheltering Sky by Paul Bowles

Ecco Press, 1998 (first published 1949)

P aul Bowles, the expatriate American writer and composer, died
in Morocco in 1999, after having lived there for more than fifty
years. Bowles is so closely identified with Morocco that many readers
believe that his best-known work, the novel *The Sheltering Sky*, is
set there. Place names are scarce in the book, and some of those
that do appear seem to have been invented. Still, the attentive reader
will find that the story begins and ends in the city of Oran, on the
coast of Algeria (also the setting of Camus's *The Plague*) and that its
characters travel as far as the vicinity of Tessalit, just over the border
with Mali. A novel of the desert, its action ranges over much of the
Sahara, of which Algeria occupies a generous portion. It is written in
a spare, incisive, balanced prose that serves its subject perfectly.

Porter Moresby and his wife Katherine – known as Port and Kit
– are psychic refugees from the massive violence and treachery of
World War II. Though Port comes from New York City, before the
war he had "felt most at home ... in Europe and the Near East." Now
he wishes to avoid any part of the world that has been touched by the
war. "Europe has destroyed the whole world," says Port in a fit of
pique. "I hope the whole place gets wiped off the map."

In some ways, Port and Kit – and their friend, a handsome and not
particularly bright young man named Tunner, who is obviously taken
with Kit – are a later version of the "lost generation" characters of
Hemingway's *The Sun Also Rises*. But while Hemingway's shell-shocked
characters begin in Paris and seek purity and forgetfulness in the dry
air and clear light of Spain, Paul Bowles's characters, reeling from the
impact of yet another world war, begin in Oran and seek oblivion in one
of the most desolate regions of the earth. Even the name "Port Moresby"
speaks of remoteness: it is also the capital of New Guinea.

To say that these people are seeking something, though, may be
putting it too strongly. By avoiding the things they despise and cutting
themselves off from their pasts – Port, we learn late in the novel,
is a writer who no longer writes – they are making themselves the

playthings of fate. The first brief chapter sets the tone, as Port stretches out on a bed in a stifling hotel room. "Now he could only lie as he was, breathing slowly, almost ready to fall asleep again, paralysed in the airless room, not waiting for twilight but staying as he was until it should come."

The stoic Port and his tense and neurotic wife Kit travel ever deeper into the desert, in search of some place without the "taint" of Europe, and seemingly pursued by a corrupt and devious American named Eric Lyle and his travel-journalist mother. But as they immerse themselves in landscapes and cultures that are increasingly alien to them, they risk losing their mental and spiritual bearings. "It takes energy to invest life with meaning," thinks Port, "and at present this energy was lacking." The sky itself begins to appear as a fragile curtain between humanity and the impersonal vastness of the universe.

Though the real subject of *The Sheltering Sky* is the souls of its rootless characters, Bowles describes the land and people of the Sahara with authority. The Algerian characters are described from the outside, yet they seem to have an inner life, and their behaviour, though sometimes cruel and violent, seems motivated by consistent albeit dimly perceived cultural codes. Apart from one "Negro urchin" who is portrayed as a cunning clown, Bowles accords them a measure of respect, if only because they know how to live in an environment that gradually destroys the foreigner.

⌐

The café had a complicated entrance. They went through a low arched door, down a dim hall into a small garden. The air reeked of lilies, and it was also tinged with the sour smell of drains. In the dark they crossed the garden and climbed a long flight of stone steps. The staccato sound of a hand drum came from above, tapping indolent patterns above a sea of voices.

"Do we sit outside or in?" the Arab asked.

"Outside," said Port. He sniffed the invigorating smell of hashish smoke, and unconsciously smoothed his hair as they arrived at the top of the stairs. The Arab noticed even that small gesture. "No ladies here, you know."

"Oh, I know."

Through a doorway he caught a glimpse of the long succession of tiny, brightly-lit rooms, and the men seated everywhere on the reed matting that covered the floors. They all wore either white turbans or red chechias on their heads, a detail which lent the scene such a strong aspect of homogeneity that Port exclaimed: "Ah!" as they passed by the door. When they were on the terrace in the starlight, with an oud being plucked idly in the dark nearby, he said to his companion: "But I didn't know there was anything like this left in this city." The Arab did not understand. "Like this?" he echoed. "How?"

"With nothing but Arabs. Like the inside here. I thought all the cafés were like the ones in the street, all mixed up; Jews, French, Spanish, Arabs together. I thought the war had changed everything."

Algeria

The Savage Night by Mohammed Dib ♫
Translated from the French by C. Dickson
University of Nebraska Press, 2001

Mohammed Dib was born in Algeria in 1920 and was deported for his nationalist views in 1959, during the country's long and bloody war for independence. Though he is a prolific and honoured writer in France, where he now lives, his work has been almost unavailable in English. The University of Nebraska Press, which published this collection of thirteen stories, calls it "the first book-length English translation of Dib's work." (A novel entitled *Who Remembers the Sea*, however, was published by Three Continents Press in 1985 and is now out of print.)

The subject of nearly every story in the collection, as the author points out in an afterword, is the violence and injustice of the twentieth century, particularly violence that is carried out coldly because it is motivated by ideology rather than personal emotion. In many of these stories, relatively straightforward action is coupled with psychological subtlety.

In the title story, "The Savage Night," a young man named Nédim and his sister Beyhana travel by trolley through the midday heat of Algiers. Nédim and Beyhana are physically and emotionally spontaneous, similar in looks, and with a mutual understanding so deep that they seem more like lovers than brother and sister. Their shifting thoughts and emotions are rendered with sensitivity and sympathy, even as Nédim begins to think that the other passengers on the trolley are mannequins that will soon "be offered up to the flames, reduced to smoke." These two young people, we gradually realize, are on their way to commit an act of terrorism for which we never learn the exact reason. In a remarkable demonstration of authorial control, the narrator retains his intimate and sympathetic tone toward his protagonists through the commission of their bloody deed and its messy aftermath. Told from their point of view, the story is one of regret and self-sacrifice, rather than the record of an outrageous crime.

In "A Game of Dice," a terrorist is forced to answer to his would-be victim. Two young men burst into a courtyard, intending to assassinate an old man from whom they expect no trouble. The old man, however, is ready for them, and once he has killed one of the attackers and trapped the other, he conducts a lengthy interrogation of the surviving youth that is intended partly to torture him but also to get to the bottom of what motivates him. Who has ordered him to do this? Does he believe it is the will of God? Now that the tables are turned, does he believe it would be fair for him to die? Does he really understand the meaning of death? The old man proposes that the young man play dice with him for his life, and as the game favours first one player and then the other, the conversation becomes more impassioned.

"I'm nothing but pain as far down as you can reach," says the would-be terrorist. "I'm nothing but an open, festering wound." The old man hazards his own interpretation: "Essentially, you – all of you, you and your kind – are nothing but our own personal demons. ... And because we weren't skillful or clever enough to keep you chained up where you should have been, here you are, free to move about, free to infest the earth and, like howling wolves, forever call up the past."

"A Game of Dice" tantalises us by hinting at motivations for the seemingly mindless atrocities that ravage modern societies. But as Dib points out in his afterword, "it is not a writer's job to mete out lessons but to reverse the learning process. He does not prescribe responses but rather poses questions."

Not all the stories in *The Savage Night* take place in Algeria – others are set in Paris and Sarajevo, and the heartbreaking "Paquita, or The Ravished Gaze" takes place somewhere in Latin America – but the troubling questions this book asks are inescapable no matter the location.

⌒

They had shown them the door. Two boys – one eighteen, the other, maybe twenty. Eighteen and twenty years old, no more. They had said to them, "There it is." They had said to them, "It's never locked." It was closed. They pushed it. It opened. They went in. Or rather they burst into the courtyard,

a large patio. It would be light for quite some time yet – the curfew would sound, and it would still be light. Here it was lighter than day – one couldn't tell why – lighter than it was out in the city. And that silence. It was impossible to explain what it was like. The patio was shimmering with muteness and solitude. They had said to them, "He lives alone."

They had said to them, "With this man, there'll be no problem. You just go there. He lives alone. An old man. And everything will go smoothly."

They had said to them, "It'll be a piece of cake."

Algeria

Algerian White by Assia Djebar

Translated from the French by David Kelley and Marjolijn de Jager

Seven Stories Press, 2000

*A*lgerian *White* was written as a tribute to three men. Each was a friend of the author, the eminent writer Assia Djebar. Each was a writer himself, in addition to his regular profession. All three were killed in the space of less than a year, and the stories of each of their deaths are at the emotional heart of the book.

M'Hamed Boukhobza, a sociologist, worked late one night on a report for a meeting the next day. In the morning, three men rushed into his apartment, tied up his daughter, and left her to listen in another room while they tortured M'Hamed to death. She found him with his chest cut open, but although she was a medical student, she could not save him.

Mahfoud Boucebi, a psychiatrist, arrived at his clinic one day to find the driveway blocked. Two men forced their way into his car and stabbed him in the chest and abdomen. He died at the hospital during surgery.

Abdelkader Alloula, a dramatist, was warned that a group had targeted him for murder. He did not tell his wife, mother, or sisters, and he did not change the date of a lecture he was scheduled to give. On the day of the lecture, he was shot twice at the bottom of his staircase. He lingered for several days in a coma, then died.

"All I do in these pages," writes Djebar, "is spend time with a few friends." But in remembering them she also reflects on the many other Algerian writers who have died before their time, and on the painful history of modern Algeria.

Some of the writers mentioned (there are nineteen in all, listed in the back of the book) were killed by the French in the struggle for independence. Others were assassinated by religious or political extremists, or – as in the case of the gay poet Jean Sénac – by parties unknown: "a one-night stand, a robber, or perhaps a police spy." Some died in other ways: Albert Camus in a car crash, and Frantz Fanon from leukaemia.

However they died, each of these writers disappeared into what Djebar pictures as the "Algerian white." Like Melville in *Moby-Dick*, she plays a series of sinister variations on the meaning of whiteness: the whiteness of death notices and of targets, "the white of dust, of sunless light, of dilution ..." The artist Kandinsky, she writes, believed that "White acts on our soul like absolute silence."

Djebar is given to "fine writing," and her memory of her lost friends is sometimes vague or indirect. She describes them as images swaying on the horizon, "in the midst of a meadow or in a sharp ray of sunlight." Often, though, she describes moments – like a glimpse of Kader, the actor, leaping across the stage in a production of *Diary of a Madman* – that for a short time bring them back to life. And always, she conveys the continuing and ever-changing pain of their absence.

———

As this friend died so suddenly, I didn't take the plane from Paris to Algiers to be with his people – to convince myself that he was gone: emerging from the sheets of love, barely twenty-four hours later swallowed in the white shroud, in the bottom of a grave, opposite the Bay of Algiers towards which he had come for the first time, twenty years before, hurried, silent and solitary. I didn't go. I should have.

Throughout the following year I passed often by the building, in front of his sitting room balcony: he would no longer come and wait for me at the airport, then find the time, a few days later, to take me back. I did not want to go inside his apartment: his widow was no longer there. Relatives undoubtedly would have taken it over. ... And turning my head towards the Bay of Algiers (that he contemplates from the depth of his tomb, very close by), I persist in telling myself that he, Malek, is not dead: that he is away: that he is going to come back. That he is going to speak to me ("To you alone," he would say, in his extraordinarily refined Arabic, "to you alone can I say how life, happiness ...!"). He will come back. And I, what can I say to him, I cannot conceive of his death in the frozen Algeria of those days, where a cold fever was lurking, where already hatred was seeking its wraps of despair in the darkness ...

Angola

Mayombe by Pepetela

Translated from the Portuguese by Michael Wolfers

Heinemann, 1996 (first published 1983)

In some ways the novel *Mayombe* resembles an old World War II movie. A rugged military officer and his closest friend are fighting for a better life, but their passion for the same woman tests their friendship and their commitment to the struggle. However, this time the two men aren't GIs in Normandy but guerrillas in the Angolan enclave of Cabinda, and they are battling not the Nazis but the colonial power of Portugal.

In the late 1960s, Artur Carlos Mauricio Pestana, whose pen name is Pepetela, fought in Cabinda for the MPLA, one of several movements struggling to expel the Portuguese and gain control of the country. He wrote *Mayombe* while the war was still going on, several years before the MPLA became the ruling party of an independent Angola. Despite its frank discussions of racial and tribal conflict among the ranks, and even its prediction of MPLA authoritarianism after independence, the book was published with the support of Agostinho Neto, Angola's first president.

Pepetela's firsthand war experience lends authenticity to his descriptions of combat and of life behind the lines. The forest of Mayombe is almost a character in its own right, and the author doesn't forget the mundane, unheroic details. The guerrillas' Pepesha machine guns, for instance, sound like sewing machines. The names adopted by the guerrillas – Truth, Struggle, New World, Miracle, even Theory – may sound like the allegorical figures in *Pilgrim's Progress*, but these men are thoroughly human: they make mistakes, struggle with their fears, and act for the most part without false bravado. They are philosophical warriors, though, and their bookish conversation is flavoured with Marx, Lenin, and Freud.

The Commander of the Mayombe guerrillas is known as Fearless, a name that sits uneasily on him (he was previously called Sphinx) and that strikes some of the men as a little too much. Fearless or not, he is certainly brave, and he inspires loyalty through example and through his sensitivity to the personal qualities of his troops. Though

he considers himself a Marxist, he struggles with the remnants of a Christian upbringing, and his approach to problem solving is far from doctrinaire. He finds fulfillment in the struggle against the Portuguese, and cannot imagine what role he would play in a free Angola.

Fearless's friend and right-hand man is referred to as the Commissar, though in intimate conversation the Commander calls him João. Steeped in Marxist ideology, the Commissar insists that his men risk their lives to return a small sum of money stolen from a local worker, and he describes his troubled relations with the tumultuous and beautiful Ondine in terms of dialectics. His hard ideological shell hides some violent emotions, however, and these erupt most dramatically in the second of two battles that (contrary to Marx) play out the first time as farce and the second time as tragedy.

Fearless recognizes that the Commissar is the model for the post-independence Angolan leader, the type responsible for the creation of a rigid government machine. "What is more tragic," Fearless tells him, "is that you will be right. Objectively, it will be necessary to tighten vigilance inside the Party, improve discipline, make purges. ... But these purges will provide pretexts for ambitious men to confuse counter-revolutionaries with those who criticize their ambition and their mistakes." Though Fearless, and apparently the author, appear to have reservations about this stark future, both seem to believe it is unavoidable.

—

By five they reached the top of the mountain, in a state of exhaustion. After a brief rest, they began the descent, since the cold made it impossible to sleep on the mountain at night. The descent, although quicker, was more dangerous than the climb. The Commissar slipped and tumbled on mud, until he managed to grab hold of a creeper. Legs shook, from the effort of standing up. Knees ached. Knapsacks pushed men forward, towards the abyss. Rain continued to fall. At six it was pitch black and they had not yet descended the mountain. The remainder was almost a crawl, in the darkness of the treacherous mountain, with rain beating back into faces. If anyone should fall, the others could not be sure

of finding him again. Finally they reached the river. Night did not allow them to look for a reasonably dry camp site. They let themselves fall in a kind of clearing, and checked the group to see if all were present. Fortunately, no-one was missing. They opened their packs, where everything was soaked, sleeping cloth, food, ammunition, took out tins of milk and drank the milk cold, as no fire could be lit in that heavy rain.

Angola

Another Day of Life by Ryszard Kapuscinski

Translated from the Polish
by William R. Brand and Katarzyna Mroczkowska-Brand

Harcourt Brace Jovanovich, 1987

For a few days in 1975, the future of Angola depended on two men, a pilot and an engineer. The Portuguese colonists had left, the precarious coalition government had broken up, and the South African army had invaded the country. Flying an ancient two-engine DC-3, the pilot – the only one available to the MPLA faction governing in Luanda – carried information, soldiers, and ammunition to remote areas of the country. The engineer, for his part, tirelessly repaired the pumps supplying Luanda with water each time they were bombarded. Without either of these people, the South African assault might easily have succeeded even before Angola had celebrated its independence. Like Namibia to the south, Angola would have become a puppet of the apartheid regime in South Africa.

One of the few Europeans in Angola to witness these events was the Polish journalist Ryszard Kapuscinski. Kapuscinski went to Angola when almost all Europeans there were leaving it. "Many were convinced that the country would turn into a hell," he writes, "and a closed hell at that, in which everyone would die without any outside help or intervention." He watched as the Portuguese, after 500 years of colonial rule, packed all they owned into wooden crates, creating a makeshift wooden city that was ultimately loaded onto ships and carried away. Expecting chaos, the Portuguese took everything. Meanwhile, guerrilla armies backed by Zaire and South Africa fought to capture Luanda from the MPLA before Angola was officially independent and could call on help from the outside world.

Deluged by rumour and propaganda, Kapuscinski relied as much as possible on what he could see, and on simple deductions. When ships were loading in the harbor, the situation was relatively stable. When they stood off on the horizon, an attack might be on the way. When the MPLA radio gave straightforward reports, things were going well, but when it feverishly praised its own troops and

vilified the enemy, something had gone wrong. Kapuscinski stayed in the capital until the police disappeared, followed by the firemen, the dustmen, and finally the abandoned dogs that roamed the city in packs before vanishing as well. It was only when the city was effectively dead that he went in search of the war.

In a country as big and vacant as Angola – it was emptied by the slave trade and has been underpopulated ever since – the war had a sketchy, informal quality. Fighting stopped at midday because of the brutal heat, and bodies lay unburied after each battle. Terrified young soldiers fired wildly to calm their nerves and scare the enemy, and for a time it worked: the enemy ran away. Uniforms were scarce, so was authority, and anyone who set up a roadblock controlled his own little piece of Angola. Kapuscinski is especially discerning when he describes the etiquette of the roadblock – the need to brake gradually some distance from the barricade, to wait patiently for the guards to approach, to avoid being either aggressive or suspiciously easy-going, and mostly to weigh the question of whether to greet the guards with *camarada* or *irmão*, when the wrong choice could mean death.

Everybody was busy building crates. Mountains of boards and plywood were brought in. The price of hammers and nails soared. Crates were the main topic of conversation – how to build them, what was the best thing to reinforce them with. Self-proclaimed experts, crate specialists, homegrown architects of cratery, masters of crate styles, crate schools, and crate fashions appeared. Inside the Luanda of concrete and bricks a new wooden city began to rise. The streets I walked through resembled a great building site. I stumbled over discarded planks; nails sticking out of beams ripped my shirt. Some crates were as big as vacation cottages, because a hierarchy of crate status had suddenly come into being. The richer the people, the bigger the crates they erected. Crates belonging to millionaires were impressive: beamed and lined with sailcloth, they had solid, elegant walls made of the most expensive grades of tropical wood, with the rings and knots cut and polished like antiques.

Benin

The Viceroy of Ouidah by Bruce Chatwin
Summit Books, 1980

In 1971 Bruce Chatwin travelled to Benin when it was still known as Dahomey, and when the capital of Cotonou was "a town of belly laughs and French brasseries." Six years later he returned to research a biography of Francisco Felix de Souza, a Brazilian who rose from the direst poverty in the early nineteenth century to become a friend of the kings of Dahomey and the unchallenged slave master of the region. While Chatwin was in Benin, a coup broke out against the newly formed People's Republic, and Chatwin was held as a suspected mercenary while the real mercenaries made their escape. "The next two days I would prefer to forget," he wrote, though he eventually described them in the British literary magazine *Granta*. His research cut short, and less than eager to make another trip to Benin, Chatwin changed the name of his subject to Francisco Manoel da Silva "and went on to write a work of the imagination."

Whatever documents he might have missed when his research was cut short, Chatwin's knowledge of the "Slave Coast" was clearly extensive, and by telling his story in fictional guise he was able to make use of his firsthand observation of the country. The narrative that emerges is a kind of mosaic. Certain events are told in brief, vividly sensual scenes, but many of the logical connections and motivations are missing. The result is as puzzling, sinister, and highly coloured as a fever dream.

Though Da Silva is far from being a sympathetic character, he does emerge as a three-dimensional one. A child of the "dry scrubby cattle country" of north-eastern Brazil, he is orphaned at an early age and taken up by a Portuguese priest. As he grows into manhood he drifts through the Brazilian backcountry, "taking jobs as butcher's apprentice, muleteer, drover and gold panner." He marries on impulse, abandons his wife just as suddenly, and finally meets Joaquim Coutinho, the son of a rich plantation owner. At the Coutinhos' sugar plantation he gets his first look at large-scale slave labour, witnesses a ceremony for the Yoruba goddess Yemanja, and conceives the idea of going to Dahomey.

"He landed at Ouidah between two and three of a murky May afternoon smelling of mangrove and dead fish. ... He brushed aside the krumen who helped him from the canoe. He refused to 'dash' the outstretched hand of the fetish-man. He refused to let the porters carry him across the lagoon, and with black ooze coating his thighs he strode up the track to the Captains' Tree." Da Silva has the good fortune to arrive during a vacuum in power, when the king is in disrepute and enemies are threatening to invade the territory. He impresses an octogenarian official, the Yovogan, with his determination and his willingness – unheard of in a white man – to work hard in the hot sun. The Yovogan sends prisoners to help Da Silva rebuild the Fort of St John the Baptist on the coast, and before long a flag is flying to advertise new slaves for sale.

There is relatively little about the actual mechanics of slavery here – how slaves were captured and bought, chained, and transported to the coast, housed for weeks or months in pestilential barracoons – or about the horrors of the Middle Passage. The sense of moral decay, however, is overwhelming: not so much for Da Silva himself, who arrives in Africa already a hard and sometimes cruel man, but for the kings of Dahomey and the society they ruled. Corrupted by the trade goods unloaded from slave ships, including guns that escalated any conflict with neighbouring peoples, they came to depend on human flesh for their prosperity and human sacrifice for their spiritual protection.

The cruelty of the court of Dahomey as Chatwin describes it, the number of executions and the size of the king's collections of human skulls, would be unbelievable if they were not attested to by the historical records of nineteenth-century explorers and officials.

⟞

The King lay lounging on a bolster of carmine velvet, thronged by naked women, who fanned him with ostrich feathers and wiped the perspiration from his forehead.

He was a tall sinewy man with dry red eyes, automatic gestures and the bonhomie of the seasoned slaughterer. The rising sun shone on his chest. His fingernails curled like cocks' feathers. His loincloth was purple and his sandals were of twisted gold wire. At his feet were the heads of

a boy and girl, sent half an hour earlier to tell the Dead Kings that their descendant had woken up. He glared at the Brazilian and spat.

All the commoners lay on the ground and, when he lifted his baton, they rubbed their noses in the dirt and bellowed, "Dada! Breathe for me! Dada! Steal from me! Dada! Dada! Break me! Take me! My head is yours!"

A troubadour crawled forward, pointed at Da Silva, and said in a hollow voice, "The bird who leaves her nest cannot carry away the eggs."

An albino dwarf jumped up, saluted crazily, screeched white man's talk and gurgled as if he were being garrotted.

The executioner ran his fingers up and down his knife-blade.

But the prisoner knew better than to show fear and, as if by suction, drew the monarch's mouth into a cracked tobacco-stained smile.

By the end of the audience he was the King's friend.

Botswana

When Rain Clouds Gather by Bessie Head

Heinemann, 1995 (first published 1969)

The daughter of a white woman and a black man, Bessie Head was born in the South African mental institution where her mother was an inmate, and shuttled from a white foster family to a black one when she began to look less white. She worked as a journalist, and in 1964, when she was still in her twenties, she took a teaching job in Botswana and stayed there as an exile. In this way Botswana gained one of the best writers in southern Africa.

If Bessie Head had stayed in South Africa, she might eventually have written a memorable protest novel about life under apartheid. Instead, her first book was this clear-sighted but disarmingly hopeful novel about her new home. Though it contains its share of suffering, *When Rain Clouds Gather* is optimistic without being naive, politically as well as psychologically aware, and remarkably free of bitterness.

The story begins when a handsome and taciturn young man named Makhaya crosses a barbed wire fence into Botswana, evading the patrols of the South African border police. In his pocket is a plan to blow up a power plant. He meets up with a kindly old man who is surprised when Makhaya tells him he is a Zulu but no tribalist. "And what's wrong with the tribe?" the old man asks. "I have a list of grievances against it," Makhaya answers. "I haven't got time to go into them now ..."

The man leads him to a village where, as it turns out, the traditions of tribe and family are unusually weak. Golema Mmidi, a village of about four hundred, is a place where refugees like Makhaya have washed up, "individuals who had fled there to escape the tragedies of life."

When Rain Clouds Gather is about making a new start in a new land. Though Makhaya is an African from just across the border, he is fascinated by what is strange and different in the landscape, plants, and traditions of Botswana. There are thorn bushes with pods that throw their seeds like coiled-up springs, and "strange freakish daisies" with stems that are "one inch wide and flat as rulers." When

wedding guests bring potatoes for the feast, the cooks tie them in colourful checked cloths and wear them as decorations.

Strangest of all, though, is the freedom Makhaya feels, and the sudden absence of the racial tension that thickened the air in South Africa. Botswana is on the verge of becoming an independent country. The local police officer is a white man named George Appleby-Smith, a friend of the local chief, a teller of jokes, and an enemy of pomposity. The policeman sizes up Makhaya as a good man, and, although the refugee won't agree to keep away from politics, tells him, "I'll still stick my neck out for you."

Makhaya forms an alliance with the only other local white man, a restless giant in khaki shorts named Gilbert Balfour. Balfour is an agricultural expert, who devotes his considerable energy to helping the local villagers farm more productively and profitably. Politically naive, he fails to see that his efforts are being hindered not only by tribalism and tradition – the villagers won't eat millet because it's the food of the "inferior" desert people – but also by the active opposition of the arrogant local sub-chief.

The sub-chief's temporary absence gives Makhaya and Gilbert the chance to begin changing the way things are done. Together they organize the construction of water reservoirs and begin cultivating tobacco to be sold for extra income. Most importantly, they change the way this village of misfits feels about itself, so that when the sub-chief returns he finds that his power has melted away.

The old man was silent for a while then continued, "In this world are both evil and good men. Both have to do justice to their cause. In this country there is a great tolerance of evil. It is because of death that we tolerate evil. All meet death in the end, and because of death we make allowance for evil though we do not like it."

"I might like it here," Makhaya said, wistfully.

"This country appeals to few people," said Dinorego. "There is too much loneliness. I stay alone with my youngest child. Her name is Maria. She likes all things modern. Because of this she is also taking lessons from Gilbert in English. One day she was looking at pictures in a book

which Gilbert gave her. There was a kitchen with shelves. So she carved the shelves in the mud wall. Then, too, she cooks goat meat with curry powder and this improves its taste. Now all the women round about have shelves in their kitchens and cook the meat with curry powder."

Botswana

Whites by Norman Rush
Vintage, 1992

Norman Rush is best known for his award-winning novel *Mating*, a love story that brings together two hyper-articulate anthropologists on the grounds of an experimental community in Botswana's Central Kalahari Game Reserve. *Mating* is a tour de force: a wide-ranging, funny, and linguistically inventive book-length conversation packed with anecdotes of African life and observations on socialism, capitalism, society, and the relations between men and women.

But for readers who want more drama, a greater variety of characters, and a less speculative take on life in Botswana, *Whites* is the book to begin with. Drawn from Rush's experience as the co-director of the Peace Corps in Botswana, *Whites* is a sharp investigation of how the white people who come to the country, mostly on short-term contracts – missionaries, aid workers, government employees – encounter the Africans who live there.

Despite the book's title, *Whites* is just as discerning in its description of the ways of the Tswana and San as it is in that of the Americans, British, Dutch, and Afrikaners. One story is narrated by an African boy named Paul, a member of the despised Mokgalagadi ethnic group. It conveys the boy's conflicted conscience and religious fixation in language that captures many of the peculiarities of English as spoken by Africans, yet without undermining his dignity. Through his eyes we get an unvarnished picture of some of the whites, his employers, who make their homes in Botswana – such as the anti-apartheid activist who hires Paul to steal some political posters for his collection. "That man was strong for Africans, I may say. Without fail at morning he would shower curses on the news reader of Springbok station from Johannesburg, as You are murderers, or cretins, at times."

"Bruns," the first story in the collection, marks the first appearance of the bright, discursive, somewhat aimless, and unnamed female anthropologist who returns as the narrator and main character of *Mating*. As in that novel, the content of her story – in this case, the

conflict between the idealistic Dutch development worker Bruns and the wife-beating Afrikaner Du Toit – is less involving than the many asides that punctuate the tale. We learn about the belly-out "African Physiological Stance" and how it has been adopted by Afrikaners, why kissing a rabid ox is the best way to contract rabies, and how, in the absence of street lighting, the local Bakorwa visit, converse, make bargains, pour drinks, and play "those one-string tin-can violins," all in complete darkness.

"Near Pala" is a powerful and well-constructed story, in which a marriage cracks open almost as suddenly and violently as in Hemingway's "Short Happy Life of Francis Macomber." During a severe drought, two couples share a ride through the Kalahari in a Land Rover. Through a skillful use of dialogue, by the end of the story you learn more than you may want to know about the qualities of each couple and the limits of their compassion.

Nan said to Tess, "Truly, one comes to dislike the medical profession. Now I must deal with them again. Coming back here to Botswana from holiday, it was so strange and nice. We were in the plane, coming low over the land. I was happy to see Botswana again. It was so strange, Tess – the country seemed like a poor relation, someone nice who refuses gifts at first, someone you like. This country is so poor. We were flying low over it. And then all I could think of was our friend the peerless Dr. Hartogs, who said that from the air the country looks as if it has ringworm. He was saying that the brush fencing round the family rondavels and kraals looks like that. It spoiled it."

"We love the sea," Tess said. "Give us four days and we make straight for Durban. Durban isn't nice, but it has the sea to put your feet in."

"You'll be singing a different tune about Hartogs when your day comes," Gareth said over his shoulder.

Burkina Faso

Of Water and the Spirit by Malidoma Patrice Somé
Putnam, 1994

Malidoma Patrice Somé was born in Burkina Faso, in the country of the Dagara people. He lived in the village of Dano until the age of five, when he was kidnapped by a French missionary priest. After fifteen painful years of re-education in a parochial school, Malidoma escaped and made his way back to his village, where he found himself unable to speak the language of his people. In the eyes of the elders, his alien education had made him a dangerous element in the village, and because he had never been initiated he could not take his place as an adult Dagara. Only initiation could make it possible for him to stay, but the psychic changes he had undergone meant that it would be an even more hazardous passage for him than for most young men.

The bulk of this dramatic memoir deals with Malidoma's initiation experience. His account offers a rare glimpse into a closely guarded series of rituals: rare not only because of traditional taboos against the inclusion of outsiders, but also because almost no one who has moved from an oral to a written culture has taken part in one, and can describe what happens to a Western audience. Literacy, Malidoma suggests, is almost directly opposed to the nonlinear understanding that initiation imparts. In fact, he comes to believe, "literacy, from the traditional point of view, occupies a space within the psyche that is reserved for something else." Malidoma stresses the great difficulty of rendering his experience in words, and admits that he has been forced to "trick" the reader by withholding certain things the elders have forbidden him to reveal. But what remains is mind-boggling enough.

Malidoma describes a series of journeys into alternate worlds that each boy (Malidoma is twenty years old, but the others are around thirteen) must undertake. In one of these, each of them must jump into a "light hole" magically created at the centre of a buffalo skin stretched tight over a circle drawn on the ground with ash and "black medicine." The boys are told that once inside they will find themselves falling through space, and must stop themselves by grabbing one of

the many coloured filaments running alongside them. As Malidoma waits for his turn, he sees one boy after another disappear into the light hole. A few minutes later the elders lift and toss the skin, ejecting a ball of violet surrounding each boy's body. Most of the initiates beat the violet flames from their bodies and walk off unharmed, but one boy returns lacerated and screaming, lies for a while in a pool of greenish fluid that gradually coagulates, then turns rigid in death.

Readers of this book, like readers of Carlos Castaneda's books about the Yaqui Indian sorcerer Don Juan, must decide for themselves whether they consider it a truthful account of a spiritual quest, a remarkable work of fiction, or some combination of the above. Malidoma compels belief, however, in the seamless way in which he merges ordinary occurrences with seemingly bizarre or impossible ones. His years at the Catholic seminary are described with as much care and apparent interest as the strange events that surrounded his initiation, because those years too are an important part of his journey. Even the apparent silliness of some of his visions, like the talking rabbit he encounters as a child, add to his seeming veracity, and he is perfectly willing to discuss the dirt-encrusted skin of certain elders, and their terrible smell an indication of their indifference to the things of this world. As a writer and speaker who has spent years mediating between the Western world and the world of the Dagara, Malidoma must have known that many readers would find the solemn and impressive visions more believable if he suppressed the apparently silly ones, and it seems significant that he does not choose to do so.

For a while only three voices were heard: the voice of the fire responding to the voice of the elder, the sound of the elder speaking to the fire, and the voice of the drum. The last two voices were familiar – part of the ordinary world – but the voice of the fire was getting stranger and stranger. As the elder spoke, the fire grew bigger and bigger, hotter and hotter; yet suddenly a wave of cold enveloped all of us. First, I began shivering and noticed that everyone around me was too. I wanted to try to figure out how something that was so hot could be so cold, but I had no time for analysis.

The elder was now inside the fire, walking in circles and speaking. In his hand he held a hyena skull, all alight and burning with an unearthly fire.

Each time the elder's voice rose higher in the air, the drum also rose in volume, the fire grew taller, and the skull became more luminescent, light breezing out of it. All of us had our concentration glued to the center of the circle, and it felt to me as if our combined attention were producing this phenomenon we were witnessing. Soon my hearing became confused and began to register strange noises. What I heard was almost like gibberish. Voices seemed to emanate from all over the place, but a lot of the ones behind me were coming closer and closer at an alarming rate. The elder's voice was getting more and more distant, the drum more timid, and the fire had no more center. It felt as if I were in the center of it except that, instead of feeling hot, I felt very cold.

Burundi

The True Sources of the Nile by Sarah Stone
Doubleday, 2002

A nne Copeland, the heroine of this skillfully written first novel,
is a Californian in her thirties who lives and works in Bujumbura,
the capital of Burundi. After a stint at a health clinic, she has gone
to work for a tiny human rights organization, one of whose aims
is to gain the release of political prisoners. At an official reception
she meets Jean-Pierre Bukimana, a cultured and elegant government
minister allied with the Tutsi elite. Their affair is not only sexually
intense but intellectually and emotionally intimate. "I had the sense,"
she thinks, "of *seeing in tandem*, of being half of a two-part unit
of perception and analysis." Being with Jean-Pierre makes her think
about the world in a new way.

One of the novel's strengths is its presentation of the heroine's
conflicted motivations, and her awareness of them. Is her work in
Burundi noble and courageous, or is she in fact "self-righteous and
self-absorbed"? Is her proper place in Burundi or at home in San
Francisco with her ailing mother? And how much does her infatuation
with Jean-Pierre cloud her political understanding? The reader's sense
that there might be something a little tawdry about the well-brought-
up young woman's exotic affair is anticipated by Anne herself, who
wonders whether she has managed to find a love who resembles the
bold, unscrupulous military officers in the cheap romances that her
mother devours. But if this is in some sense a romance novel, its self-
awareness makes it a thinking person's romance novel.

Burundi has long been bracketed with its neighbour Rwanda in
the minds of outsiders, and frequently overshadowed. Both of these
small, hilly, densely populated countries share a complicated history
of struggle between a Hutu majority and a Tutsi minority. The Belgian
colonists of both countries took a social system in which the categories
of "Hutu" and "Tutsi" were fluid and informal and turned it into a
rigid structure in which every African had a permanent identity, and
political power and educational opportunities were apportioned to
the Tutsi ruling elite. In Burundi as in Rwanda, the result has been a
series of violent outbreaks.

This novel takes place in Burundi in 1993. A new Hutu president has been elected, promising a government of reconciliation, but within months he is assassinated by elements of the Tutsi-led army, triggering reprisals and counter-attacks. Anne witnesses a shocking episode from a bloodbath that eventually kills 50 000 Hutu and Tutsi, and before long she hears troubling rumours of Jean-Pierre's involvement in a previous violent outbreak, in 1972. She is startled to realize that for all of her time with him she had assumed that the Hutus were in the right simply because the Tutsis were the ones in power. She even finds that she gets a perverse sexual charge from making love with Jean-Pierre while interrogating him about his past, as if the do-good human rights worker can only find release with someone "bad."

The True Sources of the Nile brings Burundi out of the shadows. It includes a wealth of local colour – food, weather, folktales – that together convey a distinctive picture of the country. Pizzas in Burundi are flavoured with cumin. Infants are given temporary names like Mouse Dung or Little Whore to make them undesirable to evil spirits. The domes of the national airport resemble a row of duck eggs.

More than that, however, this is a book about the scale of things: about the enormous impact that a small, out-of-the-way country can have on a person's life, and about how a national tragedy can express itself in small ways: the loss of a friend, the planting of doubt in a love affair, the failure to save a particular human being.

—

Jean-Pierre arranged for the two of us to travel into the interior, the trip he'd once planned as a surprise, but now I knew about it ahead of time. We stayed in the hills above Muramvya, a long, steep, winding drive, up and up, as if we were driving into the sky. A Greek family had a series of bungalows and gardens on a hilltop, with a central restaurant, flower beds, a swing for the family's children, and lawns in the middle of the cultivated fields, which spread down the hills in all directions. We could stand at the edge of the gardens and look down over what seemed to be most of Burundi.

Dotted everywhere on the hills below were the round shapes of the *rugos*, clusters of round, thatched buildings that make up a homestead. The parents sleep in a central building where the family gathers for meals. The grandmother and the girls sleep in one hut (where the banana beer is kept), the grandfather, boys, and goats in another, and the cows in their own. Rippling banana trees and oil nut palms divided the green fields around the *rugos* into sections. The hills so green, so red, the sky so intensely gray. Glory.

Cameroon

Mission to Kala by Mongo Beti

Translated from the French by Peter Green

Heinemann, 1964 (first published 1957)

Mission to Kala is a happy surprise – an African novel that treats village life not only with warmth and affection but also with a healthy dose of irreverence. Though it deals with the sometimes tragic theme of the young man who loses his traditional roots after living in the city, the book is light, deft, funny, and illuminating, and in the end surprisingly moving.

Jean-Pierre Medza has just returned to his home town after failing his baccalaureate exams. Stung by his setback, wishing only to rest and recoup, he is immediately recruited on a mission to the remote bush village of Kala to retrieve the runaway wife of a man named Niam. Once there he is lionized as a city dweller and man of education, and the uncle he stays with is quick to take advantage of his prestige, loaning him out for dinners with the village elders in return for gifts of sheep and other livestock.

Even a short time away from home, Medza finds, is enough to turn him from a "native" into a kind of explorer who begins to enjoy not his similarities but his differences from the villagers: a sort of colonialist in his own country. "An *easy* adventure," he reflects, "among comparatively simple people, is the wish and aim of every adventurer. When you come to think of it, the very existence of adventurers is only made possible by the survival of primitive, simple-minded tribes. When the latter finally vanish, they will take the former with them; they are like Siamese twins, who can't survive independently."

As weeks go by and the wife of Niam fails to appear, Medza falls deeper and deeper into village life, discovering in the process that these rural cousins are not as simple-minded as he had assumed. Medza's new cronies – the Boneless Wonder, Duckfoot Johnny, Son-of-God, and his hulking yet sensitive cousin Zambo – are described with zest, and Medza's growing attachment to the young girl Edima (pursued at first because of her youth and naïveté) is shown with uncommon delicacy.

The village laid siege to me socially from the early morning onwards. First of all there were the young boys. They invaded my uncle's house loaded with books and slates. They begged me to teach them to read, write, do sums, and understand the pictures in their books. Then came the grown men, who all wanted me to write letters for them. Since my arrival they had all taken it into their heads to place orders with European-style shops. I became their public scribe, scribbling away from morning to night under the absorbed and tireless gaze of an ever-increasing crowd.

Finally, there was the weaker sex – so weak, in fact, that I never found out just why young girls and women verging on middle age came and stared at me whenever they could manage it. They did nothing else, just stared: it was a simple kind of self-indulgence.

Cape Verde

The Fortunate Isles by Basil Davidson
Africa World Press, 1989

The "Fortunate Isles," a traditional name for Cape Verde, may seem a strange description for a set of dry and desolate islands, uninhabited before they were settled by slaves and their masters, and subject to periodic drought and famines that have driven a large proportion of the population to leave. Yet Basil Davidson, who has travelled extensively through Africa in a long and distinguished career as journalist and historian, finds Cape Verde one of the most hopeful examples in the troubled history of modern Africa.

Much of this book describes the struggle of a small band of rebels to free Cape Verde from Portuguese rule, and to build a new government with broad popular support. The freedom of Cape Verde, like that of the mainland territory of Guinea-Bissau, was the aim of the PAIGC, the African Party for the Independence of Guinea and Cape Verde, which originally intended to unite the two regions in one country. Davidson's admiration for Amílcar Cabral, the PAIGC leader assassinated in 1973, comes through clearly.

Guinea-Bissau was the first to win its independence, after a tough guerrilla struggle described by Barbara Cornwall in *The Bush Rebels*. In Cape Verde, collaborators with the Portuguese regime and the comfortable middle class feared that "Sancho," a legendary wild man of the hills, would come down "flailing his tail" and wreaking havoc. In fact, the struggle in the islands mostly consisted of building local organizations and holding mass demonstrations. Independence came in 1975, after a rebellion of disgruntled military officers overthrew the Salazar dictatorship in Portugal.

A painstaking process of consciousness-raising preceded the independence of Cape Verde. Unlike the countries of the mainland, Cape Verde had no ancient traditions to draw upon. In a sense it was an artificial nation, in which racial mixing had created a unique culture of "brown Creoles." Though these Creoles developed a sense of national identity, their initiative was sapped by drought, famine, unemployment, the exodus of many young Cape Verdeans, and the rigid and sometimes brutal control of the Portuguese. Under these

circumstances, it took the efforts of Cabral and a small vanguard of rebels to organize an effective resistance.

The political history in *The Fortunate Isles* will be heavy going for some readers, though intriguing to anyone with an interest in decolonization and development. The narrative is enlivened by Davidson's portraits of rebel leaders and ordinary citizens, and his descriptions of the dramatic mountainous landscape of the islands, including the volcano that makes up the island of Fogo (Fire). Though Davidson takes a warmly partisan attitude to the rebels and the new government of the independent Cape Verde, he is not averse to pointing out the problems that remain to be addressed – notably the "huge discriminations practised by Cape Verdean men against Cape Verdean women."

Well above the 1 300-metre mark the road tops a shoulder-bone of the volcano and runs for a little space until suddenly it takes you round a cliff-hung corner and throws you into the Place of the Cauldron, Chã das Caldeiras, the vast crater itself.

The moment is worth coming a long way to experience. Before this corner you are on a high peak raised above ocean horizons: perched on a globe-revealing cloud, as it were, and easily able to imagine the whole of humanity out there in front of you. Then you are suddenly inside a monstrous container of gigantic slag that might be the churned-up leavings of a long artillery bombardment: except that what is here is no kind of mud but long-cold lava cast in tortured and fantastic clumps. Beside you the wall of the cauldron climbs sheer and jaggedly to a curtain-ridge 500 feet above, while there in the centre of the cauldron, dripping its petrified rivers of grit, goes up the inner core for another 2 000 feet. You stop the car and get out and crane back your head, and still you cannot see the top of this volcano.

"One of these days," says Carlos, "I am going to climb it." The visitor has no such thought.

Central African Republic

Song from the Forest by Louis Sarno

Houghton Mifflin, 1993

Outsiders over the centuries have gone to Africa for many reasons: adventure, wildlife, riches. Louis Sarno went there for a more charming reason. As he says at the beginning of his book, "I was drawn to the heart of Africa by a song."

Sarno, "alone in a northern European capital one winter night," turned on the radio and was immediately entranced. "The song on the air was unlike anything I had ever heard: voices blending into a subtle polyphony, weaving a melody that rose and fell in endless repetition, as hypnotic as waves breaking on a shore." By the time he identified the song as an example of Pygmy music and heard some more recordings, Sarno was determined to visit the Pygmies and record them on his own. He decided at first to visit the Mbuti of Zaire, whom Colin Turnbull described in his classic account *The Forest People*, and he wrote to Turnbull for advice and contacts. In the end, however, he decided on the more remote Ba-Benjellé of the Central African Republic. The music of the Ba-Benjellé, also known as the Bayaka, was more rhythmically complex than that of the Mbuti, and they had been more or less left alone since the 1940s.

Sarno arrives in the Central African Republic with a one-way ticket and five hundred dollars. He makes his way to the Pygmy settlement of Amapolo in the south-west of the country, and finds Pygmies who dress in tattered Western clothes, live in insect-infested shacks, and badger him constantly for money. Two of the first words he learns are *mbaku* (moonshine) and *ndaku* (cigarette). The Pygmies feed him a steady diet of tadpoles, which taste like mud, and the music they perform for him is inferior to what he has heard at home.

It is only when Sarno's money runs out that the Pygmies' attitude seems to soften, all in a single day. Someone leaves him a ripe papaya. He is invited to go fishing, then witnesses a spontaneous and beautiful dance by some of the children. In the evening the older women begin to sing, and late that night as he is recording them, he sees a giant leaf glide from the forest into the clearing. A voice comes from the leaf, addressing the women, and then the leaf moves away, "screeching a

grotesque tune, which the women took up and transformed into a melody of supernatural beauty."

This episode establishes the themes that will dominate the book: the Pygmies' music, their women, and the forest spirits or *mokoondi*, which appear as animated leaves or bushes. As Sarno learns to speak the Yaka language, makes later trips to Africa, and records the many varieties of Pygmy music, he becomes attracted by two young sisters and then, most powerfully, by a teenage girl whom he knows at first only as "the fabulous dancer." The reader may wonder about the ethics of his pursuing this attachment: Sarno is about twenty years older than the girl, he professes to value traditional Pygmy culture, and he is a very rich man by Pygmy standards. But as the dancer alternately encourages and ignores him for month after month, driving him from elation to despair, it becomes clear that she wields a power of her own.

For most of his stay among the Pygmies, Sarno takes the *mokoondi* more or less for granted, assuming that hidden behind each animated leaf, bush, or bundle of raffia is one of the village elders. After a while he believes he can recognize the voices of individuals. But then he witnesses the forest spirits doing things he can't explain. By the end of the book he begins to wonder whether the *mokoondi* have involved him in a subtle plan to move the Pygmies away from settlements like Amapolo, where they die of disease and are exploited by African villagers, and back to a healthier and more traditional way of life in the rainforest. From a discouraging beginning, *Song from the Forest* opens out into mysterious and beautiful depths.

―――――

The half-hour intervals between songs were often filled with the antics of the *mokoondi*. Sometimes one of them would invent a silly tune and insist that the women sing it over and over, while it performed an equally silly dance. Once when the women refused, one of the *mokoondi* said, "Okay, no yams tomorrow." Chastised, the women instantly complied. Occasionally two *mokoondi* got into an argument, which would end with one of them going completely berserk for several minutes. Sometimes they made us all drum the earth with our hands. Once they danced uncannily like

a Broadway chorus line, sending everyone into stitches. And one night, before my eyes, one of them turned into an antelope.

The full moon, halfway through its wacky orbit, hovered somewhere north of the zenith and bathed the clearing in bright silver light. After several minutes of clowning around, one of the *mokoondi* – a faceless albino creature – lolloped in a leisurely way across the clearing, pausing within a foot of me. I gasped, as did all the women: it was an antelope! For an instant I thought the Bayaka must have released a captured one, or somehow called one from the forest into the camp. But then the antelope reached the side of the *mbanjo* and began to beat the ground – it was a *mokoondi* after all. I promised myself then that I would never again doubt what I had seen nor rationalize it away. Now, of course, I wonder.

Chad

Komoon! Capturing the Chad Elephant
by Heinrich Oberjohann

Translated from the German by Rhoda de Terra

Pantheon, 1952

B ooks about the sparsely populated, landlocked, and arid country of Chad are hard to find. Even this one, the long-out-of-print adventures of a German animal collector, can be assigned to Chad only with some ambiguity. Lake Chad, where Heinrich Oberjohann journeyed alone in the 1930s to capture young elephants for zoos, is bordered not only by the country of Chad but also by Niger, Nigeria, and Cameroon. Oberjohann wastes no time on preliminaries in this briskly written account, but does mention that he asked permission of British colonial officials to approach the lake by way of the Nigerian province of Bornu. The village of "Kinghava," where he makes his base camp, is not included in modern atlases. But regardless of exactly where Kinghava is located, the author makes clear that he travelled extensively, on foot and on horseback, around the shores of this enormous lake, most of which (despite a border dispute with Nigeria) falls within the boundaries of what is now Chad.

Lake Chad has dried up to a fraction of its former size, and some predict that the lake may completely disappear in the foreseeable future. In the 1930s, however, an expanse of open water at the heart of the lake was surrounded by a sea of papyrus reeds in which a number of smaller lakes were hidden. Oberjohann lived here for four years as he tracked, studied, captured, and sometimes released the elephants that lived here in the swamps. (He had been told that the Lake Chad elephants were the largest in the world, but doesn't say whether he found that to be true.)

Oberjohann reveals himself to be a strange mixture of the brutal and the sensitive. His preferred method for capturing a young elephant was to separate it from its mother, sometimes by screaming at the herd to create a stampede. He would rope a young elephant or even grab it by the tail and let it tow him through the swamp until it tired. A very young elephant, disoriented and anxious for protection, would sometimes follow him willingly back to camp. Whenever possible,

Oberjohann avoids shooting adult elephants to get access to their young, and generally fires only when in imminent danger. (Most so-called elephant attacks, he explains, are only bluff.) Yet he continues to capture baby elephants even though they always die after a few days – die for a simple reason that he only discovers after eighteen of them are sacrificed. Aside from Colo, his right-hand man, he treats his Berber assistants with contempt, describing them as "children of nature," sometimes whipping them, and exhibiting no interest in their lives and culture.

The author reserves his curiosity for the elephants, and his respect for them increases during his years among them. Elephants will not attack a sleeping man, he notes, and he witnesses two of them trying to help a wounded comrade. Their intelligence is extraordinary: one herd lures him into an ambush, and he discovers that the lone elephants that he and other hunters had shot, thinking they were dangerous "rogues," were actually sentries posted to alert the herd to danger.

Komoon! contains some astute observations on elephant behaviour. Oberjohann notes the extraordinarily keen hearing of the elephants, and the "deep ventriloquist grumblings" by which they seem to communicate. Noticing repeatedly that a danger to one herd causes another herd miles away to bolt at the same moment, he wonders whether the first elephant to notice a threat "emitted a sound which was heard by the elephants but was inaudible to the human ear" – coming close to guessing at the infrasonic communication discovered years later by acoustic biologist Katy Payne and described in her 1998 book *Silent Thunder*.

◆

The herd saunters but it stays close together. In the afternoon hours you hear no quarreling among the various families; the elephants browse as they range. With their trunks, they probe the bottom of the water, tearing up big bundles of reeds, root and all. They are after the succulent reed-marrow, which is more tender the closer it is to the ground. ...

It is hard to get used to the deafening noise made by the breaking and crushing of great masses of tough reeds and the rush of masses of water displaced by two hundred

elephants. Nowhere else have I ever felt such an oppressive sensation of fear, neither on the veld nor in the dense forest. My senses were whipped to a high pitch by this diabolical elephant orchestra, and in this state of feverish excitement I could travel with the herd for days at a stretch without tiring. As a matter of fact, this was not the time for sleeping. Without any warning, a couple of living, gray mountains might suddenly pass only a yard from you. Added to this there was always the danger of a surprise attack by some solitary animal watching on the fringe of the herd.

Comoros

Last of the Pirates: The Search for Bob Denard
by Samantha Weinberg
Pantheon, 1994

It's bad news when a mercenary takes an interest in overthrowing your country, especially when he succeeds. But even worse is when the mercenary falls in love with your homeland and decides to stay for a while.

Bob Denard, a French mercenary with operations in Morocco, the Congo region, and Benin on his résumé, first took over the Comoro Islands in 1975, after Ahmed Abdallah Abderemane had led three of the archipelago's four islands into unilateral independence from France. (The fourth island, Mayotte, remains a French colony.) Three years later, Denard and his team deposed Ali Soilih, the president he had installed, and reinstalled Abdallah, who shared power with another man for a few months before taking over sole leadership. Denard bought a beach house and other properties in the islands, converted to Islam, and took a Comorian woman as the latest in an informal series of wives. Then in 1989 Abdallah was shot and killed in circumstances that remain murky, and shortly afterwards Denard and his men left the country.

In *Last of the Pirates*, Samantha Weinberg, a young British journalist with considerable experience reporting on southern Africa, sets out to learn the truth about Denard's involvement in the Comoros coups, his relationship with the islands, and his character, and if possible to interview him. In her travels around the islands, Weinberg dives to the sunken hulk of Denard's ship, explores the active volcano of Karthala, and meets a cast of characters with a variety of contradictory tales to tell, from a playboy prince to the massive, blunt-spoken leader of the Comorian armed forces. In particular, she attempts to get to the bottom of the events of 26 November 1989, when five bullets were fired into the chest of President Abdallah. If she does not entirely succeed, she does turn up a number of intriguing clues and floats some plausible theories.

Mercenaries like Bob Denard, "Mad Mike" Hoare, and "Black Jacques" Schramme played an important part in the history of decolonization in Africa, when governments and rebel factions struggled to fill power vacuums, take over territory, or even carve out new countries. A glimpse into the careers and characters of men like these sounds promising, but in the case of Denard the details add up to a fairly ordinary picture. Frustrated with his lack of advancement in the French military, Denard became a mercenary more from a love of adventure than from a sense of patriotism. Though he was seen as a tool of South Africa, he saw himself as an undercover ally of French interests and an anti-Communist crusader. Those who knew him in the Comoros described him as well dressed, polite, and mild mannered, with a limp from a wound received in the Congo region.

More interesting than Denard are the Comoros themselves, known as the "perfume islands" because of the fragrant ylang-ylang blossoms that are grown there. Bigger and more populous than the neighbouring Seychelles, the Comoros are strikingly different and much less well known. "Sure, both were beautiful Indian Ocean islands, full of natural bounty; but where the Seychellois were open and unafraid, the Comorians were wary and secretive. The Comorians habitually dressed in long robes, the Seychellois wore as little as possible." Unlike the Seychelles, the Comoros have an ancient Muslim history, and perhaps for that reason Weinberg likes the Comoros more. The Comorians, she says, "had a sense of being their own people, whereas the Seychellois were only really what the thousands of tourists who visited their beautiful islands had made them."

~

It was hard to miss Abdallah's former residence and final resting place. It was situated right in the middle of the old town, which was delineated by thick crumbling walls, relics of the era of the battling sultans and raiding pirates. I got out of the car and stared in disbelief. ...

From the outside, I could see that four, tall, gold-leafed smaller minarets stood guard over the large, gold, central dome. Marble steps led up to a sumptuous tiled and carpeted mosque under another side dome. A giant chandelier hung from its ceiling. I

gathered from my guide's somewhat explicit gestures, that this was the men's mosque. He led us – Youssouf had been sufficiently enthused to follow – to a small spiral staircase in a tiled oval tower and we emerged into a minstrels' gallery overlooking the heart of the mausoleum. The walls of the huge central building were coated with shiny blue, white and orange tiles. Below us, in the center of the room, lay the ex-president's white marble tomb, inscribed with gold Arabic writing and half-covered by a gold-embroidered, green velvet shroud. Four carved gold minarets supported the heavy, green rope which surrounded the tomb. Six Korans on carved wooden holders stood at intervals around it, in front of matching Persian prayer carpets, each one with a string of worry beads laid carefully on top.

Congo (Democratic Republic of the)

The Catastrophist by Ronan Bennett

Simon & Schuster, 1997

The Catastrophist is a novel about the violent tumultuous early days of Congolese independence, when a charismatic young African named Patrice Lumumba rose to power and a few months later was overthrown, then murdered, in a plot supported by the CIA.

James Gillespie, who narrates this story, is an Irish novelist who speaks with an English accent and who sets his dry, clever, literate books in London. He is suspicious of political engagement, and especially suspicious of the intersection of politics and literature. His creed comes from the aesthete John Ruskin: "Does a man die at your feet, your business is not to help him, but to note the colour of his lips."

Strangely or not, James is in love with a woman very different from himself. Inès is a journalist for an Italian Communist newspaper. Writing, for her, is a tool to expose the oppressors and strengthen the oppressed. Inès has come to the Congo for Lumumba. James has come there for her, but he finds it impossible to stay aloof from the political earthquake around him.

James's passion for Inès is powerful: it seems at first the only passion in his life, and he is afraid of losing it almost from the start. "I am already loving you," she tells him in her imperfect English when they barely know each other. He fears her love has flared up too soon and will die away just as soon. She all but ignores him as she follows Lumumba to meetings and rallies, and becomes closer to Lumumba's driver Auguste, one of a handful of educated Africans given special privileges by the Belgian regime. "Politics stinks," he bursts out to Inès, and begs her to return to London with him. But at the same time he sees things that change him despite himself: protests brutally suppressed, eloquent speeches by Lumumba, and the casual bigotry of the Belgians. James begins writing articles himself, some of them based on tips from a shadowy American friend named Stipe. The articles are true, as far as he can tell, but Inès believes they are planted to serve the interests of others. To James, Inès's journalism is

propaganda that disregards the shadings of the truth. To Inès, James's fiction is bloodless and his journalism dangerously naive.

As the conflict in the country comes to a head and each character chooses sides, Inès never seems to question herself, while James questions himself constantly. Even at his bravest and most honourable, even when he stands up to beatings and the threat of murder, he can always identify a selfish motive that discredits his actions. In the end, he lives a story of passion and engagement that he cannot quite believe, and that he could never have written himself.

—◆—

What should I be looking at now? The Sankuru is not as wide as the Congo, not at this point at least where the *barque* crosses, but it has the same dull mud color, the same tinge of rust after rainfall, and there are the floating tangles of water hyacinth I know from Léopoldville. I have seen them here before, I have seen them in Stanley Pool and at the cataracts below the capital, I have seen them at Matadi where they debouch to the sea. The flowers are purple or magenta, some are powder blue. They are beautiful and malign, yet more parasites for this overleeched land. The rivers will never flush away these tokens of infection. The rain fell hard in the afternoon for two hours, forcing our absurd convoy off the road – one more delay upon many. Soon after the sky cleared one of his aides claimed to have heard the engine of a spotter plane and there was general alarm, but when I looked there was nothing.

Congo (Democratic Republic of the)

A Bend in the River by V. S. Naipaul

Alfred A. Knopf, 1979

At Kisangani in the interior of the Congo region – almost at the centre of the continent – the Congo River makes a wide bend to the south. The rapids here prevent riverboats from penetrating any further into the forest. V. S. Naipaul visited the town early in 1978, describing it in an essay called "A New King for the Congo." This, he notes, was the location of the crazed and violent Mr Kurtz in Joseph Conrad's novella *Heart of Darkness*.

"It was there, in Conrad's story," writes Naipaul, "that Kurtz reigned, the ivory agent degraded from idealism to savagery ... his house surrounded by impaled human heads." Seventy years later, the graves of early white pioneers lie in terraces above the rapids, "the brown river breaking white on the rocks but oddly static in appearance, the white crests never moving: an eternal level sound of water." A variety of outsiders are on hand, offering "goods, deals, technical skills."

It doesn't seem a promising setting for a novel, but something about it must have inspired Naipaul. A year after his essay appeared he published *A Bend in the River*, one of his most celebrated novels.

The critic Alfred Kazin once praised Naipaul for writing fiction that is "the very voice of exile." Naipaul is certainly an authority on exile. Born in Trinidad of Indian parents, Naipaul early realized that he had to leave in order to be the kind of writer he wanted to be. In England he began to immerse himself in a culture that he believed was not the property of white people or Westerners but that could be claimed by anyone with the will to do so. He began a series of journeys to the developing countries of the world, bringing his unique point of view to bear. His fiction as well as his nonfiction is marked by close, unsentimental observation and by extended, deeply self-revealing monologues by a variety of ordinary people.

A Bend in the River is narrated by Salim, a young man of Indian ancestry whose family has lived on the East African coast for generations. Like Naipaul himself, he knows he has to leave: not just for himself but because his whole community is threatened by the

turmoil created by newly independent states. But instead of heading to Europe, he accepts an offer to buy a shop at a bargain price at a town in the interior.

Though Naipaul never names that town, it is clearly Kisangani – a "town at the bend of the river," reached after a long drive into mountains, past lakes, and through the "gorilla forests" of what must be Rwanda or eastern Zaire. It is 1963, and a Big Man has taken over the country. Though he too is never named, details of his biography and his dress – "a chief's leopard-skin cap, a short-sleeved jacket and a polka-dotted cravat" – identify him unmistakably as Mobutu sese Seko.

The town at the bend of the river is "more than half destroyed" when Salim arrives, much of it burnt out and deserted in the wake of post-independence "troubles." But with time people return to the town, trade resumes, and Salim meets the first of a varied cast of characters, each of whom is in some sense an outsider like himself. Zabeth trades with Salim for pencils, razor blades, and other necessities, which she carries in a dugout canoe to her home in a fishing village downriver. Zabeth's son Ferdinand sees himself as a powerful figure – the "new man of Africa" – and acts out a variety of roles before becoming a powerful but uneasy official in the Big Man's government. Metty, who belongs to a slave family attached to Salim's own people on the coast, joins Salim in the interior and finds himself more independent and sought-after than he could have imagined. Raymond, an historian, is "the Big Man's white man," a mentor and admirer of the new President who cannot admit that he has become irrelevant.

A Bend in the River is a philosophical novel, in which people try to make sense of who they are, what they are doing, and where they can make a real home. Dramatic events take place mostly offstage: the real drama is in the minds of the characters. Salim constructs a routine for himself, made up of days at the shop, games of squash, and meaningless affairs with unnamed African women. He suffers homesickness, but when he returns to the coast for a visit he finds that things have changed. By the end of the book the town at the bend of the river seems to come apart like a cheap stage set, crumbling away and leaving its inhabitants truly homeless.

The rainy-season school holidays came, and Zabeth came to town to do her shopping and to take Ferdinand back with her. She seemed pleased with his progress. And he didn't seem to mind exchanging the lycée and the bars of the town for Zabeth's village. So he went home for the holidays. I thought of the journey downriver by steamer and dugout. I thought of rain on the river; Zabeth's women poling through the unlit waterways to the hidden village; the black nights and the empty days.

The sky seldom cleared now. At most it turned from grey or dark grey to hot silver. It lightened and thundered much of the time, sometimes far away over the forest, sometimes directly overhead. From the shop I would see the rain beating down the flamboyant trees in the market square. Rain like that killed the vendors' trade; it blew all around the wooden stalls and drove people to shelter under the awnings of the shops around the square. Everyone became a watcher of the rain; a lot of beer was drunk. The unsurfaced streets ran red with mud; red was the colour of the earth on which all the bush grew.

Congo (Democratic Republic of the)

Between Tides by V. Y. Mudimbe

Translated from the French by Stephen Becker

Simon & Schuster, 1991 (first published 1973)

Pierre Landu is an African, a Catholic priest, and a guerrilla in training. This dense, overheated, even claustrophobic short novel, told in Pierre's own voice, is the record of his struggle to reconcile these three identities.

Pierre's most basic identity – that of an African – may be his most threatened and problematic. His Western education, which includes religious training in England and Italy, has so alienated him from his roots that his mother's extravagant mourning at his father's funeral does not move him but only embarrasses him. He speaks of her with chilling detachment: "I scorned that stout woman, barely covered by a loincloth, her bosom heaving as she bellowed and rolled in the sand." The villagers, for their part, regard the young African priest as something not quite human, remarking "A man without a child is a dead man."

Pierre is devoted to the Catholic Church and recalls his days in Italy warmly and frequently. He is steeped in the lives of the saints and the work of Catholic theologians and philosophers, but he has gradually become dissatisfied with the smugness and worldly comforts of his fellow priests. By joining the Communist guerrillas he believes he is not turning his back on the teachings of the Church but finding a way to apply them in the real world. But although he believes that the two ideologies can coexist within him, his new comrades are not so sure. Distrusting his motivations and questioning his loyalty, they test him harshly.

Between Tides is sometimes almost comically erudite. "I recall Anaximander's dictum," Pierre thinks to himself, "exhumed by Lefebvre in his Metaphilosophie: 'Whence things were born, thence they must necessarily die, for they must expiate their injustices and be judged for them according to the laws of the universe.'" Yet one gets the sense that much of this theorizing is a smokescreen that Pierre uses to hide basic moral questions from himself.

Early in his career as a guerrilla, Pierre takes part in an attack on a town called Kanga. His recollection of what happened is brisk, almost offhand: "Soldiers were surrendering, others were trying to escape. Bullets cropped both kinds." Immediately, he recounts, "I took refuge in pure reason," repeating lessons to himself about the ruthless requirements of the Church in the defence of truth. But these arguments are not enough to paper over his revulsion: "I felt like vomiting. My body was protesting." Then he is ordered to kill a wounded man, a test he knows will be reported to his superiors. This time his rationalizations seem more effective: "Scripture came to the rescue: The ways of God are unfathomable. Even unto the highest. *Usque ad summum.* I took up my rifle, aimed, both eyes open, and shot him in the face."

Afterwards, Pierre is strangely light-hearted: "I glided, serene." The reader waits for the rest of the novel for him to revisit his decision to kill, to come to terms with it, to acknowledge his responsibility. Maddeningly, he never really does, though his constant circular arguments with himself may be his way of avoiding the question. Whether discussing scripture with his fellow priests or discussing Marx with a ruthless guerrilla officer, Pierre remains a conflicted, tortured soul. As he says at the end of the book, "My poor self-deceptions go on."

"You're a perfectionist, Pierre."

"No, come on now. I want to join the struggle for justice. God exists. I love mankind, the quick and the dead, but mainly the quick, the living, mankind today. You and the others. We're fighting for a better world. A revolution. Listen: a Christian ought to be in a permanent state of revolution. I just want to be a Christian."

Only words? Her open face expressed a more important truth. How could I presume to preach? I was ashamed of my fine phrases and the gust of religiosity rising within me. How could I explain? I tried: "Antoinette, I'm here because I can't come to terms anymore with a history that stupidly compromised Christ and that, unfortunately, many members of my Church still stand for. Most of them, in this country. If I

stay with them, fit into their organizations and institutions, I betray. And how can I live in peace except with people who really *work*, by action, for the triumph of justice? I claim Christ for my guide. He was a revolutionary! The nice people thought so. That's why they crucified Him. As a priest, I was answerable to Him."

Did she understand me? Should I have expected a reaction? Another temptation: this need to be understood, to be approved. A slave mentality. I needed her. I was using her to find peace. An actor, I told myself. A clown? Impossible. Her silence: What was she thinking of? I hardly dared move. Dispossessed. A sacrilegious gleam stung my eyes.

Congo (Republic of the)

The Fire of Origins by Emmanuel Dongala

Translated from the French by Lillian Corti

Lawrence Hill Books, 2001 (first published 1987)

In *The Fire of Origins*, the Congolese writer Emmanuel Dongala has produced not so much a novel as a national creation myth. His hero, Mandala Mankunku (who has several other names in the course of the story), is an outsize figure whose life seems to "beat in the same rhythm as the country." Mankunku's exploits and failures span the history of the two Congos, especially the Republic of the Congo, from traditional village life through colonialism, the brutalities of the rubber trade and of the forced-labour construction of a railroad to the coast, World War II, national independence, and beyond.

Like any good epic hero, Mankunku is born in ambiguous circumstances, his identity and even his mortality open to question. His mother gives birth to him alone in a deserted banana plantation, wraps him in a banana leaf, and plants a frond in the ground to mark the occasion. Because there are no witnesses, others question whether he was ever really born and therefore whether he will ever die.

Mankunku shows early signs of being one of those annoying people who do everything well. Though his father is a blacksmith, he rejects that profession and learns from his uncle to become a great hunter who can kill "a lion as easily as a hare, an elephant as easily as a mouse." Quickly dissatisfied by this role, he becomes a blacksmith after all, and masters the craft almost at once. "How adept he was! One would have thought that all the experience accumulated in this art since the days of his most remote ancestor was flowing into his fingers." He becomes a master sculptor as well, but is still dissatisfied: not so much because he cannot find his niche but because he wants to do everything in a society "where each individual has a role to play."

Mankunku turns to another uncle, Bizenga the sorcerer, and quickly learns everything he knows about the art of healing. He also discovers the boundary between Bizenga's real knowledge and his quackery. Before long Mankunku is experimenting with roots

and herbs, discovering new medicines, and finding that he can cure patients with his remedies alone, without calling on the help of the ancestors. With the arrival of the first European invaders, Mankunku is drawn into the role of military resistance leader, and in later years he accommodates himself enough to the new regime to become the country's first "native" train conductor.

Like other epic heroes, Mankunku is a misfit in his own society, even a "destroyer." Though his conscious struggle is against the white colonialists, his great talents and great restlessness cause him to master his own people's traditions only to undermine them. Yet it may be, as his wise old mentor Lukeni says, that undermining the old ways is a necessary step for a people who have become too hidebound and conservative. Emmanuel Dongala seems to suggest that Mankunku represents a way forward for Africa that the continent never had a chance to take – a way that might have helped Africans resist colonialism more effectively. Unhappily, though, the closer Mankunku comes to the world of the white man, the more he loses his direction, and he can find no real place in the world of the corrupt "revolutionaries" that follows independence.

Among the risks of writing a modern-day myth are making the scenery and action too general and the hero too perfect. Dongala never falls into this trap. In a sense, he does the opposite: by condensing the history of the country into the life of one man, he makes it almost unbearably specific and personal. The Congolese countryside, with its weaver-birds and "acrobatic thrushes," the great river that passes through it, and the shimmering colours of the lantana blossoms, could not be more sensually described. When the first white man arrives in Mankunku's village, he is a very specific white man, "red as a cock's comb," wearing a "white long-sleeved shirt buttoned up to the neck with two fat side pockets stuffed with God knows what" and carrying strong drink in a "strange gourd made out of glass." And when the colonists' African mercenaries confront Mankunku's mother and his blacksmith father, the resulting tragedy stands for a thousand others. If *The Fire of Origins* ends on a dispiriting note, this has more to do with history itself than with any lack of skill in the telling.

—

Lukeni opened his eyes and smiled sadly.

"Last night I had a strange dream, Mandala: I saw living cadavers, their faces white as the Moon, with a strange hairiness only found in the land of shadows, arrive from under the sea in the bellies of great whales. But this is what frightened me: they scattered over our lands like a cloud of crickets, they marched over the tombs of the ancestors, destroyed their offering cups, pillaged our goods. I invoked the ancestors, I called on them to help, they didn't come ... All of this is beyond me, I'm too old. I can't wait to die."

Mankunku was shaken. He saw in the eyes of the old man Nimi A Lukeni that faint wavering, he heard in his voice that barely perceptible little trembling that you sometimes notice in very old people who are nearing the end of their lives on this earth. What did it all mean?

Congo (Republic of the)

The Seven Solitudes of Lorsa Lopez
by Sony Labou Tansi
Translated from the French by Clive Wake

Heinemann, 1995 (first published 1985)

Readers of *The Seven Solitudes of Lorsa Lopez* may sometimes feel as though they are reading not an African writer but the Colombian novelist Gabriel García Márquez. The town of Valancia, like García Márquez's imaginary town of Macondo, is a place of rumours and supernatural occurrences, where the flow of time follows different rules than in the outside world.

The unnamed country where Valancia is situated corresponds only partially to the real-life Republic of the Congo. It also has a coastline, Pygmies, and perhaps a dinosaur. The real-life Republic of the Congo is a former French colony, but the inhabitants of this country have Portuguese and Spanish names, and they eat, dance, and celebrate with a Mediterranean flair.

As in the García Márquez novella *Chronicle of a Death Foretold*, the plot of *Seven Solitudes* revolves around a murder that everyone knows will happen but no one seems able to prevent. But whereas *Chronicle* circles obsessively around the events of a single day, *Seven Solitudes* takes place over half a century of suspended animation. Estina Bronzario is the fated victim, and her murder has its roots in the murder of another woman with a similar name: Estina Benta, who is butchered by her husband Lorsa Lopez when his parrot informs him that someone has given her "lap lice." Estina Bronzario, a fiery ageing beauty, calls a meeting of local women, after which they declare a sex strike against their male oppressors.

Estina Bronzario commits other acts of defiance that gain the attention of the government. She buries (presumably with some help) the bodies of over three thousand student protesters killed by government troops and left to rot. Most serious of all, when an official offers to make her the mayor of the country's new capital of Nsanga-Norda (moved for the seventh time from Valancia itself) "she spat into his government face a mixture of tobacco, anise and pimento."

The people of Valancia spend much of this novel abusing the Nsanga-Nordans as soulless bureaucrats, "treacherous Mahometans," and meat-eaters (the Valancians eat perch). Yet their actions speak of a desire for reconciliation. The Valancians, for instance, take for granted that the body of Estina Benta cannot be put to rest until the police arrive from the capital to investigate the killing. Each time there is a rumour that the police will arrive, the mayor lays out her varnished bones at the crime scene, together with the spade, axe, and other implements used in the crime. Meanwhile Lorsa Lopez, the murderer, mourns his victim by sticking seven nails, which he calls his "solitudes," into his dewlap. Though he kills again during the long wait for the police, the townspeople's attitude toward him is strangely benign, as if he is not really guilty until the proper authorities have ratified his guilt.

A series of strange phenomena cry out that life in Valancia is out of joint. Morals have decayed, we are told, and a string of murders occur where murder was almost unknown. The cliffs groan ominously, a sea serpent is captured and killed, and a monster resembling the Beast from the Book of Revelation is born to a madwoman.

The meaning of all this is far from clear. Is the book a protest against post-colonial sloth and corruption? Against the oppression of women by men? Against the small-minded exaggeration of regional differences, or against a rigid and logical attitude to a life that is full of inexplicable wonders? In the end, *The Seven Solitudes of Lorsa Lopez* is a poet's novel, held together by its vivid language, memorable imagery, and intuitive connections.

Great crowds stream across the bayou at the place where Fr Bona of the Sacristy crossed on the day of the crime. We can't understand it: men, women and children; Mahometans, Christians, Hindus and homodeists; Orientals dressed in all the colours of the rainbow and wearing extravagant hats – all of them mounting their assault on the hill to photograph Sarngata Nola's stone monster. The sea has spewed them up like termites. The arrogant, incestuous construction, nesting place of eagles and vultures, turns its leaden back on the nine o'clock sun. The shapes and the barbaric glitter of the

walls, weather-beaten by rain and wind, dance in the glare. Always and everywhere, man has played at laying stones on top of stones, to hide the wound of his fragility. I look at the crushing smile of the citadel seated on its cliff-top plinth. I liken those laughing stones to the taciturn spirit of the water which drank and dismembered Nsanga-Norda, and swallowed the once longest bridge in the world. The khaki water innocently weaving its fleece of foam around the Island of Solitudes. The water gorged with arches, menhirs, minarets with their hard iron bones, triumphal arches, corbels and the never-ending ventriloquism of the muezzins. The water on to which, this evening, the Southern Cross will throw its dismayed gaze, while in its belly lotes and piranhas swarm like crabs, dancing the unending rumpus of that other dimension of things. We are the wounded, wrenched from the sky, the water and the hard, grey-thinking stones.

Congo (Republic of the)

No Mercy: A Journey to the Heart of the Congo
by Redmond O'Hanlon
Alfred A. Knopf, 1997

Like a modern-day *Moby-Dick*, Redmond O'Hanlon's *No Mercy* is a big, sprawling book about a quest by an obsessed, even half-demented man. O'Hanlon is his own Ahab, but instead of a white whale he is searching for *mokélé-mbembé*, a creature resembling a dinosaur that has been reported for many years to be living in the remote waters of Lake Télé in the Republic of the Congo. The reports come from the Pygmies – traditionally a reliable source. It was information from Pygmies, O'Hanlon points out, that led to the "discovery" of the okapi or forest giraffe.

As with *Moby-Dick*, the journey, not the arrival, matters. The reader who turns the pages looking for the payoff at the end will miss much of what makes this book so fascinating. *No Mercy* is a funny and harrowing adventure story, a brutally honest self-exploration, and a rich account of a little-known part of Africa.

Accompanied by Marcellin Agnagna, a moody Congolese scientist, and by his friend Lary Shaffer, a stalwart though foul-mouthed professor from upstate New York, O'Hanlon journeys upriver on a hideously overcrowded boat, undertakes an arduous looping reconnaissance of the territory north of Lake Télé, then (without Shaffer, who has bailed out) forges on to Lake Télé itself. For this journey, as on previous journeys to Borneo and the Amazon, O'Hanlon has chosen a region of the world that has been minimally affected by "Western civilization" and therefore offers the closest possible approximation to the experience of the nineteenth-century explorers: mud huts, spears, Pygmies, and sorcery in the land of the Congo River.

Where O'Hanlon transcends a certain neo-colonialist stance is in his compassion: a compassion so deep and unsettling that it eventually threatens to unseat his reason. Toward the end of the journey, perhaps frustrated at how little he can do for the people, O'Hanlon adopts a baby gorilla: cradling it, talking to it, even sleeping with it like a new mother.

The title *No Mercy* has an obvious application to the unrelenting poverty, fear, and violence O'Hanlon encounters in the Congo, but his companions make it plain that it also applies to the comfortable Western world that has caused so many of Africa's problems. "Really, the whites are terrible," says Marcellin. "They brought the guns here and now they say don't kill your wildlife. They're cruel one minute, sentimental the next." O'Hanlon appears to accept the point, but by the end of the book – sick, exhausted, impoverished, emotionally raw, and dependent on an African fetish he has carried for most of the journey – he seems more a victim of the Congo than a victimizer.

———

A dignified, middle-aged man, with a thin mustache and beard, stood behind Bague, wearing nothing but a once-white loincloth, encrusted with dirt – two filthy squares of cotton, front and back, tied to a string round his waist. … Just above his pubis was an open ulcer, a raised, black, shiny mound of infection, four inches across. The pink inner sides of the pit, one and a half inches deep, moved slightly as he breathed. …

Lary drew a tube of Savlon, a bandage and a safety-pin from his pocket. "We're out of dressings," he said, his voice constricted. "You gave them all away, in Manfouété. Yaws." And, "Here, you do it," he said. Lary was crying. He was silently crying: big, real tears ran down his cheeks, into his beard … The hole smelt of rotten fish. I filled it with Savlon, unrolled the bandage round the man's waist and fastened it with the already rusted pin. …

"He'll die," said Marcellin. "He'll die in three weeks."

Djibouti

Somebody Else: Arthur Rimbaud in Africa
by Charles Nicholl
University of Chicago Press, 1999 (first published 1997)

At the age of twenty-five, the renegade French poet Arthur Rimbaud gave up his country and career and travelled to East Africa by way of the Middle Eastern port of Aden. Little is known of the remaining twelve years of his life. A thin, laconic, prematurely greying figure, Rimbaud worked as a trader, moving cloth, gold, and rifles by caravan across Somalia and Ethiopia. He lived for a time with "l'Abyssine" – an Ethiopian woman. Outside the region, rumours sprang up about him. Some said he was a slaver as well as a gun-runner. Some said he was dead.

In *Somebody Else* the British writer Charles Nicholl reconstructs Rimbaud's African years with the help of scattered documents and background information gleaned from his own trips to the region. Nicholl's account of life in Ethiopia in the 1880s is remarkable, as are his painterly descriptions of the Ethiopian highlands, but his book is unique in its portrait of the tiny and little-known country of Djibouti, which Rimbaud passed through in 1885 when it was a French outpost. Nicholl's chapter "The Air of Djibouti" alone is more illuminating than any of the few slim volumes currently available about the country.

"In Djibouti," writes Nicholl, "one sees the last decaying remnants of the French in East Africa – the crumbling colonnades, the pitted grey walls, the street-signs in that peculiarly French shade of blue – and one hears it too, in that lovely flattened-out African French …" Though it gained its independence in 1977 (relatively late), Djibouti remains a French enclave, "propped up by French money, French soldiers and French cuisine." Barren of natural resources, it serves mainly as a strategic seaport, a gateway to Ethiopia, and a magnet for young Ethiopian girls fleeing poverty, who end up as prostitutes in the bars and clubs.

"One sees 'l'Abyssine' again and again in the bars of Harar and Dire Dawa and most of all in Djibouti," Nicholl writes. "They get hassled by the grossly underpaid police for backhanders: I saw a policeman spit in the face of an Ethiopian girl and take off his leather

belt as if to whip her. They get sneered at by the upstanding Muslim Djiboutiens. ... They live in a hostile world, a world that insults them." Nicholl befriends a 23-year-old woman named Ainalam, meaning "Eyes of Africa," and she tells him about a Belgian man in his thirties who, like Rimbaud, looked older, and who lived with her for several happy months. Her description and his own imagination give Nicholl a glimpse of Rimbaud's time with his Ethiopian lover. "He listens to her broken improvised French – *marci* for *merci*, *ristoree* for *restaurant*, *bizoo* for *baiser*. He chews the little purse-shaped parcels of *khat* which she feeds into his mouth. He looks into the large, limpid eyes of Africa."

Khat is the mildly narcotic leaf that is harvested and chewed by the ton throughout the region, contributing significantly to the local economy and blamed by governments for reducing productivity. Nicholl tries it, and offers an inviting description of "browsing" on the glossy leaves like a monkey cushioned in the forest canopy. Though this is one of the most pleasant images of Djibouti in this book, there are many other vivid snapshots of this "illusory" little country, from the pink and orange light in the side streets of the capital to the "echoing ravines and strange black dunes" of the salt lake of Assal – the lowest point on the continent of Africa.

———

The *khat* markets have something of the *joie de vivre* of a flower market. Great bunches of glossy green foliage are brandished and compared. You are invited to smell them, to bury your nose in the leaves, to lose yourself for a moment as you do in a bouquet of sweet-smelling flowers.

"*Goutez, chef. C'est comme votre whisky ...*"

The smell is slight, sweetish, herbal: something like the smell of sorrel, Waugh thought. It has a pleasant overtone of summer gardens: the clippings of an overgrown hedge, the tang of snapped wood. The tiny leaflets at the centre of the cluster have a purplish tinge.

I am sometimes invited to take *khat* with Gina [Ainalam] in her room above the Historil. One of the girls who live with her – a plump Addis girl called Million, essentially the maid

of Gina's little household – is despatched to purchase some. She brings it back in a polybag. She washes it, rolls it up in a cloth. It sits at our feet for a bit. There is a thermos of *chai*, and small cups, and a fresh pack of cigarettes on the floor between us. There is the ceiling fan, and Rahel Johannes singing that haunting Ethiopian soul music: touches of Indian *raga* and Algerian *rai* mixed up with a backing of ghostly Basement Tape keyboards and horns.

Gina unwraps the bundle, holds it up like a bouquet, smooths the leaves. "*Faut pas tomber,*" she says, with a faintly lascivious smile. The leaves shouldn't droop. Should they do so, Million the maid will be in for trouble.

Egypt

Out of Egypt by André Aciman

Farrar, Straus and Giroux, 1994

A writer, one would think, would have to be crazy to invite comparisons to Marcel Proust. André Aciman, the author of this skilled and atmospheric boyhood memoir, is at least sly enough to make his allusions indirectly.

As the author's uncle Vili is about to leave the country, he visits the boy's bedroom and, "with something like mock scorn on his face," picks up a book. "Do people still read this?" he asks. "More than ever," the boy replies. "Another Jew," says Uncle Vili. "No, a half-Jew," says André. But then, after putting the book back, Uncle Vili begins "quoting in French the long, sinuous prose of the first few sentences."

In fact, however, *Out of Egypt* is so beautifully written that it can stand the comparison. Aciman finds in sunbaked Alexandria a languid sensuality like that of Proust's Paris or Balbec, and the themes of his book – loss, regret, memory, the pleasures and cruelties of family life – will be familiar to readers of *In Search of Lost Time*. Perhaps most obviously, Aciman is writing about the end of an era, and about an Egyptian Jewish community that is both privileged and threatened, and faces the outside world with a mixture of arrogance, contempt, and frustrated love.

The author's family arrives in Egypt from Constantinople in 1905. Like many other Turkish Jews, they speak French and Italian as well as Ladino and some Arabic, and they prefer to think of themselves as Italian. The family leaves Egypt some time after the Suez war, when the nationalist government seizes the livelihood of Jews and makes it impossible to stay. This long-anticipated expulsion hangs over most of the narrative, giving it a kind of prospective nostalgia.

Out of Egypt has little plot, but it compensates with an extraordinary gallery of family portraits, beauties and grotesques alike. Om Ramadan, the washerwoman, invites young André to peer into her empty eye socket. Uncle Vili, an enthusiastic Fascist, makes his family dress in black shirts and donate their jewellery to Mussolini – but he is secretly a spy for the British. André's deaf mother is tender and loving, but capable of letting out a terrible shriek when angry or

frustrated. In a grocery store one day, she slaps a young man when she notices him mocking her, then throws him to the ground and beats him up. André emerges as a precocious and observant child, essentially solitary despite his fascination for the world of adults of all races and classes. (His father brags that André "knows every cook and servant in our building," but other relatives are less than happy about this fact.)

The family squabbles, petty treacheries, and long-standing feuds that occupy the characters take place against the intermittently glimpsed background of Alexandria, a city of great beauty, great antiquity, and extraordinary cultural richness. Even though the narrator knows his time there will probably be limited, he doesn't really see and appreciate Alexandria until it is almost time to go. At its heart, *Out of Egypt* is about leaving a place that one realizes one loves only at the last moment.

———

Often a neighbor, friends, Aunt Flora, or others would sit on the balcony outside of the Saint's dining room, and everyone would talk quietly under the delicate shade of a striped awning, hardly a breeze fluttering, with sunlight shifting so slowly that it could be hours before everyone would pick up their chairs and move to an adjacent balcony to resume conversations filled invariably with gossip, tears, venom, and self-pity. When one of the women was moved to cry, she would do so softly, quietly, her face folded into her chest, holding a crumpled handkerchief against her mouth, not because she was ashamed of crying in front of the others, but so as not to wake up Monsieur Jacques, who did not like having his naps interrupted by women whom he lumped together dismissively in the category of *sales comédiennes*, sobbing or no sobbing.

Thus the summer hours would linger, and the Sudanese boy servant, who had taken forever to bring out the rainbow assortment of sherbets, seemed to take yet another eternity to come back to clear the sticky dishes from the balcony. And even then, there were still so many of these afternoon hours before dusk set in that, in Aunt Flora's words, Egypt had the longest hours in the world.

Egypt

Mountolive by Lawrence Durrell

Dutton, 1961 (first published 1958)

As a promising young British diplomat fluent in Arabic, David Mountolive spends several months with the Hosnanis, a Christian Coptic family living in Alexandria. He becomes friends with the smooth and cultivated older brother Nessim, he is impressed by the inarticulate power of the harelipped younger brother Narouz, and for most of the summer he carries on a discreet affair with Leila, the mother – apparently with the tacit consent of her wheelchair-bound husband. Years later, after diplomatic appointments in other parts of the world, Mountolive returns as the British ambassador to Egypt, and before long he hears troubling rumours about Nessim Hosnani.

Mountolive is the third volume in Lawrence Durrell's Alexandria Quartet, but although knowledge of the first two volumes, *Justine* and *Balthazar*, will add to one's appreciation of *Mountolive*, the novel stands well on its own. The four books in the Quartet, meant by the author to examine various aspects of love, reflect on one another but don't proceed chronologically, and it is not essential to read them in sequence.

Durrell is renowned for his ability to set a scene, and his Alexandria is steeped in the exotic. A mélange of French, Greek, Italian, and Arabic influences, it resembles a medieval European city transplanted to Africa. "The Alexandrians themselves were strangers and exiles to the Egypt which existed below the glittering surface of their dreams, ringed by the hot deserts and fanned by the bleakness of a faith which renounced worldly pleasure: the Egypt of rags and sores, of beauty and desperation. ... The ambience, the social manner, everything was different, was cast in a European mould where somehow the camels and palm-trees and cloaked natives existed only as a brilliantly coloured frieze, a backcloth to a life divided in its origins."

Among the characters that populate Durrell's Alexandria are the irreverent novelist Ludwig Pursewarden, his beautiful blind sister, and Maskelyne, the lean, ascetic, hawk-like War Office official whose warnings about Nessim Hosnani go unheeded. Memlik Pasha, the

local potentate, accepts bribes in the form of rare copies of the Koran with money interleaved between the pages, and has those who oppose him "elegantly maimed or deftly blinded." Though the reader may sometimes wonder whether this cast of characters is too good to be true – too cultured, too mysterious, too bizarre – the authority of Durrell's prose style, and his evident erudition, help us suspend disbelief.

Mountolive himself, the handsome young Arabist and ambassador, is lent believability by a wealth of detail gleaned from Durrell's own Foreign Office experience. Though his knowledge of the country's language and culture enables him to pass easily for a Muslim, Mountolive feels increasingly alienated from the country and confused about the loyalties of those he thought were friends and allies. His attempt to reestablish the lost connection ends in near-disaster and cracks (at least temporarily) his smooth diplomatic façade.

He slipped lightly downstairs into the dusky street, counting his money and smiling. It was the best hour of the day in Alexandria – the streets turning slowly to the metallic blue of carbon paper but still giving off the heat of the sun. Not all the lights were on in the town, and the large mauve parcels of dusk moved here and there, blurring the outlines of everything, repainting the hard outlines of buildings and human beings in smoke. Sleepy cafés woke to the whine of mandolines which merged in the shrilling of heated tyres on the tarmac of streets now crowded with life, with white-robed figures and the scarlet dots of *tarbushes*. The window-boxes gave off a piercing smell of slaked earth and urine. The great limousines soared away from the Bourse with softly crying horns, like polished flights of special geese. To be half-blinded by the mauve dusk, to move lightly, brushing shoulders with the throng, at peace, in that dry inspiriting air … these were the rare moments of happiness upon which he stumbled by chance, by accident. The pavements still retained their heat just as water-melons did when you cut them open at dusk; a damp heat slowly leaking up through the thin soles of one's shoes. The sea-winds were moving in to invest the upper town with their damp coolness, but as yet

one only felt them spasmodically. One moved through the dry air, so full of static electricity (the crackle of the comb in his hair), as one might swim through a tepid summer sea full of creeping cold currents. He walked towards Baudrot slowly through little isolated patches of smell – a perfume shed by a passing woman, or the reek of jasmine from a dark archway – knowing that the damp sea air would soon blot them all out. It was the perfect moment for an *apéritif* in the half-light.

Egypt

Adrift on the Nile by Naguib Mahfouz

Translated from the Arabic by Frances Liardet

Anchor Books, 1994 (first published 1966)

In much of his work, Egypt's leading novelist Naguib Mahfouz is preoccupied with the social decay and spiritual emptiness that followed the revolution of 1952, when Nasser's Arab nationalists overthrew a corrupt royalist regime. (Mahfouz has been critical of that regime too, and of British colonialism in Egypt.) Mahfouz's fiction is marked by a clear, harsh view of modern Egyptian life, and his characters are frequently unsympathetic.

Adrift on the Nile, one of the brief novels Mahfouz wrote in the 1960s after completing his massive Cairo Trilogy, is an exception to the rule and a good introduction to his work. Though its theme is familiar – the absurdity and emptiness of life in Cairo, and the yearning for a serious existence – it is marked by an unaccustomed sympathy, even tenderness, for the characters.

The novel's main setting is a houseboat on the Nile where Anis Zaki, a bored and aimless civil servant, spends his leisure time in a narcotic daze induced by smoking kif (a mixture of tobacco and marijuana) in his water pipe, or using it to brew "magic coffee." An educated man with an extensive library on the boat, Anis dreams of ancient times and imagines a whale that lives in the Nile and swims to his boat to visit him

In the evenings Anis serves as master of ceremonies, tending the water pipe for a group of male and female friends who gather to smoke, banter, and flirt with one another. They have families and jobs – the group includes an actor, a lawyer, a translator, an art critic, and a writer of short stories – but their approach to life is essentially cynical and unserious. Though their gatherings are sometimes roiled by political disputes or romantic misunderstandings, the friends are not really challenged to examine their lives until a new character arrives: Samara Bahgat, an elegant woman journalist whom Ragab the actor sees as "an alarmingly serious person."

Despite its brief length, *Adrift on the Nile* is unhurried and atmospheric. Little happens for most of the book, and the relationships

71

among the characters are allowed to unfold gradually. Much of the story moves in and out of the dreamy, drug-blurred mind of Anis, slipping sometimes into a stream of consciousness, and the narrative shifts fluidly from the first to second to third persons. Mahfouz's novels sometimes read like indictments of Egyptian society, but this one conveys the sense of what it is like for an essentially decent but troubled and drifting man to live in that society.

—

Ragab poured Samara a whiskey. Anis saw Sana snatching a furtive look at Samara from beneath her curls, and he smiled. As the coals glowed, he became merry. He offered the water pipe to Samara, but she declined, and all his encouragement was in vain. Everything was silent, save for the bubbling of the pipe. Then they were swept away on a stream of diverse remarks. American planes had made strikes on North Vietnam. Like the Cuban crisis, remember? And as for the rumors, there was no end to them. The world was teetering on the brink of an abyss. The price of meat, the problems of the government food cooperatives – and what about the workers and the peasants? And corruption, and hard currency, and socialism, and the way the streets were jammed with private cars? And Anis said to himself: All these things lie in the bowl of the pipe, to go up in smoke, like the vegetable dish, *mulukhiya*, which Amm Abduh cooked for lunch that day. Like our old motto, "If I were not, I would wish to be." And when a light like the light of these embers blazes in the heavens, the astronomer says that a star has exploded, and in turn the planets around it, and everything has been blown to dust. And one day the dust fell onto the surface of the earth and life sprang from it …

Egypt

In an Antique Land by Amitav Ghosh

Vintage Departures, 1994 (first published 1992)

The Indian writer Amitav Ghosh approaches Egypt from a combination of perspectives that you are unlikely to find anywhere else: that of a Hindu living among Egyptian Muslims, and that of a scholar researching the world of twelfth-century Egypt (and India) while living in a twentieth-century village. The result is a quiet, graceful, and illuminating book about the interplay of cultures and the enduring influence of the individual.

Ghosh goes to Egypt to enroll as a graduate student at the University of Alexandria, but he tells us almost nothing about the university or the city. Instead, we learn more than one would have thought possible about the tiny village of Lataifa where he finds a home. Ghosh lives at first under the roof of the enormous and overbearing shopkeeper Abu-'Ali, one of whose first acts is to try to "lay claim" to Ghosh's radio. He discusses religion with the local imams, and gets to know the caretaker and part-time sorcerer 'Amm Taha, who wrings the neck of a hoopoe that flies into Ghosh's window, saying he needs the blood for a fertility spell. So immersed does Ghosh become in the details of life in this village of four hundred people that he hardly seems to look beyond it. He refers a few times to a somewhat larger village called Nashawy, and it is startling to learn, after he has been living in Lataifa for many weeks, that Nashawy, to which he has not yet travelled, is only about a mile away.

One of the main themes of *In an Antique World* is that even the lives of those who live in a tiny Egyptian village radiate far across the globe, and that the worlds of the twelfth and twentieth centuries may come together more closely than one would have believed possible. While living in Lataifa, Ghosh begins to investigate an intriguing clue in a medieval document: a reference to the Indian slave of a Jewish trader whose papers had been found in a Cairo synagogue. Ghosh is afraid at first that he will be unable to decipher the medieval texts he needs for his research, only to find that the rural dialect of Arabic he has learned to speak is the perfect preparation for the task.

73

Ghosh first learns of the slave's existence because a friend of the Jewish trader once sent "plentiful greetings" to the slave in two letters to the trader. "It is nothing less than a miracle," writes Ghosh, "that anything is known about him at all." Abraham Ben Yiju, the slave's master, was a rabbi's son from Tunisia. He had lived in Egypt and the Middle Eastern port of Aden, and had spent seventeen years in India. "A man of many accomplishments, a distinguished calligrapher, scholar and poet, Ben Yiju had returned to Egypt having amassed great wealth in India." Well educated, he wrote "a clear, carefully crafted prose, with some arresting images hidden under a deceptively plain surface" – not a bad description of Ghosh's own prose style.

Much less is known about Ben Yiju's slave, but by working with a few scattered clues and by drawing on his firsthand knowledge of Indian culture as well as an impressive and lightly worn erudition, Ghosh builds up a plausible (though still sketchy) portrait of a "toddy-loving fisherman" called Bomma, who comes from the Tulu ethnic group of southern India. In so doing, he rescues this man from the undifferentiated, politically simplified morass of what he calls History (using a capital H) – just as his closely observed and sympathetic portraits do the same for the inhabitants of present-day Lataifa.

~

"This is Ustaz Mustafa," said Jabir. "My uncle. He studied law at the University of Alexandria."

Ustaz Mustafa smiled and, nodding vigorously, he addressed me in classical, literary Arabic. "We are honoured," he said, "to have Your Presence amongst us."

I was dismayed to be spoken to in this way, for in concentrating on learning the dialect of the village I had allowed my studies of classical Arabic to fall into neglect. I stuttered, unsure of how to respond, but then, unexpectedly, Jabir came to my rescue. Clapping me on the back, he told his uncle: "He is learning to talk just like us."

Ustaz Mustafa's face lit up. "Insha'allah," he cried. "God willing, he will soon be one of us."

I noticed that he had a habit of flicking back the cuff of his jallabeyya every few minutes or so to steal a quick

look at his watch. I was to discover later that this gesture
was rooted in an anxiety that had long haunted his everyday
existence: the fear that he might inadvertently miss one of
the day's five required prayers. That was why he looked
much busier than anyone else in Lataifa – he was always in
a hurry to get to the mosque. "I have read all about India,"
said Ustaz Mustafa, smiling serenely. "There is a lot of chili
in the food and when a man dies his wife is dragged away
and burnt alive."

Egypt

The Map of Love by Ahdaf Soueif

Anchor Books, 2000

The Map of Love is an ambitious and subtle novel that looks at Egypt through the double perspective of two story lines: one that takes place at the beginning of the twentieth century and one that takes place at the end. Though the heart of the novel is a love affair between a cultured Englishwoman and an Egyptian nobleman, and the prose is often lushly romantic, the book has more on its mind than moonlight in the desert. The relationships between the lovers and their descendants unfold in the context of social and political questions that echo down the generations.

The novel begins with the meeting of two women. Amal is an Egyptian translator, and Isabel is an American journalist who knows Amal's brother, an orchestra conductor and political writer who lives in New York. Isabel travels to Egypt with a trunk full of old papers – some in English and some in Arabic – that once belonged to Isabel's mother. Amal's brother thinks his sister might be willing to help Isabel with translations.

The contents of the trunk prove that the two women are distant cousins. The letters, journals, and articles tell the story of Anna Winterbourne and Sharif Basha, their common ancestors. Fascinated by the documents, Amal slowly sorts them into a coherent story that begins to shed light on her own life and times.

Anna Winterbourne arrives in Egypt as a young widow. Her husband, a victim of empire, has sickened and died returning from the Sudan, where British troops committed atrocities against the rebel Dervishes. After months of depression, Anna is persuaded to travel to Rome and then to Alexandria, where she is looked after by a young British officer and her lady's maid. An educated woman, curious about her surroundings, she begins to learn Arabic and even enlists the young officer to help her travel into the Sinai Desert on horseback, disguised as a man. A group of nationalist Egyptians kidnap her as a hostage and are mortified to find that they have captured a woman. Since neither Anna nor the kidnappers want it to be known what has happened, she is allowed to continue on her journey to the Sinai,

accompanied by Sharif, an reliable older man in the household where Anna has been held.

So begins the relationship of Anna and Sharif. Their encounter might seem the stuff of pulp romance – the well-born Englishwoman and the haughty, dashing Arab – except that we see it from the other side of the cultural divide. Sharif's political views, including his resentment toward the British occupation and his disquiet at the plans of the early Zionists, are explored in leisurely conversations. Anna's marriage to Sharif causes her to be ostracized from the expatriate community, and she is sometimes frustrated by the constraints of Egyptian and Islamic convention: for instance, when she finds she cannot go to the bank alone without causing malicious gossip. But she also makes the surprising observation that – sometimes, at least – a veil can be liberating. "While I was wearing it, I could look wherever I wanted and nobody could look back at me." When Anna learns Arabic, we discover things about the language that a Western writer might not know, such as the link in sound and meaning between words such as *qalb* (heart), *qalab* (to overturn), and *inqilab* (a coup).

The present day, in *The Map of Love*, sometimes seems like a poor imitation of the past. Political divisions have deepened with the years, and the almost gentlemanly kidnappings have given way to random bombings and the killing of tourists. Even love is struggling. Isabel loves Amal's brother, and Amal is courted by a long-time friend, but both relationships are fraught with obstacles. In a sense, *The Map of Love* reaches back to the hopefulness that marked the beginning of the twentieth century in an effort to recreate it at the beginning of the twenty-first.

A story can start from the oddest things: a magic lamp, a conversation overheard, a shadow moving on a wall. For Amal al-Ghamrawi, this story started with a trunk. An old-fashioned trunk made of brown leather, cracked now and dry, with a vaulted top over which run two straps fastened with brass buckles black with age and neglect.

The American had come to Amal's house. Her name was Isabel Parkman and the trunk was locked in the boot of

the car she had hired. Amal could not pretend she was not wary. Wary and weary in advance: an American woman – a journalist, she had said on the phone. But she said Amal's brother had told her to call and so Amal agreed to see her. And braced herself: the fundamentalists, the veil, the cold peace, polygamy, women's status in Islam, female genital mutilation – which would it be?

Equatorial Guinea

Tropical Gangsters by Robert Klitgaard
Basic Books, 1990

Equatorial Guinea, once a colony of Spain, consists of the island of Bioko, where the capital is located, a few smaller islands, and a chunk of mainland territory wedged between Cameroon and Gabon. It is a poor country even by African standards, with a reputation in development circles for "backwardness." "Equatorial Guinea is the worst of the worst," a World Bank economist tells the author of this book.

Robert Klitgaard, a Harvard-trained economist with experience in Asia and Latin America, went to Africa because he believed that that was where the action would be for experts in economic development. He chose Equatorial Guinea because it was an interesting test case: a country with serious economic problems that was small enough to have a limited number of officials and institutions to work with.

In recent years the World Bank and International Monetary Fund have promoted a model for economic development known as structural adjustment. Under structural adjustment, currencies are devalued, export agriculture is encouraged at the expense of domestic food production, and food subsidies are cut. The short-term effect is often devastating for the poor – in Zambia and elsewhere, sudden increases in the price of staple foods have led to riots – and these plans have come under intense criticism.

Klitgaard is surely one of the most charming characters to have peddled this approach in Africa. Ranging widely in his free time from the picturesque dilapidation of Malabo, the capital, he seeks out the few beaches where he can ride his beloved surfboard. He plays the guitar in jam sessions with members of the local rock star's band, and writes a Spanish version of Woody Guthrie's "This Land Is Your Land" that becomes a hit with local children.

As a consultant to the Equatoguinean government, he gets to know many of the government ministers, and uses his influence to help one who is imprisoned and tortured by the authoritarian regime. Rather than dictating policy, he conducts seminars on policymaking and tries to adapt his proposed remedies to local conditions. Though

cocoa had been the country's traditional export, for instance, he reluctantly concludes that the world market for high-quality cocoa doesn't justify the expense of rehabilitating the neglected plantations. After a while, he begins referring to the people of Equatorial Guinea as "we," and he concedes that the term "tropical gangsters" applies not only to the corrupt local officials but also to the profiteering expatriate "experts" and the condescending development officials who fly in for a day or two to lay down the law.

Readers interested in economic development will appreciate the author's insights into the thinking and planning behind one ill-fated plan for economic revival. But the book is so loaded with local colour that even those with no interest in economics will enjoy it for its portrait of a little-known corner of Africa. Though Klitgaard has some blind spots – he blithely equates "indigenous healers" with "witch doctors" and even cannibals – his book is full of surprises, from the mountains of Rio Muni that recall Chinese landscape paintings, to meals of porcupine and enormous land snails, to the career of Francisco Macías Nguema, a former dictator considered by experts to be worse than Idi Amin or Jean-Bedel Bokassa, but whose bloody reign is less known because it took place in this out-of-the-way part of West Africa.

The afternoon cleared up as I unpacked, worked at odds and ends, assembled documents, and made a long list of things to do. At about six in the evening, I took a break and walked to the corner of the house overlooking Malabo. In the gorgeous light of late afternoon, the dilapidated wooden houses of colonial times looked like proud exhibits in a living museum. In the distance, the volcano was in full regalia, its verdant slopes satiny against the sunset, crowned by a pink and mother-of-pearl cloud that crested westward like a giant plume. This natural exultation contrasted with my own ominous forebodings, which I couldn't shake. Later I drove aimlessly around the darkened town. I didn't feel like seeing friends, only somehow reabsorbing my surroundings. It was Saturday night at the end of the world. Beneath the town's available sources of illumination, clumps of men played cards

and checkers, little girls squealed as they hopscotched, boys kicked around small, dirty, half-inflated soccer balls. On the streets slow-moving cars skirted potholes as if performing an elaborate minuet. The palm trees waved wearily in the tropical wind.

Eritrea

To Asmara by Thomas Keneally

Warner Books, 1989

Timothy Darcy, the hero of this novel by the author of *Schindler's List*, is a middle-aged social worker and journalist. While living in the Australian outback, he loses his wife to a man from an alien culture. To forget, he travels from an Australian desert to an African one, and attaches himself to the rebels who are fighting for the independence of the mountainous Red Sea territory of Eritrea. There he finds a cause to believe in, and a woman from another alien culture whose beauty and suffering attract him powerfully.

Like Ethiopia, Eritrea was able to preserve its independence much longer than other countries in Africa. First occupied by Italy in 1889, it fell under British administration after the defeat of Italian forces in 1941. In 1952 it was federated with Ethiopia, giving that land-locked country access to the sea. Ethiopia gradually exerted its power over Eritrea, prompting the formation of the Eritrean Liberation Front (ELF), which led a struggle for independence until its dominance was challenged in the 1970s by the breakaway Eritrean People's Liberation Front (EPLF). Backed by the Soviet Union, Ethiopia deployed tanks and MIG fighter-bombers against the EPLF rebels, torturing and executing those they captured.

To Asmara takes place in late 1987 and early 1988. It follows its hero Darcy into rebel-controlled Eritrea by way of the Sudan, and beyond the front line on a clandestine mission into Ethiopian-occupied territory. Darcy is accompanied by Lady Julia, a veteran British campaigner against female circumcision; Mark Henry, a foul-mouthed American aid worker whose Somali fiancée is being held by the Ethiopians; and Christine Malmédy, who is searching for her father, a legendary filmmaker documenting the war. Together they see how the rebels are not only fighting but also running schools, pharmacies, and hospitals – even performing cosmetic surgery – in caves and in bunkers dug out of the desert.

The novel has been criticized for glossing over some uncomfortable history (including the virtual civil war between the ELF and EPLF) and for its admiring descriptions of the EPLF rebels. In truth, the rebels

as presented here are almost too good to be true. The supposedly hard-headed Lady Julia raves, "They are jumping a gulf which no other race has jumped … A new level of moral being!" They even smell nice: "Two of them, a girl and a boy, climbed aboard with us. I smelled their somehow pleasant musk of sweat and antique dust." The Ethiopians, on the other hand, are as evil as B-movie villains: bombing and napalming civilians, hacking the arms off their captives, and even "plucking" the gold nose bands from the faces of massacred Eritrean women "as if they were gathering fruit."

But despite its likely exaggerations, the discipline and fanaticism of the Eritrean rebels rings true when compared with real-life accounts of other African guerrillas, like the Guinea-Bissau fighters described in Barbara Cornwall's *The Bush Rebels*, as well as with fictional accounts based on personal experience, like the Angolan novel *Mayombe*. The taut, patriotic, and sometimes authoritarian society that has sprung up in Eritrea since independence is another sign that Thomas Kencally essentially got it right.

I saw black ambulances, inching slowly along ahead of us, occupied most of the valley floor now. Moka, Salim, the kinswoman Amna, and I abandoned the truck and began walking toward the terraces outside the operating theater, where the stones were covered with wounded on stretchers.

I found myself shivering at the sight. I flexed my jaw to keep my teeth from giving away my condition of terror. As a reporter of fact, I counted perhaps fifty litters set down there. It was all reminiscent, I thought, as the trembling spasm gave out, of the tent of the Afabet women. There was a notable lack of protest, of moaning. I thought at first that this was because the wounded must all have been sedated for their ambulance journey. But then I noticed certain signs of the usual mannerliness of the Horn. For example: A boy lowered from the back of one of the ambulances onto the stone terrace insisted on reaching his thin arm up and shaking hands with each of the stretcher bearers. The next soldier lifted down did exactly the same.

"Why do they all shake hands?" I asked Moka.

But it was Salim who answered absently. His eyes were darting for a sight of his wounded niece. "Pride. They don't wish to die without having thanked everyone they should."

Ethiopia

The Emperor by Ryszard Kapuscinski

Translated from the Polish by William R. Brand
and Katarzyna Mroczkowska-Brand

Harcourt Brace Jovanovich, 1983

"Few people had heard anything, and those who had did not know what to think about the whole affair. For them it was a Palace matter, and the Palace had always been inaccessible, unreachable, impenetrable, beyond understanding, on a different planet." These words could have come from Kafka's novel *The Castle*, but in fact they come from *The Emperor*, an account of the last days of the reign of Emperor Haile Selassie.

The Polish journalist Ryszard Kapuscinski arrived in Ethiopia after the death of the Emperor, and sought out as many members of Haile Selassie's court as he could to create this concentrated, even poetic account. Much of the book is told in the voices of Kapuscinski's informants. To protect their identities we are given no descriptions of their homes or their personal appearance, and each of them is identified (in Kafkaesque style) by initials: T. K.-B., a clerk in the Ministry of the Pen, or G. S.-D., the Emperor's pillow bearer. The effect is ghostly. Though the long quotations from the author's informants seem worked over, more shapely and literary than a literal transcription, they carry conviction.

The court of Haile Selassie, as it emerges in this book, is like something out of a sinister fairy tale. Lions guard the palace, and the Emperor's day begins with reports from his informers (many of them assigned to inform on one another), which the Emperor commits to memory, along with all other facts about his kingdom that he feels it is necessary to know. The day continues with the Hour of Assignments and the Hour of the Cashbox. One servant is assigned to carry the Emperor's lambskin purse, one to arrive and bow to the Emperor when it is time for his next appointment, and another to wipe the dignitaries' shoes with a silk cloth when the Emperor's Japanese dog urinates on them. High officials are chosen and rewarded for their loyalty and their lack of personal initiative. All decisions must come

from the Emperor (or be seen to come from him), all questions must be asked from the top down, and the Emperor must be consulted on even the most trivial of financial expenditures. To bring the poverty and starvation of the countryside to the Emperor's attention is dangerous, and when the Emperor can no longer deny that these problems exist, he responds not by taking action but by bestowing his "highest concern" on the problem. Though dissenters in the kingdom continue to be imprisoned and sometimes beheaded, the Emperor considers himself a reformer because the hands and legs of minor offenders are no longer lopped off.

The Emperor is a fascinating study in how absolute power can leak away imperceptibly, step by step. Even as they plot to depose him, the conspirators in the army of Ethiopia profess their love and undying loyalty to the Emperor. The Emperor, for his part, smoothes over this challenge as he does every other, continuing to praise the loyalty of his military officers and to meet with them. One by one, high court officials are arrested by the army and taken away, without any real protest by the Emperor or any real resistance by his spineless dignitaries. The minor officials go next, then the Emperor's last elderly servant, and finally the tiny, frail Emperor himself, who is packed into the back of a green Volkswagen and taken to the Menelik Palace (the Emperor has fifteen palaces in all), where a few months later he dies.

The greed and cruelty of Haile Selassie's regime, papered over by the ceremony of the court and the Emperor's personal charm and dignity, are forcefully conveyed in this small book. The sympathy one feels for the officers who depose the Emperor – a military council known as the Dergue, led by the taut, solemn young officer Mengistu Haile Mariam – is tempered by the knowledge that these officers would bring in a regime that was even worse.

❧

I was His Most Virtuous Highness's pillow bearer for twenty-six years. I accompanied His Majesty on travels all around the world, and to tell the truth – I say it with pride – His Majesty could not go anywhere without me, since his dignity required that he always take his place on a throne,

and he could not sit on a throne without a pillow, and I was the pillow bearer. I had mastered the special protocol of this specialty, and even possessed an extremely useful, expert knowledge: the height of various thrones. This allowed me quickly to choose a pillow of just the right size, so that a shocking ill fit, allowing a gap to appear between the pillow and the Emperor's shoes, would not occur. In my storeroom I had fifty-two pillows of various sizes, thicknesses, materials, and colors. I personally monitored their storage, constantly, so that fleas -- the plague of our country – would not breed there, since the consequences of any such oversight could lead to a very unpleasant scandal.

Ethiopia

Notes from the Hyena's Belly by Nega Mezlekia
Picador USA, 2001

otes from the Hyena's Belly is the memoir of an Ethiopian, from his birth in the provincial town of Jijiga to the day he leaves the country as a penniless young man. The sardonic voice with which Nega Mezlekia tells his story brings alive the years in which Ethiopia was wrenched away from its ancient traditions and the rule of its seemingly immortal Emperor and thrust into a world of revolutionary violence and crazily shifting allegiances.

Ethiopia would seem to be too subtle a country to be drawn into the crudely polarized ideologies of revolution. A country that had escaped colonial rule and developed a distinctive culture for thousands of years, it existed on an everyday plane and a mythic plane at the same time. When Mezlekia is born – at the same time that Haile Selassie's queen is dying – the nun who assists with the birth announces that there are actually two children in the womb, wearing golden crowns. She calls in a second midwife who, though she arrives drunk, has an impressive reputation. "Tsege had once helped a passing angel, caught between the two worlds, with the agony of childbirth, successfully delivering her young with wings intact."

As a young boy, Mezlekia is taught by a legless instructor in a shack made of twigs. The classes cover nothing but Amharic language and poetry, but the children are exposed to a literature of amazing sophistication. The Amharic alphabet contains 268 characters – some of them duplicates for the same sound, because the characters used to spell "celestial" or "imperial" people or objects must be distinct from those used to spell ordinary things. A form of poetry called a *kinae* carries both a "bronze" or obvious meaning and a "gold" or hidden one, and there is even a puzzle-like form called a "stranded" poem. "One can draw a jagged line through a stranded poem, from top to bottom, breaking it into two independent pieces. Each of these halves rhymes and has its own meaning; put together, the two pieces form a body that gives a third and entirely different meaning."

As he grows older, Mezlekia becomes conscious of the corruption and brutality in Ethiopian society. His friendship with a boy from the west of the country opens his eyes to a medieval system of serfs and feudal lords that has persisted into the twentieth century. He takes part in demonstrations for land reform and is repeatedly jailed, whipped, and tortured. He is shocked to learn how the Emperor's regime tried to cover up the massive famine of 1973 – even to the extent of hiding starving people in camps where they could die in secret.

The military junta that overthrows the Emperor soon shows that it has its own methods of repression. Mezlekia's father, a former clerk who has risen through the ranks of government service, is summarily executed as an official of the old regime. Two new parties emerge: the EPRP, which wants power turned over immediately to a civilian government, and the Meison, which prefers to have the junta stay in charge until the people are educated politically. Both parties resort to rape, torture, and even death squads to strengthen their influence.

Although many students and the intelligentsia support the EPRP, and although the party opposes the junta as he does, Mezlekia has no illusions about them. "These intellectual gangsters," he writes, "would prove to be a far more horrific threat to dissenters than the enemy in uniform." Simply to avoid being killed by one faction or another, Mezlekia and his childhood friend Wondwossen finally leave Ethiopia for Somalia, where they join a rebel movement that is fighting for control of the Ogaden desert.

This brief summary covers barely half – and the least traumatic half – of Mezlekia's adventures and sufferings. Remarkably, he tells his story without self-pity, though not without feeling. Throughout his book, Mezlekia's dry narrative voice finds the interest and even the humour in what might otherwise seem an unrelenting tale of misery. The folk tales interspersed with the narrative – stories in which clever peasants get the best of kings, and monkeys find a way to defeat a lion – hint that his grounding in Ethiopian tradition may have helped provide the courage and flexibility he drew on to survive.

Mr. Alula proceeded to shed light on the morality of wandering hyenas. He explained not only why it was moral to permit the hyenas to reclaim the town at night, but why

89

we should encourage them to do so by throwing discarded bones into the streets after the compounds were locked. He persuasively argued that without hyenas, the city would be forced to hire street sweepers to remove the carcasses of goats run down by speeding trucks, or the remains of street dogs hacked by angry butchers, or the vultures killed in battle over decaying meat. Without timely intervention by the hyenas, the city might even have a homelessness problem.

Sleeping outdoors in Jijiga was the ultimate suicide. It was a vanishing act. The hyenas would cut you up into pieces quicker than the gods could put you together. They would devour you, your shoes, bracelets, linen and anything else you had touched. Beggars know this; they might go hungry, but they always had shelter. They would pull together their slim resources with ten or more of their colleagues and rent a room with a strong door and eighteen latches. Mr. Alula did not enjoy the spectacle of people being eaten by hyenas; but he was a moral man, and had to make tough decisions. He was willing to sacrifice a few individuals so that the rest would have homes. Homelessness, concluded Mr. Alula, is a vivid indication of a shortage of hyenas.

Gabon

Travels in West Africa by Mary Kingsley

Beacon Press, 1988 (first published 1897)

The sheer length of this book has probably put off many potential readers. Photos of the author, looking plain and severe in a high-necked Victorian dress, may have put off others. But it is worthwhile tracking down an unabridged edition, because this is one of the liveliest, funniest, most insightful, and most humane volumes of African exploration ever published.

At the time of her first journey to West Africa, in 1893, Mary Kingsley had made only two overseas trips: one to France and one to the Canary Islands, where she went to recover from the death of her parents the previous year. For years she had looked after her depressed mother and her "delicate" and supercilious brother, and had acted as a researcher for her father, a world traveller and amateur scientist, who paid for her brother's entire education but only for Mary's German lessons. When her brother went to Burma in 1893, leaving her with "five or six months which were not heavily forestalled," she made the brave and unusual decision to travel to Africa, where she would collect specimens of fish and study African religious beliefs, referred to as "fetish."

Travels in West Africa is based on Mary Kingsley's second African voyage. It begins with colourful vignettes of Sierra Leone, the Gold Coast (now Ghana), Fernando Po (now part of Equatorial Guinea), and Lagos, and ends with her ascent of the "Great Peak of Cameroons." She is the twenty-eighth person to have climbed this 13 760-foot mountain, and almost certainly the first woman, though she characteristically makes no mention of this second distinction.

Mary Kingsley's explorations in the French territory that is now Gabon make up most of this book. From the capital of Libreville she travels up the Ogooué River, past Lambaréné where Albert Schweitzer would found his hospital in 1913, to a point beyond the village of Talagouga. Reversing course, she and her party go back down the Ogooué some distance before travelling overland to Lake Ncovi and returning to Libreville by way of the Rembwé River. Much of this territory is occupied by the Fang people (referred to here as the

Fans), who have a well-deserved reputation as warriors. The natural environment presents an array of hazards, too, which Kingsley meets with fortitude and good humour – whether crossing a swamp with a "collar" of leeches around her neck, or extracting herself from a pit lined with ebony spikes. ("It is at these times," she notes, "you realise the blessing of a good thick skirt.")

Though many African ethnic groups have been unjustly described as cannibals, the Fangs did in fact practise ritual cannibalism, eating the remains of relatives in order to absorb their virtues. Noticing a "violent smell" in a hut where she is staying during the overland part of her journey, Kingsley opens one of the bags that are hanging from the roof pole and shakes the contents into her hat. "They were a human hand, three big toes, four eyes, two ears, and other portions of the human frame. The hand was fresh, the others only so so, and shrivelled." She ties up the bag again, replaces it, and writes, "I subsequently learnt that although the Fans will eat their fellow friendly tribesfolk, yet they like to keep a little something belonging to them as a memento."

This may sound like sarcasm, or a calculated attempt to make us shiver, but it is really one of many examples of the sympathetic curiosity that is one of Mary Kingsley's most attractive qualities. "I like Africans in my way," she says, and she makes it clear that she prefers "my friends the Fans" to the demoralized, half-Christianized Africans of the coastal settlements. "The Fan is full of fire, temper, intelligence, and go; very teachable, rather difficult to manage, quick to take offence, and utterly indifferent to human life." Though she wears it lightly, she comes to her travels with the benefit of many years of ethnological research, and she is properly sceptical of what she hears from European officials and missionaries.

On the cover of this book, Rudyard Kipling is quoted as saying of Mary Kingsley, "Being human, she must have been afraid of something, but one never found out what it was." A close reading of this book will reveal that she is afraid of caves, of bees, and of direct confrontations with leopards. But unlike such violent and even murderous explorers as Mungo Park and Henry M. Stanley, she never allows her fears or frustrations to make her brutal. "My chief pride in West Africa," she notes in passing, "is that I have never raised hand nor caused hand to be raised against a native."

—

The first day in the forest we came across a snake – a beauty with a new red-brown and yellow-patterned velvety skin, about three feet six inches long and as thick as a man's thigh. Ngouta met it, hanging from a bough, and shot backwards like a lobster, Ngouta having among his many weaknesses a rooted horror of snakes. This snake the Ogowé natives all hold in great aversion. For the bite of other sorts of snakes they profess to have remedies, but for this they have none. If, however, a native is stung by one he usually conceals the fact that it was this particular kind, and tries to get any chance the native doctor's medicine may give. The Duke stepped forward and with one blow flattened its head against the tree with his gun butt, and then folded the snake up and got as much of it as possible into the bag, while the rest hung dangling out. Ngouta, not being able to keep ahead of the Duke, his Grace's pace being stiff, went to the extreme rear of the party, so that other people might be killed first if the snake returned to life, as he surmised it would. He fell into other dangers from this caution, but I cannot chronicle Ngouta's afflictions in full without running this book into an old-fashioned folio size. We had the snake for supper, that is to say the Fan and I; the others would not touch it, although a good snake, properly cooked, is one of the best meats one gets out here, far and away better than the African fowl.

The Gambia

Our Grandmothers' Drums by Mark Hudson
Grove Weidenfeld, 1990

On a brief visit to the village of Dulaba in The Gambia, a young Englishman named Mark Hudson met three African women walking along a path. They greeted him and disappeared into the bush, but the image of them – brisk, bold, purposeful, almost threatening – haunted him afterwards. "What had they been going so eagerly to do, out there in that thin, featureless forest, on that dismal afternoon?"

Life in England, Hudson finds after returning home, seems "extraordinarily lacklustre, and what was most difficult to bear was the thought that those women's lives were continuing in that other world, and that I would never know anything more about it." Hudson makes up his mind to return, and to investigate the "essential mystery of the lives of the women of Dulaba." The result is one of the most sensitive and graceful books ever written about the lives of African women.

Basing himself at a British medical research centre established in Dulaba years before, Hudson soon attaches himself to one of the *kafo* societies to which women of the same age group belong. As an honorary member of the Saniyoro Kafo (meaning "golden chain") he spends his days hoeing fields with the women, shelling groundnuts, learning the Mandinka language as they banter with each other, and listening to the drumming that drives their work and the songs in which they comment on people and society. Before long the women have written a song or two about him.

Much of what is hidden in the lives of the women is gradually revealed, including their religious beliefs, the rivalries between the kafos, marital strains and infidelities, and "the five main vices of the Gambians: cigarettes, kola nuts, black mints, sugar and Chinese tea." Hudson also learns that as a European he is regarded as a "kind devil," able to "give people things and make them wealthy." All Europeans are believed to have refrigerators stocked with soft drinks and beer, and since Hudson does not have these things, "they assumed I must be hiding them in some secret, inner part of my house, and

that it was only through my wickedness that I was not prepared to part with them."

It may seem inevitable that a young Englishman bored with his life at home and fascinated with the lives of Gambian women should become sexually involved with one. Hudson is strongly attracted to several of the women, particularly the pretty and independent-minded Sona, but after some time he seems to absorb the worldview of the kafo: their sense of connection with one another and their belief that the important events of their lives are fated. When Sona proves unattainable he turns his attention to other women, and the "connection" he eventually forms with the woman he calls "my person" proves unexpectedly fulfilling. In a sense, he has fallen in love with the kafo as a whole.

Perhaps the most controversial chapter of this book is "The Crocodile," in which Hudson describes what he was able to observe of the initiation ritual in which the village girls are subjected to "circumcision." Hudson is disturbed by the thought of the physical ordeal the girls will undergo, especially when he sees some of the girls lying on a mat afterwards, "almost inert, as though numbed with shock." He is more disturbed when he learns that the local version of circumcision is not the "ritual incision in the clitoris" that had been reported but a much more painful and extensive operation. But even more unsettling is his discovery that the local women regard circumcision as an absolute necessity and an essential part of a ceremony without which no girl can become a real woman or a "pure Muslim." Their knowledge that the Koran does not mention the practice makes no difference to their belief.

Mark Hudson has a painterly eye, and scenes of life in Dulaba sometimes remind him of the old masters. Dressed to attend a special prayer at the mosque, he writes, "I wore a long gown and a curious tall cap, both of a deep bottle green. I looked like some vaguely ecclesiastical figure from the background of a quattrocento genre painting; in a word, I looked absurd." Watching the village women at a funeral, "their bodies racked, bent double with suffering," he is reminded of "one of those medieval paintings of Doomsday, in which the timeless village calm is riven by apocalyptic chaos." More often, though, his vivid pictures of a Gambian village are centred in the experiences of those who live there. Hudson scarcely mentions his life in England throughout the entire book, and compared to the

immediacies of hunger, struggle, death, and desire in the village, that life seems to have become a distant dream.

———

At the beginning of September the maize harvest began, and the period of hunger came to an end. The maize was much harder than the European and North American varieties, and unsuitable for boiling. Instead it was roasted over braziers, and everywhere the young children could be seen sinking their teeth into the frizzled cobs.

When I went into Natoma's compound, I found her mother and all the children of the compound sitting deseeding the raw cobs into a huge enamel basin. It was difficult work, as I discovered when I joined them, and soon my nails were bleeding. But they worked with great enthusiasm. Mariatou, the niece, was sitting on the opposite side of the basin. She smiled. "*Kongko a tata,*" she said, gesturing off into the middle distance. "Hunger has gone."

The raw grain was pounded into a fine flour which was steamed to make *futo*. Some evenings we would gather round our basin in Demba's room, and lift the lid to find it full of this futo, which in this state reminded me of the granular substance used to fill cracks in window frames. To the excitement of all, water would be added – not too much and not too little – and mixed into it. Then Sirrah or Ndey-Touti would come in with a bowl of thin leaf sauce – like algid pond slime – or a thin, hot groundnut sauce, and pour it over the mixture. We dug our hands into the sludgy mass, piling it into our mouths with our fingers. There was something marvellously satisfying and reassuring about this food, and we ate it with a sense of exultation, for the appearance of the futo signified the end of hunger – the end of suffering.

Ghana

All God's Children Need Traveling Shoes
by Maya Angelou
Vintage, 1991 (first published 1986)

Perhaps because they come with more expectations, or because they take the failings of African society more personally, African-American writers have produced some of the most harshly critical books on Africa, from Richard Wright's *Black Power* to Keith Richburg's *Out of America*.

Many of these books are written soon after a stay on the continent, when shocks and disillusionments are still fresh. Maya Angelou's memoir *All God's Children Need Traveling Shoes*, on the other hand, was written almost twenty-five years after Angelou – a poet, singer, actor, and single mother in her early thirties – arrived with her son in Ghana. Though some details may have faded in the author's mind, the meaning of the experience is clear, and the joys and heartaches of the experience are conveyed in prose that has the balance and simplicity of a fable.

Angelou's stay in Ghana happened literally by accident. After three days in the country, en route to Liberia, Angelou's teenage son Guy was seriously injured in a car accident. While his mother, angry and frightened, looked after him, she was gradually drawn into the band of "Revolutionist Returnees": black Americans who had been attracted to Ghana by the promised welcome of the charismatic socialist leader Kwame Nkrumah. When that welcome failed to materialize, the Returnees, wounded by the experience of racism in America and with a deep need for a new and more nurturing home, used their imaginations to convince themselves that they were living in the Ghana of their dreams. "I was soon swept into an adoration for Ghana as a young girl falls in love, heedless and with slight chance of finding the emotion requited."

Angelou takes a job at the University of Ghana, makes Ghanaian friends, and finds romance with a rich and handsome businessman from Mali. The gestures, vocal rhythms, and traditional customs of the Africans she meets reveal unexpected links to the ways of black Americans. Though she does not encounter the open-armed welcome

many Returnees first expect, what she does find is in some ways better: an implicit belief that as a black woman she cannot be a stranger. "To many Africans only Whites could be strangers. All Africans belonged somewhere, to some clan." She is taken for a Bambara and an Ahanta, and in an eerie and powerful scene toward the end of the book she experiences a sense of déjà vu on approaching an Ewe village, and is struck with an electrifying sense of mutual recognition on meeting the villagers, the descendants of children whose parents were taken away by slavers.

This historical link has a more sinister side. In Accra she asks herself, "Were those laughing people who moved in the streets with such equanimity today descendants of slave-trading families? Did that one's ancestor sell mine or did that grandmother's grandmother grow fat on the sale of my grandmother's grandmother?" Treated by an African receptionist as rudely as by a white clerk in America, she reflects that history may have had a larger role than she suspected in the way she and other black Americans were treated, both in Ghana and at home. "Was the odor of old slavery so obvious that people were offended and lashed out at us automatically? Had what we judged as racial prejudice less to do with race and more to do with our particular ancestors' bad luck at having been caught, sold and driven like beasts?"

Though this book includes a number of memorable episodes, including the visit of Malcolm X to Ghana on his return from Mecca, it is perhaps most compelling in the way it addresses what the novelist David Bradley called "the question at the heart of the African-American dilemma: what's in a hyphen?"

⁓

I drank and admitted to a boundless envy of those who remained on the continent, out of fortune or perfidy. Their countries had been exploited and their cultures had been discredited by colonialism. Nonetheless, they could reflect through their priests and chiefs on centuries of continuity. The lowliest could call the names of ancestors who lived centuries earlier. The land upon which they lived had been in their people's possession beyond remembered time.

Despite political bondage and economic exploitation, they had retained an ineradicable innocence.

I doubted if I, or any Black from the diaspora, could really return to Africa. We wore skeletons of old despair like necklaces, heralding our arrival, and we were branded with cynicism. In America we danced, laughed, procreated; we became lawyers, judges, legislators, teachers, doctors, and preachers, but as always, under our glorious costumes we carried the badge of a barbarous history sewn to our dark skins. It had often been said that Black people were childish, but in America we had matured without ever experiencing the true abandon of adolescence. Those actions which appeared to be childish most often were exhibitions of bravado, not unlike humming a jazz tune while walking into a gathering of the Ku Klux Klan.

Ghana

No Sweetness Here by Ama Ata Aidoo

The Feminist Press, 1995 (first published 1970)

*N*o *Sweetness Here*, a collection of short stories, is the first book by the novelist and playwright Ama Ata Aidoo. Satisfying in itself, the book is also intriguing in the way it shows the rapid development of the author's talent.

Aidoo is concerned with the contradictions of life in a newly independent Ghana. In "Everything Counts," the first story in the collection, a young woman studying abroad argues with her expatriate friends about the wig she wears. She finds it more convenient than fussing with her hair, but her friends tell her that to wear a wig means "we have no confidence in ourselves." By the time she marries and returns home, she has agreed to wear her own hair, "lightly touched to make it easier to comb" – but she returns to a country that seems superficial and mercenary, where the girls in the first class she teaches are all wearing wigs.

"Everything Counts" is a solid, workmanlike story that makes its points clearly. In the stories that follow, the author continues to address social and political issues, but with more depth, more concern with character, and occasional flashes of eloquence.

In the second story, "For Whom Things Did Not Change," Aidoo leaves behind the distancing third person and begins to make her points in dialogue. A husband and wife discuss the problem of young girls who sleep with "big men" – with acute observation but a little didactically, as if they were performers in an educational play. Later in the story, an educated young man struggles to convince a rural cook to make him ordinary food, not the braised lamb's liver and other English dishes he is used to making. But Zirigu the cook takes pride in the dishes he has learned to make – and in fact has forgotten how to make the traditional food of his people. "Massa, I beg," he pleads in pidgin. "Don't make so. I no wan' vex you. This here chop, 'e be white man's chop. 'E be the chop I cook for all massas, for fifteen years."

It is a moving scene, but the story rises to a new level before it is done. In the last few pages Zirigu speaks his mind in a lengthy

100

soliloquy to the young "massa" (an African, though his education makes Zirigu think of him as white). Zirigu, we gradually realize, is no longer speaking in pidgin, as if we are listening not to his words but to his listener's understanding of them – or even as if we are listening directly to Zirigu's thoughts. For six or seven pages Zirigu describes his life and his experience of independence, in a simple direct English in which long phrases contain only words of one syllable. He joins the army, travels throughout West Africa, becomes a yam trader with his brother, and is cheated of his savings. He gets a job as a cook and servant at a government rest house, serving white men and then a few black men who have been given positions of responsibility. When independence comes, he hopes and expects that the servants' quarters will be given electric lights and a toilet. Eventually the walls are painted and a set of steps repaired. There are no electric lights and no toilet, but the old pail in the lavatory is taken away and replaced with a new one. The pail itself is never described – is it made of galvanized steel or colourful plastic? – but it stands as a powerful symbol of the betrayals and disappointments of the new order.

In the stories that follow, Aidoo develops her mastery of dialogue and monologue. "In the Cutting of a Drink" is a simple but powerful monologue by a young man who has just returned from searching for his sister in Accra. "Something to Talk About on the Way to the Funeral" reconstructs a woman's life in the unsparing commentary of the mourners on the way to her funeral. And in the final story, "Other Versions," the author returns to the theme of the African abroad in a story that culminates with a touching encounter on a subway car.

I asked Duayaw if people who did not know me would dance with me. He said "Yes." I lifted my eyes, my uncles, and looked at those four young women sitting round a table alone. They were sitting all alone, I say. I got up.

I hope I am making myself clear, uncles, but I was trembling like water in a brass bowl.

Immediately one of them saw me, she jumped up and said something in that kind of white man's language which everyone, even those who have not gone to school, speak in the city. I shook my head. She said something else in the

language of the people of the place. I shook my head again. Then I heard her ask me in Fante whether I wanted to dance with her. I replied "Yes."

Ei! my little sister, are you asking me a question? Oh! You want to know whether I found Mansa? I do not know. ... Our uncles have asked me to tell everything that happened there, and you too! I am cooking the whole meal for you, why do you want to lick the ladle now?

Yes, I went to dance with her. I kept looking at her so much I think I was all the time stepping on her feet. I say, she was as black as you and I, but her hair was very long and fell on her shoulders like that of a white woman. I did not touch it but I saw it was very soft. Her lips with that red paint looked like a fresh wound. There was no space between her skin and her dress. Yes, I danced with her. When the music ended, I went back to where I was sitting. I do not know what she told her companions about me, but I heard them laugh.

Guinea

The Dark Child by Camara Laye

Translated from the French
by James Kirkup and Ernest Jones

Farrar, Straus and Giroux, 2000 (first published 1954)

The Dark Child by Camara Laye is one of the classic accounts of growing up in West Africa. Told in a pure, sometimes biblical style, and suffused with a piercing nostalgia for a world that is slipping away, *The Dark Child* would seem to be a memoir written by an old man looking back after many years. It is startling to realize that the author was still in his twenties when he wrote it.

Camara Laye grew up in the town of Kouroussa on the inland plain of French Guinea. Though his father was a blacksmith and goldsmith, and a man of tradition, he wanted a Western education for his son and never passed on much of what he knew of his people, the Malinké. Even as a child, it seems, Camara Laye was haunted by the sense that he was losing something. "What words did my father utter?" he asks himself about the incantations his father murmurs as he is smelting gold. Watching the start of the rice harvest in a rural village, he sees that the head of each family goes out at dawn to cut the first swath from his field. The old villagers no doubt knew the reason for this custom. "But I was not old enough nor curious enough to inquire, nor did I become so until I was no longer in Africa."

At the centre of this book are the chapters in which Camara Laye describes his initiation into adulthood at about the age of thirteen. Together with the other boys he sings, beats his *coro* (an instrument shaped like a miniature canoe), then enters the forest where he kneels with the others, eyes closed, while the roar of many lions surrounds them. On his return he sees white threads connecting the village huts and the tops of the bombax trees, which are too thick and too thorny to be climbed. Later he discovers the "rational" explanations for these frightening and mysterious events, but he is wise enough to recognize that for the boys who take part in it, the ceremony is still a true test of courage, and a real division between childhood and adulthood. The actual circumcision comes later, which he describes as "a really dangerous ordeal, and no game" (but without

103

referring to the probably more painful and dangerous circumcision to which Malinké women would have been subjected). He returns proudly with the other boys to the village, where they are greeted by relatives holding up the symbols of their future professions, and he is embarrassed to see his father's second wife displaying an exercise book and a pen – the marks, along with the school clothes he is made to wear in the country, of what divides him from traditional society.

Still, although Camara Laye is on the threshold of leaving traditional life, he has the sensitivity to recognize the hidden power it contains. His mother's totem is the crocodile (he never learns his own totem) and he watches her draw water from the crocodile-infested banks of the Niger, where the other women are afraid to go. He observes a "little black snake with a strikingly marked body" that comes and goes around his father's workshop and that his father explains is the "guiding spirit of our race." The snake, which has chosen to reveal himself to the boy's father, tells him what will come and gives him authority over all the other blacksmiths – an honoured profession among the Malinké.

The boy's departure from his village, when it comes, is heart-rending yet inevitable. Camara Laye has been fated, by his own talents and personality, by the way his parents raised him, and by the changes in Guinean society, to make his way in a wider world. Like his initiation into manhood, what he calls his "exile" is a painful yet necessary part of his development.

—

My playmates were extremely kind. They were excellent companions though stronger than I and, indeed, rather tough. In deference to the city boy sharing their country games, they gladly kept their high spirits in control. Furthermore, they were full of admiration for my school clothes.

As soon as I had dried myself in front of the fire, I dressed. Filled with envy, my playmates watched me put on my short-sleeved khaki shirt, shorts of the same color, and sandals. I also had a beret, which I hardly ever wore. The other clothes made enough of an impression. These splendors dazzled country boys whose sole article of clothing was a short pair of drawers. I envied them their freedom of movement. My city

clothes, of which I had to be careful, were a great nuisance, for they might become dirty or torn. When we climbed to the lookout posts, I had to keep from getting caught on the rungs of the ladders. Once on top I had to stay away from the freshly cut ears of corn which were stored there, safe from the termites, and which would later be used as seed. And if we lighted a fire to cook the lizards or field-mice we had killed, I dared not go too close lest the blood stain my clothes or the ashes dirty them. I could only look on as our catch was cleaned and the insides salted, preparatory to being placed on the live coals. And I had to take all sorts of precautions when I ate.

Guinea-Bissau

The Bush Rebels by Barbara Cornwall

Holt Rinehart Winston, 1972

The small West African country of Guinea-Bissau has produced few books and attracted few European settlers or tourists. Perhaps for those reasons it is one of the least-known corners of the continent to the outside world: even more obscure than countries like Burkina Faso and Chad, which are in danger of being famous for their obscurity. Raided for slaves as early as the 1440s and later exploited for its rice and peanuts by Portugal, which deliberately discouraged the building of roads, schools, and hospitals, Guinea-Bissau is known to those who know it at all for its charismatic leader Amílcar Cabral, who led the country to independence as head of the PAIGC (African Party for the Independence of Guinea and Cape Verde).

Barbara Cornwall, an American journalist based in the Middle East, went to Mozambique and Guinea-Bissau to live and travel with the guerrillas who were seeking the overthrow of Portuguese rule. Unlike other accounts from the front lines of Third World revolutions, Cornwall's is refreshingly free of false bravado and Marxist rhetoric. Her admiration for the guerrillas of both countries is based as much on their discipline, their tolerance for hardship, and their consideration for her – a heavy smoker whose inability to keep up with the column sometimes put them in danger – as with their ideological purity. Her attention to landscape and wildlife, her patient questioning of the guerrillas on their lives and motivations, and her willingness to discuss the everyday details of life in the bush add immediacy to her story. She even offers fourteen "ground rules for ladies regarding bush survival," from the advantages of tennis shoes to the best way to handle stinging ants.

The second and longer section of this book takes Cornwall across the swamps, rivers, and forests of Guinea-Bissau. Along the way, she and the guerrillas inspect a downed Portuguese jet and negotiate a minefield where a disposal team is clearing the area and saving the mines for reuse against the enemy. While the Portuguese receive aircraft and heavy weapons from their NATO allies, all of the rebels'

weapons and supplies enter the country on foot or by canoe. They visit a mobile bush hospital where "two guerrillas, two civilian hernia cases, and a child burned by hot palm oil" are treated in a facility that has medicines and equipment but no refrigerator, autoclave, or electricity. The journey culminates with an attack on a Portuguese fort: one of the few small centres of colonial power in a country that is already about three-quarters liberated.

Struggling with language difficulties – one woman's comments are translated from a dialect called Nalou into "Balante, then Creole, then Portuguese, and finally into French" – Cornwall takes many opportunities to question guerrillas about their previous lives, their reasons for joining the struggle, their training, and their hopes for the future of the country. Carmen Pereira, the political commissar who accompanies Cornwall, had left a comfortable life as one of the "small, privileged group of blacks in the capital," but like others Cornwall talks to, seems surprised when asked why. "Although my own life was not unpleasant," Pereira says, "I could see the sufferings of my compatriots all around me. At the same time, my husband had become a secret member of the party, and eventually I was drawn into the revolution myself."

By stifling development, demanding forced labour, buying up crops at artificially low prices, and putting down protests with massacres of civilians, the colonists had made rebellion inevitable and created a patriotic consciousness where none had existed before.

"The road is mined from here onward," said Pansao. At first I thought that it must be some ghastly mistake, but then recalled that the Portuguese had always mined the approaches to their forts.

"We have been lifting them out of here for some time," said Pansao, "but we started on this part only this morning and we cannot tell how many are left."

At this point, the demolitions man pointed to a metal slab along the roadside on which lay rows of small, dark objects, like square iron cakes on a confectioner's tray. Each was topped with a tiny, plastic button like the decorative blob on a petit four. Just underneath lay the attached detonator and if stepped upon the explosion could tear the legs off or rend

the crotch or split open the abdomen, depending upon the angle of the victim and at which point he had stepped. ...

As we inched toward the fort, the men absolutely quiet, I was gripped not with fear, surprisingly, but with a steadily rising sense of an evil so awesome and proximal, a peril so acute, that it blocked all emotions of terror or despair or panic. There was only an all-pervading and insupportable tension which seemed to originate in the calves of the legs and unfold in layers as it rose, like a large, black rubber flower, finally to settle in the brain where it lay flopping and breathing.

"Walk where the terrain is hard," cautioned Barry. "Follow exactly in my footsteps. Don't go near any loose patches of earth. Step exactly where I step."

Ivory Coast

The Suns of Independence by Ahmadou Kourouma

Translated from the French by Adrian Adams

Holmes & Meier, 1981 (first published 1968)

Fama is a handsome prince of the Malinké people, but he spends his days in the capital city, far from his people, wandering from one funeral to the next as an uninvited, sometimes unwanted orator. Salimata, his beautiful wife, supports her angry and frustrated husband by selling porridge and cooked rice to the workers by the waterfront.

Traditional life was hard. Colonialism was harder. Independence is hardest of all. This is the message that emerges from *The Suns of Independence*. But although no one could call this an especially cheerful novel, the feisty spirit of the characters and the cynical bite of the language make it a bracing rather than a depressing one. Even the chapters have names like this: "His neck was hung about with collars bristling with magic charms, like the spike-studded collars worn by baboon-hunting dogs." Fama may be downtrodden, but he still has the pride of a prince, willing to fight rather than accept a slight. Salimata, too, still has enough spirit and idealism to make a grand but poorly considered gesture, such as giving away all her rice to the beggars at the market. (She is not only robbed as a result, but also precipitates a riot that nearly destroys the place.)

Fama's opportunity comes when his cousin Lasina dies, leaving Fama the heir apparent of his branch of the Dumbuya dynasty. Leaving Salimata in the city, Fama travels to his home village, but finds his people in a state of "decrepitude and decay." The village straddles what is now a national boundary between two fractious countries eager to wield their new powers. "Independence had suppressed the chiefdom, dethroned Fama's cousin, and set up a committee in the village, with a president. A sacrilege, a disgrace!" Fama rallies the support of two old men, a fetish priest and a praise singer, but he is not even sure if it is worth the effort to claim power over the place. This is a village where hyenas routinely raid the graves, where days drop identically one by one "like the eggs of one guinea fowl," and

where good Muslims greet each other "for about as long as it would take a leper to thread a needle." (The book abounds in pungent expressions, many of which are unrepeatable in polite company.)

At dramatic moments in the story – a sacrifice, an act of divination, or an outburst of violence – the colours red, yellow, and green appear together. The flags of many African countries use these colours, and one might assume that they symbolize Fama's country. The flag of the Ivory Coast, however, is red, *white*, and green. But then, this corrupt and violent land is not exactly the Ivory Coast. Unnamed for most of the book, it is eventually called the Ebony Coast, as if the author is signalling that this is a darker version of his homeland, strategically shadowed so as to bring out its flaws.

In keeping with its title, *The Suns of Independence* pays close attention to suns, skies, and weather. The schemes and squabbles of the characters take place against towering skies that make them seem even pettier, and the struggle between the sun and the clouds nearly turns them into characters in their own right. Sometimes the effect is grand: "The huge sun, blazing like a blacksmith's forge, had climbed high in the sky, and a broad band of copper ran from east to west across the lagoon." Other times it is more subtle: "The morning was damp and millet-coloured, like morning in a wood after a stormy night."

Salimata entered the compound through the front door. In the middle of the courtyard, under mango-trees swarming with weaver-birds, amidst scattered calabashes, children and chickens, some women were pounding grain. They had spent a peaceful night, was their response to Salimata's greetings, along with loud bursts of laughter. Fama was sitting in the room, useless and empty at night, useless and empty in the daytime, a weary worn-out thing like an old chipped calabash. Yet the look of him was still pleasing: tall as a silk-cotton tree, with shoulders, arms and face still likely to win an oh! of admiration from a woman who didn't know him.

"Salimata, did you do well at the market?"

As if deaf, she busied herself with household tasks, tidied utensils, changed into one of the cloths she wore for

110

cooking, carried a pot outside. The pestle beat out a rapid rhythm. She returned, carrying a basin. Still he waited for an answer to his greeting.

"Yes, I did well at the market. What about you? Tell me! Are you going to spend the whole long day like that, sprawling on a chair?"

Ivory Coast

In the Shadow of the Sacred Grove by Carol Spindel
Vintage Departures, 1989

C arol Spindel goes to Africa with the simplest possible motivation: to live there for a year and to try to understand what life in an African village is like. Though she has been to the continent before, backpacking from Morocco to Tanzania, she ends up in the Ivory Coast almost accidentally, because her boyfriend Tom lands a grant to do agricultural research there. Unlike a researcher or a Peace Corps volunteer with classes to teach or wells to drill, Spindel has no "project" to come between her and village life.

Perhaps because she has no agenda, or because she learns languages quickly, it doesn't take long before Spindel is in better touch with the community than Tom, who had arrived several months before. After passing through the early stages of adjustment, struggling to learn the local etiquette and striving to think the best of everyone she meets, it dawns on her that Yardjuma, the translator and assistant Tom hired on his arrival, has been using his position to take advantage not only of Tom but also of people in neighbouring villages – using Tom's name to wangle loans he has no intention of repaying. This realization spurs her to learn the Dyula language and assert her independence as soon as possible.

With time and increasing fluency, Spindel begins to feel accepted, and she is gradually drawn into the community of women, gaining a deeper understanding of their strength as well as of the limitations they face in a patriarchal society. The women of one group make and sell water jars and cooking pots, travel from village to village to sell them, and keep the money they earn. It is not easy to be part of this privileged group, however. Members must be born into a particular ethnic subgroup, and with rare exceptions all the women potters are married or widowed. For a single woman to have so much economic independence is seen as threatening.

The pleasures of this book come not so much from dramatic events as from an accumulation of small, affecting details. A herniated belly, we learn, is considered a sign of beauty because it emphasizes one's connection to the ancestors. An old man is horrified at the thought

112

of building a second storey on his house, saying that only the houses in paradise are meant to have more than one storey. Tom devises an ingenious way to remove a kernel of corn stuck in a girl's ear, and Carol begins to see the subtle differences that distinguish one woman's pots from another's.

A lesson that sinks in only after some time concerns the villagers' mortality. Early in Spindel's stay a man dies from snakebite, then the "very old wife of a former chief" passes on, but it takes a year for her to understand that hunger is constant in the village, and that the end of the dry season is always a time of deaths, some of them unexpected. "How can Carol joke with me every day when her stomach is full and mine is empty?" one woman asks pointedly, yet by the end of her stay Spindel is trusted enough to be invited into the village's sacred grove and told the secrets of the communal power known as *poro*.

In the past, adultery was severely punished. If a man slept with another man's wife – or with his unmarried daughter – he was severely beaten. But now times have changed, and these traditional laws are no longer enforced. Adultery has become just another aspect of the system of arranged marriages.

The way Adama described it, the village at two in the morning sounded like a game of musical huts. The favorite gift for a man to give his lover was a flashlight so that she could find her way to him on dark nights. "But what do you do," I asked Adama, "when everyone is going around the village at two in the morning with their flashlights? You must bump into one another."

"Oh, we do!"

"What do you do then?" I asked.

"Oh, well, we greet one another."

"Then what? Do you ask them where they're going?" People were always asking me where I was going.

"Oh, no," said Adama. "Because if I asked them, they'd ask me. Oh, no! We just greet one another politely and then we keep going!"

Kenya

A Grain of Wheat by Ngũgĩ wa Thiong'o

Heinemann, revised edition 1986 (first published 1967)

A Grain of Wheat takes place in the uneasy interval between the victory of the liberation struggle in Kenya and the country's independence. The white colonizers have been defeated but they have not yet left the scene. Imprisoned rebels, battered in mind and body, are making their way home. Politicians are scrambling to maintain their power and possessions. Justice is being meted out to the collaborators, and myths are growing up around the heroes.

Nothing, however, is exactly as it seems. An old man who brags of losing a leg in battle was actually injured by a truck. A husband who treats his unfaithful wife coldly fails to understand the whole story. A hero risks his life to protect a pregnant woman from a savage beating, but he is tortured by a guilty secret.

A Grain of Wheat takes its title from a New Testament verse about the meaning of sacrifice. Unless a grain of wheat falls into the ground and dies, says the verse, it remains alone – but if it dies, it brings forth much fruit. In the same way, the African characters who sit out the struggle find that they have lost their souls, while those who sacrifice themselves pave the way for freedom and a new society.

Ngũgĩ's novels, and especially this one, may be more like the great Russian novels than any other works to come out of Africa. Dense and challenging, *A Grain of Wheat* sometimes suggests Dostoyevsky, with its many characters, its stormy confrontations and feverish soliloquies, its atmosphere of society in upheaval, and its themes of sacrifice and redemption. Manual labour is described lovingly, as when the carpenter Gikonyo sets to work repairing a panga or machete for the woman he loves. "Worms of wood wriggled along the cyclic grooves of the drill-bit and heaved themselves on to the table. The holes were ready. Next he cut three nails with which he riveted the two pieces of wood to the panga. As he hammered the thin ends of the nails into caps, another wave of power swept through him. New strength entered his right hand."

Like many Russian novels, this one is polyphonic, shifting from one character's point of view to another's. Even by the end, it may be

impossible to say who is the main character: The stalwart, misguided Gikonyo? The tortured ex-prisoner Mugo? The martyred rebel Kihika? The morally compromised Karanja? Perhaps it is the entire local community of Kikuyus (or Gikuyus, in the author's preferred spelling) or the Kikuyu nation itself, whose Mau Mau rebellion led the way to a wider liberation struggle, and who suffered heavy losses at the hands of the British. Almost everyone in the story, it seems, has sacrificed love, life, reputation, or honour. Almost everyone has suffered as Kenya moves to a new era in its history.

———

In the afternoon the sun appeared and brightened the sky. The mist which in the morning lingered in the air went. The earth smoked grey like freshly dropped cow-dung. The warming smoke spread and thinned upwards into the clear sky. The main ceremony to remember the dead sons and bless foundations for a new future was to be performed in the afternoon. It seemed that everybody had been waiting and making themselves ready for this occasion. Except for the old women and a few other people who were ill or lame, most people from our village came to the meeting. This was Kihika's day; it was Mugo's day; it was our day.

Other people from Ndeiya, Lari, Limuru, Ngeca, Kabete, Kerarapon, came in lorries and buses, and filed out into Rung'ei market place. There were the schoolchildren in their khaki uniforms of green, red, yellow – of every colour in the rainbow; the village children in tattered clothes with flies massed around their sore eyes and mouths; women, dressed in Miengu and Mithuru, with beads around their necks; women in flower-patterned calicos that showed bare their left shoulders; women, in modern frocks; women, singing Christian hymns mixed with traditional and Uhuru songs. Men stood or talked in groups about the prospects opened up by Uhuru.

Kenya

A Primate's Memoir by Robert M. Sapolsky
Scribner, 2001

K enya, more than any other country in Africa, has a certain glow in the Western imagination. Writers of talent or even genius, from Ernest Hemingway and Isak Dinesen to Beryl Markham, have celebrated its wildlife and its natural beauty, and created a larger-than-life country populated with such figures as the noble Masai warrior, the great white hunter, and the intrepid scientist. Even the Mau Mau rebellion and the country's eventual independence failed to shatter the golden myth, and Kenya's durable status as the continent's most popular safari destination has helped keep the myth alive, as Western tourists come to witness the herds of wildebeest and the Masai with their spears and scarlet robes.

A book like *A Primate's Memoir*, which deftly dismantles many of these cherished myths, is long overdue. *A Primate's Memoir* is one of the funniest books ever written about Africa, and one of the few books to deal intelligently with both the continent's wildlife and its human inhabitants. Sometimes, in fact, the distinction seems to disappear.

Each section of the book begins with a chapter on the colony of baboons that Sapolsky studied over the course of twenty years. Even those of us who accept that chimpanzees and gorillas have personalities may find it startling to be told that a baboon he calls Obadiah "looked like a dissipated fin de siècle Viennese neurotic" or that Rebecca, daughter of Bathsheeba, "lacked the classic looks of her mother, but had a fresh baboon-next-door quality to her." But while we are being entertained we are also learning how baboons handle stress (the initial subject of his research), as well as how they play, hunt, choose their mates, and struggle for status.

Sapolsky learned a great deal about what motivates baboons, or how typical baboons will behave in certain situations. But every so often a baboon would do something completely unpredictable. Male baboons, for instance, will protect their own children, or at least those with a reasonable chance of being their own children – a calculation that requires some brainpower, as female baboons may

mate with different males at different times when they are more or less fertile. But when two young baboons are threatened by a lion, these considerations make no difference to a male named Benjamin. Although "there was no way in hell either of these kids was his," Benjamin faces down the attacker, "yelling, threat-grunting ... snarling like a lunatic," until the lion retreats. Benjamin, understandably, is one of the author's favourite baboons. He is less fond of characters such as the "mean, stupid, and untalented" Nebuchanezzar, who likes to snatch infant baboons from their mothers.

Writing about the people he encounters in Africa, Sapolsky exhibits the same mixture of scepticism and admiration that he shows in his field research. Regarding the Masai, his neighbours in the field, he doesn't so much attempt to demythologize them as to add perspective to the usual picture. When his research began, young Masai men still had to kill a lion with a spear to become warriors, and "wedding parties still always featured big tureens of coagulated cow's blood for dessert." But Sapolsky is frank about drunkenness among Masai men, and reflects on the fact that warrior nomads are less popular among peaceful farming peoples than they were to the romance-seeking British settlers.

Taking a swipe at those settlers and at the modern-day expatriates who have followed them, Sapolsky notes that today's tour operators "follow the grand British tradition in Kenya Colony, which was to instantly become alcoholic adulterers and, worse, insufferably boring popinjays." He is impatient with the legend of the great white hunters, many of whom responded to bans on hunting by becoming game wardens and safari operators. "I definitely don't have any careful statistics on the subject – how many became conservationists, how many simply liked blowing away animals, what percentage really did manage to look taciturn and handsome at dawn on the savanna. I'm just clearly not crazy about the whole scene."

To his credit, Sapolsky is perfectly willing to poke fun at himself, especially at the ignorant, idealistic, semi-hippy from New York City that he was when he first appeared on the savanna. He catalogues his qualifications for field research in Africa point by point, noting that in addition to having read a great number of books he had "backpacked extensively in the Catskill Mountains" and even "managed to make a campfire once, allowing me to melt my Velveeta cheese on my crackers, instead of eating them cold, as was my typical meal on a

backpacking trip." In Kenya he subsists on a diet of rice, beans, and canned mackerel.

Like many of the funniest books, this one has a hidden core of grief and rage. In this case the grief stems from a preventable tragedy that befell his baboons, and the rage is at those who were responsible. Sapolsky's animus for the tourist industry is more understandable when we discover the role of a local game lodge in what happened. The heartbreaking finale of the book attests to the author's love for Kenya and for the primate relatives who accepted him as an honorary savanna baboon.

———

Solomon was good and wise and just. Actually, that's nonsense, but I was an impressionable young transfer male at the time. Nevertheless, he was a pretty imposing baboon. For years, the anthropology textbooks had been having a love affair with savanna baboons and their top-ranking male, the alpha male. According to the books, the baboons were complex social primates living in open grasslands; they had organized hunts, a hierarchical rank system, and at their core was the alpha male. He led the troop to food, spearheaded the hunts, defended against predators, kept the females in line, changed the light bulbs, fixed the car, blah blah blah. Just like our human ancestors, the textbooks ached to say, and sometimes even did. Most of that turned out to be wrong, naturally. The hunts for food were disorganized free-for-alls. Furthermore, the alpha male couldn't lead the troop to food during a crisis, as he wouldn't know where to go. The males transferred into the troops as adolescents, while the females spent their whole lives in the same troop. Thus, it would be the old females who remembered the grove of olive trees past the fourth hill. When predators attacked, the alpha male would be in the thick of it, defending an infant. But only if he was absolutely certain that it was his kid who was otherwise likely to become someone's dinner. Otherwise, he had the highest, safest spot in the tree to watch the action. So much for Robert Ardrey and 1960s anthropology.

Lesotho

Singing Away the Hunger
by Mpho 'M'atsepo Nthunya

Indiana University Press, 1997

Singing Away the Hunger is one of the few full-length oral histories to be published by an African woman. It is the product of a remarkable collaboration between Mpho Nthunya, a housekeeper at the National University of Lesotho, and K. Limakatso Kendall, a Fulbright scholar who came to Africa to teach creative writing and English literature. (The name Limakatso, meaning "someone who brings surprises, wonders, even miracles," is given to her by Nthunya.)

After recruiting Nthunya to help her elicit stories from others, Kendall discovers that Nthunya herself is a better storyteller than anyone else she has found. Though she has little formal education, Nthunya speaks eight languages and "has a knack for generating suspense at the beginning of her stories and for tying them together at the end with a line or two that harks back to the beginning." Nthunya finds it harder to tell her stories in English than in Sesotho, but Kendall believes that "her struggle to translate the stories verbally into English condensed them, tightened them, and may have made them more powerful in some ways than the Sesotho originals." Kendall takes down the stories in shorthand, transcribes them onto a computer, then organizes and polishes them until both she and Nthunya are satisfied.

The result is a roughly chronological tale of a woman who is born in rural Lesotho, spends several years in a brawling South African township near Benoni, marries and returns to Lesotho, gains and loses a fortune in livestock, and eventually makes a meagre living as a housekeeper. It is a tale of extraordinary hardship and suffering – much of it caused or worsened by the cruelty and neglect of family members.

Lesotho – one of two small mountainous countries embedded within the territory of South Africa – is a poor country even by African standards. Nthunya's mother is poor even by the standards of Lesotho. While her mother, dressed in a rough sack, grinds corn for the chief's wife and gathers wild greens to eat, Nthunya is left with her

119

grandmother, who feeds her brother but starves her. When the child's dress catches fire one day, her grandmother does nothing. Nthunya is saved when her mother hears her cries, but she is permanently scarred from the burns.

There is more pain to come: the death of Nthunya's first child (the result, in part, of a misunderstanding with a hurried doctor), her husband's lingering death from exposure, the theft of the government's disability payments by her husband's cousin, her brother-in-law Joseph's cruel treatment of her surviving children, and (as she believes) his use of witchcraft to murder her three sons. Nthunya's response to these tragedies is muted but not unfeeling. She does not strike back or waste energy in grief when she thinks it will do no good. She values her ability to endure. "I was not angry," she says after one injustice. "I was 'M'e 'M'atsepo, who never changed."

The supernatural is an important and unquestioned element of Nthunya's story. She talks with her dead mother in her dreams, and when she is pregnant, dreams tell her the sex of the child. More often, though, the supernatural is used as a weapon: children are killed by malevolent ghosts, and "wizard snakes" are implanted in a victim's chest, where they move "up and down" until they are expelled by magic or the victim dies. Sangomas can identify an enemy or prescribe a cure, but one must guard against fake sangomas who may make things worse.

African writers often focus on family and community and ignore the landscape (while Western writers in Africa often do the opposite). Nthunya's memoir is remarkable for its almost painterly descriptions of the highlands of Lesotho, which she obviously loves. Though her husband complains that the hard life of the mountains makes her dark and thin, Nthunya responds to it on a deep level – perhaps in part because it offers an escape from the cruelty and treachery she so often encounters from other people.

"I liked the colours," she writes, "the shapes of the mountain-tops, the way the shadows from the clouds fall and move across the mountains so everything is always changing. Everywhere I could smell wild sage. I like the wild sage and clean mountain wind, the colours of the wildflowers: bright blue, deep yellow, or maybe red and orange like flames of the fire. I like the sounds, the birds and the crickets, the waterfall near the house, the music of sheep-bells and cow-bells, the silence. Most of all I like the silence."

After Tseliso died, Joseph started to work on Motlatsi. Motlatsi also went to the gold-mines in the Republic, and Joseph used to frighten Motlatsi in a dream which came many times. In the dream Joseph comes to him and growls deep in his throat like thunder in the mountains, "Let's go home, *uena*!"

Joseph is on a horse and is pulling a small black dog on a rope behind him. He's got a green blanket, and he wears black trousers and black shoes. When he says, "Let's go home," Motlatsi will wake up and be frightened and sick. He gets cold and hot just like a flu. He has this dream for two months. So they take him to the hospital in the Republic. He goes to the hospital four times, coming back, going again. Every time he has that dream, he has the flu but it's not the flu.

One day an old miner says to Motlatsi, "My child, this is not a sickness which white people can heal. White people cannot help you because this is our sickness, Basotho sickness. You must go home. When you arrive at home, tell your mother to take you to the Basotho doctor. Maybe he can heal you. If you don't do this, you are going to die in the Republic without seeing your mother again."

So Motlatsi came home. When he arrived here he told us about the sickness. After that flu there is something moving up and down in his chest. We could look at him and see he was in pain. It blocks his breathing. We see that it throbs under his ribs.

Liberia

Journey Without Maps by Graham Greene

Penguin, 1980 (first published 1936)

In 1935 Graham Greene, thirty years old and already the author of about a dozen books, took his first trip outside Europe. Together with his cousin Barbara, he crossed roughly four hundred miles of the backcountry of Liberia on foot – or, for short periods when he was sick and exhausted, by hammock. *Journey Without Maps*, his account of that trek, demonstrates that the themes of his novels were also those that obsessed him in life. Like the Haiti of *The Comedians* or the Mexico of *The Power and the Glory*, Graham Greene's Liberia is a realm of seedy surroundings, religious anxiety, and moral ambiguity.

At first glance *Journey Without Maps* is a striking example of the bad old school of neo-colonial travel writing. Like many books of African travel, it begins with a list of local diseases and parasites: "elephantiasis, leprosy, yaws, malaria, hookworm, schistosomiasis." Greene dwells on the discomforts of the journey – the heat, the rats, the cockroaches, the dwindling supply of whisky – and on the shortcomings of his porters. He stresses the alien quality of African culture, writing of two Senegalese men holding hands that "it wasn't love; it wasn't anything we could understand." His language is sometimes appalling, as when he describes a "moron dwarf" who is made to dance with "a couple of picaninnies of three years old who were as tall as he … he swayed a great inflated head, like a blister a pin would burst, to the beat of the rattle, and then howled and wept to be released."

Unlike other Westerners in Africa, though, Greene's jaundiced view doesn't arise from an attitude of smug superiority. Flashbacks to England make it plain that he finds many "civilized" English characters at least as grotesque as any Liberian he meets, and eventually he confesses that life itself has struck him as deeply unsatisfactory. "I had always assumed before, as a matter of course, that death was desirable." He has come to Liberia, in fact, to immerse himself in a culture that predates modern "civilization," and to "recall at which point we went astray."

Though he notes that Liberia and Ethiopia are the only two African countries never colonized by Europe, Greene has no very high opinion of the African-Americans who did colonize it. Beginning in 1822, an American philanthropic society began sending freed slaves to settle the "Grain Coast": some of them, Greene says, the illegitimate children of slave owners among the society's directors. As these "half-caste settlers" began to dominate the indigenous people, Liberia was marked by "the same broken contracts, the same resort to arms, the same gradual encroachment" that characterized the European colonies.

Unlike most visitors to Liberia, Greene arrives overland, sees the interior of the country before the coast, and gets to know and respect the indigenous peoples before encountering the comic-opera society of the Americo-Liberians. Walking through the forest from one isolated village to another, he encounters "only gentleness, kindness, an honesty which one would not have found, or at least dared to assume was there, in Europe." Despite the exhaustion, boredom, sickness, and fear that he also experiences in the interior, when he leaves the forest for the coast Greene feels "disappointment with what man had made out of the primitive." He arrives in Monrovia on the ove of a fixed presidential election, and describes the capital as packed with drunken, corrupt lawyers and politicians addicted to rhetoric and self-interest. The Americo-Liberian rulers, he finds, show no concern for the indigenous people except to pacify rebellious villages or to round up forced labourers, some of whom are sold to the Spanish to work on the island of Fernando Po. *Journey Without Maps* succeeds in conveying the texture of traditional life in Liberia as well as some of the seeds of the bloody conflicts that would eventually erupt there.

⸺

When the sun was low a clamour of voices brought me from bed. The population of Sakripie was pouring into the compound behind two huge stilted and masked devils. They must have stood more than eighteen feet high. They wore tall witches' hats rimmed with little shells; their faces were black, the masks looked as if they had been made out of old cotton stockings, they wore striped pyjama jackets, with the sleeves sewn up to hide the hands, and pyjama shorts, while the stilts were wound with a thinner striped material. Their performance

was humorous and sophisticated. They sat down on the roof-tops and idly fanned themselves with their legs crossed, then stretched a leg right across the thatch and pretended to fall asleep. They had a sense of climax which would have earned the applause of the most sophisticated music-hall audience as they leaned back their whole stiff inarticulated length at an angle of about twenty degrees and just recovered as they began to fall. They had the usual interpreter with them. He lay on the ground while they hopped on one stilt towards him, so that it seemed almost inevitable that the wooden hoof would be planted on his face; but always at the last moment they cleared him. When the entertainment was over, they left the compound by the wall; the gateway was too low for them. They sat on the ten-foot wall and lifted over each stiff leg in turn like old men crossing a stile, and for a long while after their witch hats were visible bobbing away above the huts toward their own compound.

Liberia

Mississippi in Africa by Alan Huffman
Gotham Books, 2004

Alan Huffman's journey to Liberia began with a piano. The piano had belonged to Isaac Ross, a slave owner and veteran of the American Revolution. Ross lived in Jefferson County, Mississippi, on a plantation called Prospect Hill. He was a supporter of the movement to resettle freed slaves in West Africa, and his will stipulated that after his death his plantation would be sold and the proceeds used to send any slaves who wished to go to begin new lives in Liberia. (Those who decided not to go would remain slaves, though their families would not be broken up.)

Isaac Ross's will was contested bitterly by his heirs, particularly by his grandson Isaac Ross Wade. When nine years passed and his slaves were still in bondage, they rose up and burned the Prospect Hill mansion to the ground. Somehow the grand piano was rescued – though a young girl died in the fire – and years later it ended up in the home of Gwen Shipp, a descendant of Isaac Ross, who kept it at Holly Grove, an "early kit house" made in Cincinnati and transported to Jefferson County. When the house fell into disrepair, Gwen Shipp gave it to Alan Huffman, a journalist who "took the house apart, board by board," reassembled it on his own property, and retrieved the piano from where it had been taken for safekeeping.

Huffman's curiosity about the piano led to curiosity about Prospect Hill, about Isaac Ross and his grandson, about the slave revolt, and about the 142 Prospect Hill slaves who travelled to Liberia in 1849 and settled in an area they called Mississippi in Africa. They were the largest of any group of freed slaves to make this journey.

Huffman gradually realizes that understanding the full story of Prospect Hill requires a trip to Liberia, and in 2001 he flies to Monrovia in search of the descendants of the Prospect Hill settlers. His first impressions include fires in the jungle, a bombed-out airport, and checkpoints manned by drunken young men with automatic weapons.

Huffman's plans to visit Greenville, the centre of the Prospect Hill settlement, are quickly thwarted. The overland trip is far too

dangerous, he is told, and the antebellum-style mansions built by the settlers in imitation of their former masters have all been burned down. In any case, the descendants he is looking for have most likely left, many of them for Monrovia itself.

Huffman meets several Liberians with the surname Ross or other names that may link them to Prospect Hill, but the needs and the tragedies of the present day come to seem more urgent. "Sad stories," writes the author, "are the real hard currency for Liberia ... the brother who is dangerously ill with malaria, with no money for medication and no public hospital to go to since the only one in the country closed a few weeks ago ... the children selling candy or peanuts on the street to try to pay their way through elementary school."

Though the US has all but abandoned Liberia, and though the Americo-Liberian elite is small and widely resented, Huffman finds that this is a "nation of America-philes," awash in American T-shirts, decals, bumper stickers, and fashions. The affinity is more than superficial. So many place names and customs are imported from the US that a Liberian talking about his own country may sound as if he's in the Deep South: "He says he remembers the soldiers torching the columned mansions of Mississippi during the civil war, remembers eating crawfish in Louisiana, and collard greens and okra. He remembers crossing the languorous river that flows between Mississippi and Louisiana in a canoe." Another woman describes the Liberian Louisiana this way: "It's just a small farming community, with wooden houses. No jobs. The women mostly just sit on the porches and enjoy the breeze. Sunday, go to church. All the men go deer hunting on Sunday." Deer hunting? Huffman asks. The woman nods.

Huffman is often the only white person on the street, and knows that by local standards he is rich. "I have more money in my belt than most people here will see in a lifetime. I am a flash of hope in their world that will fly away in a few brief days." Yet the Liberians he meets approach him so gently that he soon begins to feel surprisingly safe.

"Liberia is not a bad place, not completely bad," says a guard at a local convent. "You, a white man, could walk all the way across Monrovia at night and no one bother you. Only when the heat is on, then you have trouble." By the time his trip ends, Huffman is genuinely sorry to go. Where else, he wonders, could he inform a

group of black guys that he comes from Mississippi and be greeted with delighted handshakes and high fives?

———

I stroll onto the terrace to watch the sun set over the Atlantic. Boys are playing soccer on the beach with a ball fashioned from a tightly stuffed canvas bag. Children climb atop two statues of lions surmounting the grand staircase of the ruined mansion next door, where perhaps a score of families are encamped.

The mansion is one more indication that there is no such thing as an abandoned building in Monrovia. All over town, families squat in roofless buildings with blown-out windows and doors, the most dramatic being the marble ruins of the Masonic temple, situated on the heights overlooking the city, not far from Mamba Point. Gunfire, mortars, and scavengers have stripped away most of the temple's architectural adornments, which makes the massive, Greek Revival building even more darkly imposing. Children balancing five-gallon jugs of water on their heads scurry in and out while mothers prepare meals of rice and whatever else they can find on coal stoves, crouching under the shelter of tarps stretched between nails in the walls.

Libya

The Bleeding of the Stone by Ibrahim Al-Koni

Translated from the Arabic by May Jayyusi and Christopher Tingley

Interlink Books, 2002

Fiction from Libya is hard to find in English translation. *The Bleeding of the Stone*, a slender but hard-hitting novel by an author said to be Libya's leading novelist, gives us an idea of what we've been missing.

The Bleeding of the Stone takes place in the desert of south-western Libya, not far from the town of Ghat. Those who live there, however, owe their allegiance more to the Sahara than to any country. Casual references to Kano (Nigeria) and Agades (Niger) indicate that trade routes and oases count for more than national capitals or boundaries.

Asouf is a Bedouin who has made his life where the sandy desert meets the mountain desert. The son of a gazelle hunter, he has grown up herding goats and trading for supplies with passing caravans. His solitary life becomes even more solitary with the deaths of his parents: his mother in a flash flood and his father at the foot of a cliff, while hunting in the mountains for the rare and elusive wild sheep called the *waddan*.

As the story opens, Asouf is serving as a guide to the ancient rock paintings of the area, many of which – paintings of gazelles, *waddan*, oxen, and hunters – he has discovered on his own. Asouf is a religious man: a devout Muslim who has also learned Sufi chants from his father. He feels a deep religious response to the rock paintings, and recognizes a similar reverence in the Christian tourists who drive into the desert to see them.

Whether or not you could call it religious, Asouf feels a powerful psychic or even magical link to the desert gazelles and especially to the *waddan*, to which both he and his father attribute intelligence and even a soul. As a child, Asouf begs his father to take him on a hunt for the *waddan*, but his father makes one excuse after another. Finally Asouf's mother explains: a *waddan* once saved Asouf's father's life, and he vowed never to kill the animal again. Driven by starvation to break his vow, he promised that his son would never hunt the *waddan*.

When Asouf, like his father, is saved from death by the mysterious wild sheep, his psychic link to the animal strengthens and he loses all taste for meat of any kind. This is when he encounters a man named Cain, an orphan like himself but his opposite in every other way: cruel, worldly, with a voracious hunger for meat that borders on addiction.

Skilled in modern weapons and technology, Cain has slaughtered hundreds of desert gazelles with the help of Land Rovers, helicopters, and high-powered rifles, devouring their flesh raw. As a baby, he survived a waterless caravan by licking the blood from a slaughtered gazelle – a gazelle that may have sacrificed itself to save him. But rather than gratitude, this experience leaves him with a hunger that is likened to a restless worm in his teeth. When the gazelles are gone, Cain tastes the dried meat of a *waddan*, carried over the desert from Agades, and he makes up his mind to kill more fresh meat for himself.

In very few pages, the author sets up a confrontation between the two orphans – the desert mystic and the ruthless hunter – that is also a conflict between the old and the new, religious awe and technological arrogance. Themes of sacrifice, loyalty, and retribution resonate in highly charged language that is sometimes biblical or Koranic. Though it is possible to situate the story in time – it's around 1935, for instance, when the Italian troops occupying Libya attempt to recruit Asouf to help in a planned attack against Abyssinia – the novel is most successful in describing a timeless way of life: the jinn-haunted caves and wadis and rocky cliffs of the Sahara, and the harsh, precarious lives of the hunters and herdsmen who live there.

—

Asouf still took pleasure in the jinn faces in the mountain caves. Fleeing the scorching heat, he'd take refuge, panting, among the hollows of the rocks. There he'd lie for a time, then crawl to the rocky wall and start taking off the layers of dust, until the lines painted in the rocks would begin to appear. Still he'd go on, wiping away at the mighty walls, until at last the faces would appear, masked or long, or else animals fleeing from the arrows of the masked hunters: *waddan*, gazelles, oxen and many others, huge in size, with long legs he never saw in the desert today.

In time he began calling the wadis and chasms and mountains by the names of the figures painted on their rocks. This was the Wadi of Gazelles, that the Path of the Hunters, that the *Waddan* Mountain, that, again, the Herdsmen's Plain; until, finally, he'd discovered the great jinni, the masked giant rising alongside his dignified *waddan*, his face turned toward the *qibla*, awaiting sunrise and praising Almighty God in everlasting prayer.

Madagascar

The Eighth Continent by Peter Tyson

HarperCollins Perennial, 2001

In the nineteenth century, when explorers travelled to African countries that were largely unknown to the outside world, they returned to write compendious volumes that seemed to cover every aspect of where they had been: landscape, geology, plants and wildlife, food, clothing, family life, and religious practices. Today most African countries are well enough known not to require this kind of encyclopedic treatment, but Madagascar may be an exception. An island a thousand miles long, it was uninhabited until only about two thousand years ago, and it receives few visitors even today. It is home to so many plants and animals found nowhere else on earth that there is an argument for considering it to be, like Australia, a continent of its own.

The Eighth Continent accepts the challenge of the all-inclusive approach, and it is packed with odd and intriguing facts. Tenth-century Arab geographers knew Madagascar as the Island of the Moon. Marco Polo wrote that it was the home of the Roc, a giant bird that could snatch up elephants in its claws. Yet Madagascar has no elephants, or any of the other "signature wildlife" of Africa. It did, though, have a giant bird (now extinct): the *Aepyornis*, the largest of which stood ten feet tall. Today it is home to many species of lemurs, a primate found nowhere else in the world. They include the golden bamboo lemur, which each day eats bamboo shoots and leaves containing so much cyanide that it should be killed twelve times over.

Many of the ethnic groups of Madagascar resemble Indonesians more than Africans in their appearance and customs. Taboos abound on the island. "One should not sing while eating, for it causes the teeth to grow long, while to skin a banana with the teeth results in extreme poverty." It is taboo to say that anyone is dead: one must instead say that someone is "wounded," "broken," "lost," or "seriously ill." The Sakalava, who live along the west coast, are prone to possession by the spirits of their ancestors, or by the spirits of Malagasy who died far from home. The Merina and

Betsileo have a ceremony called "turning the bones," in which the bodies of family members are removed from their graves, wrapped in new silk shrouds, and carried around town to check out new developments before being returned to the tomb.

The book, however, is not just a collection of odd facts. It is primarily a scientific travelogue in which the author accompanies four scientists on their investigations in Madagascar. With Chris Raxworthy, a herpetologist, he searches the forest for leaf-tailed geckos and the elusive *Zonosaurus boettgeri* (pronounced "butchery"). With Dave Burney, a paleontologist, he crawls through a cave in quest of the fossilized remains of giant lemurs and pygmy hippos. With Bob Dewar, an anthropologist, he uncovers fragments of pottery at ancient tomb sites. And with Pat Wright, a primatologist, he watches golden bamboo lemurs darting through the trees in a national park that Wright created "almost singlehandedly."

Madagascar suffers from deforestation and erosion on a massive scale. "Mile after mile after mile," writes Tyson, describing the view from a plane approaching the capital, "you see below you bare, treeless hills or plains, often gouged by erosion gullies and blackened by brush fires." Others have said that Madagascar's rivers carry so much red earth into the Indian Ocean that the island looks as if it is bleeding to death. Yet along with a nineteenth-century curiosity and appetite for detail, the author has a bracing sort of nineteenth-century optimism. Though Pat Wright runs her park with a heavy hand, Tyson finds that the Malagasy staff who roam the park and monitor its ecology are knowledgeable and caring. "Looking at these modest men, I think if anyone will save Madagascar it will be these people."

⌒

"The Malagasy have a lot of rumors about this snake," Raxworthy says now, cinching down the mouth of a large cloth sack with one hand while reaching in carefully with the other. It is the morning after my arrival at Lokobe Reserve, and Raxworthy is giving the Earthwatch team a live-animal briefing at our oceanside camp. The talk should give us a good feel, he says, for the spectacular radiation that has occurred among Madagascar's herps.

"When missionaries translated the Bible into Malagasy, they made this the snake that tempted Eve," he continues. I can see why. The large brown-and-yellow snake he pulls out looks evil. It is the menarana, and it bears the pugnacious upturned snout that gives hog-nosed snakes their name, a long forked tongue like an animated strand of linguini, and a pair of shiny black eyes that, due to a fold of skin pressing down from the forehead, makes the serpent look downright pissed off.

"That's one mean-looking head," I say.

"I think he's got a sweet head," Raxworthy responds as he eases the snake back into the bag.

Malawi

The Chattering Wagtails of Mikuyu Prison
by Jack Mapanje
Heinemann, 1993

Jack Mapanje published his first collection of poems, *Of Chameleons and Gods*, when he was in his thirties. The book won a prestigious award and was reprinted three times. It was less popular with Dr Hastings Kamuzu Banda, Malawi's President for Life. The book was banned in Malawi, and in 1987 Jack Mapanje was detained by order of President Banda. Senior police officials, not wanting to question the president's order, met with the poet and asked him who he was and why he thought he had been arrested. Mapanje was held in Mikuyu Prison near Zomba for three years, seven months, and sixteen days.

The Chattering Wagtails of Mikuyu Prison includes work written before and after his imprisonment, as well as poems about the experience of imprisonment itself. Mapanje's poems are unrhymed. Many of them are divided into short stanzas of two or three lines, while others are unbroken blocks of as many as thirty-four lines. But although they have a minimum of formal structure, these poems never seem loose or casual. Each line is tightly knit and driven by powerful emotion: fury against tyranny, grief for the dead, and sorrow for the poet's country.

It is sometimes said about African literature, most of which is written in ex-colonial languages like English and French, that it is aimed at a foreign readership. That cannot be said of *The Chattering Wagtails*. Though there are surely not many readers of serious poetry in Malawi (there are few enough in the United States), Mapanje's ideal reader is clearly a fellow Malawian. The poems abound in references to political figures and events from the life of President Banda (never mentioned by name) that not many outsiders will fully understand.

It's not necessary, though, to know the history of the country to feel the impact of Mapanje's images of life and suffering in Malawi. In "Baobab Fruit Picking (or Development in Monkey Bay)" he describes how the women of Monkey Bay manage to survive while their husbands are working in the mines of South Africa and local shorefront land is being seized for the benefit of tourists and expatriates.

Shoving dead cassava stalks into rocks, catching
Fish in tired *chitenje* cloths with kids, picking

Baobab fruit & whoring. The bark from the baobab
They strip into strings for their reed wattle,

The fruit they crack, scoop out the white, mix with
Goat milk, 'That's porridge for today, children!'

The heart of this collection, though, is the verse that describes Mapanje's imprisonment. In "The Famished Stubborn Ravens of Mikuyu," Mapanje pays grudging tribute to the ravens, as hungry and tenacious as the prisoners, who arrive each day at dawn, "hammering at the corrugated / iron of this cell, drilling at the marrow of our / fragile bones ..." In "Scrubbing the Furious Walls of Mikuyu," the poet gets a close-up view of the walls of the prison, encrusted with urine and marked with the blotches of squashed mosquitoes. He discovers the scrawls of prisoners who have come before him and refuses to wash them out, thinking "We have liquidated too many / brave names out of the nation's memory." And in "To the Unknown Dutch Postcard Sender (1988)," he honors the anonymous supporter whose brightly coloured tourist postcard somehow made it past the prison censors to bring "waves of hope and reason" to his cell.

Perhaps most moving is a poem called "Your Tears Still Burn at My Handcuffs (1991)." Addressed to the poet's mother, the poem recalls her protests when her son was arrested, the ceremonies with which he imagined she would greet him when he returned, and the stories he would tell her about his time in prison. It was not to be: Mapanje's mother died two months before her son was released.

———

From "Your Tears Still Burn at My Handcuffs"

... After that constant care
Mother, I expected you to show me the rites
Of homing in of this political prisoner,

A Basket of Leaves

Perhaps with ground herbal roots dug by
Your hand and hoe, poured in some clay pot
Of warm water for me to suffuse, perhaps

With your usual wry smile about the herbs
You wish your mother had told you about.
Today, as I invent my own cleansing rites

At this return of another fugitive, without
Even dead roots to lean on, promise to bless
These lit candles I place on your head and

Your feet, accept these bended knees, this
Lone prayer offered among these tall unknown
Graveyard trees, this strange requiem mustered

From the tattered Catholic Choir of Dembo
Village. You gave up too early, mother: two
More months, and I'd have told you the story

Of some Nchinji upstart who tamed a frog at
Mikuyu Prison ...

Mali

The Heart of the Ngoni
by Harold Courlander with Ousmane Sako

University of Massachusetts Press, 1994 (first published 1982)

The present-day country of Mali was home to several of the great West African kingdoms of antiquity. As Harold Courlander explains in the introduction to this book, the kingdoms of Ghana, Mali, and Songhay were followed by that of Segu, whose territory stretched along the Niger River (known to the Segu as the Joliba) from Bamako to Timbuktu.

Segu was a Bambara kingdom, but as it expanded it came to include Soninke and Fula land and cities. Though the Bambara held to their traditional religious beliefs, they were influenced by the Islamic faith of the Soninke and Fula. The citizens of Segu consulted the *filelikela*, the traditional Bambara diviner, as well as the *morike*, a "practitioner of the mystic sciences" who derived additional power from his knowledge of the Koran.

The Heart of the Ngoni is a collection of tales from the oral tradition of the Segu, as told by the *djeli*, the "professional bard-historians" who "sang the chronicles of the noble families, were consulted on questions of genealogy, and often were used as family emissaries." The stories, originally accompanied by the plucked strings of the *ngoni*, deal primarily with the deeds of the Segu kings and heroes. They stretch in time from the founding of the kingdom, at a site where a *morike* on pilgrimage found a golden stone guarded by an invisible devil, to the final brief account of an uneasily resolved encounter with a French colonial administrator, at a time "after the white men came and assumed power over everything."

The heroes of Segu are individuals with a believable mixture of virtues and character flaws: among them jealousy, which is the motivating force for many of these tales. When a hero becomes too popular with the people, or a neighbouring city gains too much power, the chiefs in these stories look for an excuse to undermine their rivals. If such an excuse is lacking, an insult can elicit an angry response, or a provocation can be manufactured in some other way.

Yet once the conflict has been initiated, it proceeds according to a code as stylized as that of the medieval knights. The chiefs agree upon a date for the challenge, and in the meantime consult their diviners for advice or to strengthen their spiritual power. If the challengers arrive too late in the day for battle, they are welcomed into the enemy city for feasting and revelry, and begin the fight the next morning. Often the heroes of two cities meet in single combat, and one will offer the other the first blow, or even three shots from a rifle: a test of power, since spiritual protection may cause the bullets to fall harmlessly from the end of the barrel. If a hero discovers that his opponent is afraid of him, he may even refuse to fight on the grounds that it is dishonourable. Defeated warriors are enslaved, but slaves often stand up for themselves, reminding their captors of their noble origins.

The *djeli* make no apologies for the sometimes treacherous or overweening behaviour of the heroes, perhaps because all things are controlled by destiny in the world of the Bambara. "If you are born to be great, you will be great. Therefore let us not concern ourselves with questions." The story of Ngolo Diara illustrates this belief in destiny, and suggests other ancient tales in which a boy (Oedipus, or Joseph, or Moses) is abandoned or given away to a strange people, only to reach his destiny by unexpected paths. A chief named Yiara, learning that the son of his poor and sickly brother is fated to become the king, has the boy sent to the king in lieu of the brother's annual tax. The king makes Ngolo a servant, then learns of the predictions about his future. Needing an excuse to punish him, the king decides to "help him commit an offense" by entrusting the boy with a piece of gold, thinking he will soon lose it. But when the king's sons find the gold, which Ngolo has sewn into his clothes for safekeeping, and throw it into the river, fate takes a hand. "He who is born to be a blacksmith will be a blacksmith. He who is born to be a hero will be a hero." Ngolo catches a carp, and when he is ordered to clean the fish to make soup for the king, he discovers the cloth with the lump of gold inside.

Da Monzon's djeli said to him, "Great Da Monzon, what you have done to Chiaro will always be remembered in the songs of the djeli. What you do now to these people of Chiaro also will be recalled. Remember that they are not Fula or Manding or Maraka. They are Bambara, they are true citizens of Segu. If you are harsh with them, the ngoni of the djeli will speak of it. If you are generous with them, the ngoni of the djeli will speak of it. The ngoni retains everything. It is like a treasure chest from which nothing is ever lost. Everything that happens in the world is stored in the ngoni, and when a djeli plays this instrument he only liberates what is stored there. If you can be generous to these people of Chiaro, be generous. If you cannot, then it is destiny that you cannot."

Da Monzon was moved by the words of his djeli. He said, "I swore to the Twelve Fetishes of Segu that I would raze Chiaro, and this I must do. But these people can go elsewhere, and I will give them land to build a new town." So Chiaro Mamari's son and the other captives were set free.

But as for the city named Chiaro, Da Monzon ordered it destroyed. It ceased to exist, and in time there was nothing there but land covered with grass and other wild things.

Mali

Segu by Maryse Condé

Translated from the French by Barbara Bray

Penguin, 1987 (first published 1984)

If *The Heart of the Ngoni* presents the mythic, courtly aspect of the Segu kingdom – the kingdom as imagined and glorified by generations of djelis – then Maryse Condé's novel supplies the crowded, tumultuous context of everyday life there.

Beginning in 1797 and spanning a half-century, *Segu* tells the story of a Bambara nobleman's four sons and their very different fates. Tiekoro, the oldest son, is entranced at an early age by the newly introduced religion of Islam and by the mysteries of reading and writing that its followers know. He sets out for Timbuktu, accompanied by his brother Siga, to learn at a Koranic school, but when the infidel Siga is turned away, the two boys are separated. Siga becomes a donkey herder and eventually a trader, while Tiekoro starts on the path to becoming a man of learning.

With his older brothers gone, the third son, Naba, makes friends with a handsome and popular young hunter. While on a hunting expedition Naba strays from his companions and is captured by Bambara kidnappers and sold as a slave. Meanwhile Malobali, the youngest son – the child of his father's Fulani concubine, who has returned to her people – is growing into a spoiled and impetuous young man. Offended by the sanctimoniousness of his oldest brother Tiekoro, who has returned to Segu and seems headed for Muslim sainthood, Malobali leaves his home on horseback and becomes a mercenary in the army of the Ashantis.

Segu is as crowded with incident and character as a novel by Dickens or Dostoyevsky. Though the events of the novel take place not only in Segu but also in Timbuktu, Jenne, Fez, and the Gold Coast – even in England and Brazil – the Bambara kingdom remains at the centre. Like Dickens, Condé relies on coincidence to hold together the narratives of the far-flung brothers. They get news of each other through chance encounters, eked out by supernatural communication in the form of dreams, premonitions, or creatures like the "*urubu* of death," which appears in the form of a bird.

Tiekoro, the oldest son, gradually emerges as the most significant. Though a respected figure in Segu, he symbolizes the forces that will eventually destroy his home. In succumbing to the lure of Islamic art and learning, Tiekoro illustrates the blindness of those societies that realized only too late that Islam carried a potent political and military threat.

Though the reader sometimes wishes for fewer incidents, fewer characters, and a more leisurely exploration of the characters' inner lives, what Condé never fails to provide is a deeply researched and vividly sensual description of the lives of noblemen, hunters, fetish priests, traders, slavers, and scholars. From the very first page, when the father of the four boys eats his favourite breakfast of "millet gruel mixed with curds and honey," then cleans his "fine filed teeth" with a twig whose sap will increase his strength and potency, Condé places us in a convincingly detailed and fascinatingly alien world.

———

Koumare got into a little straw boat and rowed toward a small island in the middle of the river.

It was nightfall, for he needed darkness and secrecy for what he had to do. As they saw him embark, the last of the Somono fishermen taking home their catch prudently averted their gaze, for they recognized the redoubtable fetish priest and knew that what was about to happen was outside the ken of ordinary mortals. As Koumare plied his oars, the walls of Segu vanished in the gathering dusk. Hordes of vultures sat motionless on the walls, indistinguishable from the tall stakes protruding at intervals. There were vague shapes on the rocky beach below. Koumare drew closer around his shoulders the goatskin he wore against variations in the temperature, for the air was growing cooler. He took a pinch of snuff from an antelope horn and put it up his nostrils. Then he took up the oars again.

He was soon at his destination. Hiding his boat among the reeds, he went over to a little hillock on which there stood a straw shelter like those of the Fulani herdsmen. But everyone knew that this one was a temple where strange conversations were held with the unseen.

For the last three days Koumare had abstained from all sexual intercourse with his wives: he did not want to dissipate his strength by spilling his seed. He was also chewing *daga* for second sight. He lost no time before starting to search among the plants growing around the hut for those he needed in his work.

Mauritania

The Fearful Void by Geoffrey Moorhouse
J.B. Lippincott, 1974

Geoffrey Moorhouse, a foreign correspondent turned author, set out to cross the Sahara from west to east, by foot and by camel: a feat never accomplished before, though the north-south crossing had been made many times. He did not succeed, as the two maps at the beginning of the book make plain. The "Planned Route" begins in Nouakchott, Mauritania, touches at Timbuktu, Mali, then Tamanrasset, Algeria, then Murzuk, Libya, and ends on the banks of the Nile at Luxor, Egypt. The "Actual Route" stops at Tamanrasset, about 2 000 miles into what would have been a 3 600-mile journey.

But whatever the loss to the record books, the delays and red tape and illness and other hardships that prevented Moorhouse from completing his mission mean that roughly half of his book is devoted to Mauritania, a country little written about. It could be, too, that an adventurer tough enough to have gone the distance could not have written as feelingly about the joys and miseries of Saharan travel. Moorhouse was motivated in part by a desire for a "giddy and unique success," but much more importantly he wanted to face and overcome his fear, which he had come to see as "the most corrosive element attacking the goodness of the human spirit." His own deepest fears, he writes, "were those of annihilation, of being surrounded by what is hostile, of being unwanted, of loss and of being lost." What better place to encounter these fears than the Sahara?

After studying Arabic, consulting with desert legends such as Wilfred Thesiger and Theodore Monod, and spending nights on Hampstead Heath practising navigation with a bubble sextant, Moorhouse found himself in Nouakchott, which struck him as a "queer amalgamation" of a deserted beach resort in England and the "decayed small town of Texas" from The Last Picture Show, only with men in sky-blue boubous and women in black ones walking the sand-muffled streets.

Moorhouse offers snapshots of the country's desert outposts as well. Chinguetti, dominated by a crenellated fort from colonial times, is "a village of mud houses and tents made of hides stretched

domelike over latticeworks of palm branches." Tichit is a collection of box-shaped stone buildings, including a mosque with a tower that looks "quite ridiculously like that of an Anglo-Saxon parish church at home." Tidjikja straddles an empty riverbed that, when the water flows, becomes a river two hundred yards wide. When he sees it, though, the riverbed is "an expanse of bare sand on which camels sat couched in twos and threes, and across which figures in blue sometimes moved, their heads swathed up to the eyeballs against the dust and wind ..."

Moorhouse finds dealing with the local people nearly as wearing as the harsh environment. Children shout at him, and young men lecture him on Islam. Buying every camel and every item of food or equipment requires arduous negotiation. He gradually finds that Mohamed, the guide on whom he depends to help him cross the desert safely, has little more stamina, expertise in desert travel, and knowledge of the terrain than he does. As Moorhouse gains in confidence and understanding, a battle of wills develops between the traveller and his guide, with Mohamed using any ruse to gain the upper hand – even pretending that some harmless fellow travellers are bandits about to attack them.

Despite his new confidence, Moorhouse begins to appreciate the folly of his plan to cross the desert entirely by himself. "Thrice now, sitting in an oasis just before departure, I had experienced a deep primeval fear of the void around. ... Wilfred Thesiger has told me that he would most certainly be crushed by the immensity of the desert if he found himself in it alone." Fortunately he is able to find more congenial guides than Mohamed. In Néma, the friendliest town he has so far encountered, he hires Sid' Ahmed and bids a welcome farewell to Mohamed. Moorhouse is "very sharp" with his new guide at first, distrusting the "awful, wheedling tilt of his head." But after many miles of stalwart service from the guide, who leads him safely past the border of Mauritania and into Mali, he sees his real worth. One day, after his guide has unloaded the camels, collected firewood, brewed tea, and offered the badly spent Moorhouse the first glass, Moorhouse declares, "You're a good man, Sid' Ahmed."

"His head tilted to one side in that mannerism I had associated with wheedling," Moorhouse writes. "I realised now that essentially it betrayed embarrassment. 'You're a good man yourself, *sayyid*,' he replied.

"Quickly, I turned my head away from him. I could feel the tears springing into my eyes, starting to roll down my scarecrow cheeks. There had been something terrible but very beautiful in that gesture of his. It was as though the thought that he was a decent human being had never crossed his mind before."

With Gul Mahomed leading the beast by its headrope, we lolloped off across the sandy scrub, in a rocking motion that could easily, I guessed, become soporific once your body became accustomed to the hard wooden edges of the saddle. Gradually I began to learn things. You carried a long riding stick, and with this you tapped the camel on the right side of his neck if you wanted him to veer left. If you wanted to break into a trot, you cut him smartly on the rump, or dug your dangling heels into his neck, like a jockey. To stop him, you hauled hard on the headrope. To make him couch so that you could dismount, you tapped him on the back of the head and hissed at him until he went down on his knees.

After a couple of hours, it seemed to me that the discomforts of camel-riding had been greatly exaggerated. True, it was tricky work rising from the ground, when you were flung heavily backwards, then forwards, then backwards again, as the animal came up onto its knees, then to the full extent of its hind legs and finally all-standing on its front feet too; and vice versa when coming to ground. Otherwise, it seemed largely a matter of allowing the body to sway back and forth with the beast's motion, flexibly, without straining to sit tight – though at the trot one bounced and bumped ungracefully in the rahhla, the huge saddle, with its great butterfly wings at each side. The tendency was then to hold on to these.

Mauritius

Journey to Mauritius
by Jacques-Henri Bernardin de Saint-Pierre

Translated from the French by Jason Wilson

Interlink Books, 2003 (first published 1773)

Though he is little known today, the author of *Journey to Mauritius*, the oldest work in this collection, was a best-selling writer in the eighteenth century.

Jacques-Henri Bernardin de Saint-Pierre was the author of *Paul et Virginie*, a romantic tale of star-crossed lovers on a tropical island. The island was Mauritius, where he had spent twenty-eight months from 1768 to 1770. But before spinning his experience into fiction, he wrote this book, which with all its earnestness, patchy construction, and oddly charming digressions, provides a valuable glimpse of the early days of this Indian Ocean nation.

Well-travelled though rather naive, Bernardin arrived on Mauritius at the age of thirty-one – as the translator tells us, "heart-broken by his affair with a Polish princess while working as a spy for France in Warsaw." Offered a job as a military engineer in Madagascar, he quarrelled with his employer on the way there and left his ship in Mauritius after a harrowing journey in which the ship's mainmast was shattered by lightning and almost a dozen sailors died from scurvy. On Mauritius he worked as a master mason and made ends meet by trading money on the black market.

In writing about his stay on the island, Bernardin is well aware that he is breaking new ground. None of the greatest French writers, he points out toward the end of his book, have written a travel book: neither Voltaire, nor d'Alembert, Buffon, or Rousseau (who later became his friend). "I think that the travel genre, so little attempted," he continues, "is packed with problems. You need universal knowledge, order in your plan, warmth in your style, and sincerity. You must speak about everything."

Early in this book the reader gets the uneasy feeling that Bernardin does indeed intend to speak about everything. He begins with a description of the dodo, which even in 1768 he was too late to see

in the wild. The Dutch explorers, he writes, "found extremely odd birds as big as swans, without wings and in their place three or four black feathers. They could not fly. They called them nausea birds partly because they were so tough that they could not be cooked." Then come accounts of the soil ("a reddish colour, mixed with veins of iron"), plants (including a "prickly kind of asparagus" that grows twelve feet high), insects (including three species of cockroaches), sea turtles, parrots, the extremely prolific rats, and much more.

Perhaps because of his precarious finances, Bernardin appears willing to eat almost anything. He writes that "monkey flesh has a boring taste," that manatees taste like beef, and that parrots are "rather good to eat." Before reaching Mauritius he offers the startling observation that the remora, the fish that attaches itself to sharks by a sucker on its head, tastes "like fried artichokes."

Bernardin seems unsure what form a travel book should take, and alternates between excerpts from journals, letters to a friend, and straight narrative. Cataloguing gives way to storytelling when Bernardin describes his walking tour around the island and the characters he meets. Though he buys a slave to travel with (naming him after a friend, treating his wounded foot, and freeing him at the end of his journey), Bernardin is keenly aware of the suffering of the slaves, and recounts the story of forty maroons – escaped slaves – who threw themselves into the sea rather than be retaken. "For myself," he writes, "bearing in mind the blacks, I can think of nothing worse than slavery."

The murmuring of the springs, the beautiful green of the sea waves, the steady breeze, the scent of the *veloutier* trees, the harmonious plain, and the shaded hills seemed to spread happiness and peace around me. I regretted being alone; I invented plans, but from the rest of the world I would have only wanted some beloved objects to spend my life here.

I left this beautiful place in sorrow. I had hardly taken two hundred paces when I bumped into a troop of blacks armed with rifles. I walked towards them and recognized them as a detachment, a sort of island police force. They halted when they came up to me. One of them carried two small puppies in a gourd; another one dragged a woman

with rope made of rushes tied around her neck. This was the booty that had been taken from a camp of black maroons that they had just routed. They had killed one, whose *gris-gris*, a kind of talisman made like a rosary, they showed me. This black woman seemed overwhelmed with grief. I asked her some questions, which she refused to answer. On her back she carried a bag made from the vacoas tree. I opened it and was appalled, alas, to find a man's head inside! The beautiful scenery vanished, and I was faced with a land of abominations.

Mauritius

The Book of Color by Julia Blackburn

Vintage International, 1996

Written by a British novelist with family roots in Mauritius, *The Book of Color* is a memory novel, though the memories it relates are intertwined with imagination and speculation. (The talking pig that appears in the early pages is a hint that not all should be taken literally.) The narrator, whose sex is unspecified, relates the recollections of his or her grandfather, who trembles with Parkinson's disease and who carries with him a collection of boyhood mementos. These mementoes – a snail shell, a silver crucifix, a white feather, a piece of coral, a crab claw, the enormous nut from a *coco de mer*, and a tin box containing a musty powder – are the touchstones for the story that follows.

The old man's earliest memories come from the island of Praslin in the Seychelles. His missionary father, an avid hunter and an angry man obsessed with sin, has set out to wipe out "fornication" among the Seychellois. Various hints suggest that his zeal is rooted in a sinful secret whose nature the son absorbs unconsciously long before he learns the truth. The missionary's wife powders her face and shuns the sun, and a local woman named Evalina Larose lives with the family, though the boy doesn't know "if she was a servant or a distant relative." The shape of the *coco de mer* nut reminds the boy of a woman's body, and he lies in bed with it nestled on his pillow, "his lips close to the shining black skin."

When the missionary finds a local man in the act of copulation and shoots him in the arm, the victim's curse rebounds on the missionary's wife, who falls ill and appears to be losing her mind. The boy, the wife, and Evalina Larose are sent away to Mauritius, where the wife is admitted to a hospital and the boy goes to live with his uncle. Uncle Julius, the owner of a sugar plantation, is an angry man like the missionary father but a far less guilt-ridden one. The boy realizes very quickly that the servant his uncle refers to as "my mulatto" is in fact his uncle's son. When he meets his new tutor, he learns the secret of his own heritage.

149

The Book of Color portrays the Indian Ocean world of the narrator's grandfather as brightly coloured yet cruel and claustrophobic. The descriptions of Praslin and Mauritius have the freshness of a sensitive boy's perceptions, but the overpowering sense of sin he inherits from his father gives everything a second, often sinister, meaning. Land crabs are like hairy red hands, the long-tailed white birds suggest angels, and even after he has grown up, his mental image of the devil is that of "a black man with a pink tongue, pink fingernails, and the soles of his feet and the palms of his hands are pink as well." It is understandable that years later, remembering a storm that wreaked havoc on this sinister island, the old man confides, "I rather enjoyed it."

—◆—

My grandfather lapses back into silence and at first I think that he must have fallen asleep, but as I look at him I realise that he is walking through the streets of Port Louis, inspecting the damage that was inflicted by the storm. He wrinkles his nose at the stench of decay that hangs in the air. He crosses his feet in their felt slippers as he steps carefully over the swollen corpse of a dead dog, over the bales of brightly coloured silk that have burst out of a shop window and now lie derelict in the gutter, over all the rubble and confusion that surrounds him. Down by the market there is a cargo ship that has been swept bodily out of the sea and thrown on to the street, spilling its load of polished rice that is already beginning to ferment in a huge stinking heap. My grandfather goes to the Hotel Universe and is glad to see that it has survived even though it looks very battered. Somebody tells him about the horse that managed to swim to safety through one of the bedroom windows and they found it there in the morning, standing between two beds. He laughs to himself when he thinks of that.

Morocco

The Sand Child by Tahar ben Jelloun

Translated from the French by Alan Sheridan

Harcourt Brace Jovanovich, 1987

A wealthy Moroccan potter has seven daughters. According to tradition the lack of a male heir shames him and will cause his property to pass to his brothers. He decides on a bold step: the next time his wife becomes pregnant the child *will* be a son. When that child is born, his father gives a great feast and publishes a notice in the newspaper. The secret of the child's true sex is kept by the father, his wife, and the midwife. Before long the father has almost convinced himself of his own story.

The Sand Child is the story of Mohammed Ahmed, the "son," who senses early that something is wrong and whose entire life is shaped and distorted by the knowledge. Tahar ben Jelloun treats this potentially comic situation with beautiful gravity, peeling back one layer of deception, desire, and identity after another. In keeping with its theme, the story is told through a series of masks. A storyteller begins the tale, reading to his listeners from what he claims is the notebook of Mohammed Ahmed. He is not far into his account, however, when one of his hearers takes it over, claiming that *he* has the true words of Mohammed Ahmed, written on the pages of a cheap edition of the Koran. The second storyteller comes to an untimely end, and rather than let the story run into the desert without a resolution, two more men – and one woman – devise conclusions, each according to his or her understanding of what has gone before.

With its preoccupation with the nature of narrative, and its slightly antique atmosphere, the novel suggests the work of Jorge Luis Borges, and in the last pages of the book there appears what seems to be a tribute to Borges: the arrival from Buenos Aires of a blind writer and traveller, the owner of an extensive library, who intrigues all the listeners in the marketplace with his own additions to the tale of the "sand child."

The Sand Child is written in a rich and lyrical style that never becomes heavy and static, with a wealth of psychological subtlety

and a sympathetic understanding of the difficult role of women in Moroccan society.

———

The secret was there, in those pages, woven out of syllables and images. He entrusted it to me just before he died. He made me swear not to open it until forty days after his death, long enough to allow him to die completely. Forty days of mourning for us and of journeying through the darkness of the earth for him. I opened it on the night of the forty-first day. I was overwhelmed by perfume. I read the first sentence and understood nothing. I read a paragraph and understood nothing. I read the whole of the first page and was illuminated. Tears of astonishment came to my eyes; my heart pounded. I was in possession of a rare book, a book containing a secret, spanning a brief, intense life, written through the night of a long ordeal, hidden under large stones, and protected by the angel of malediction. This book, my friends, can be neither borrowed nor loaned. It cannot be read by innocent minds. The light that comes from it will blind those who are unprepared. I have read this book. I have deciphered it for others. You can gain access to it only by traversing my nights and my body. I am that book; I have paid with my life to read its secret. Having reached the end, after months of sleepless nights, I felt the book become embodied within me, for such is my aim.

Morocco

The Road to Fez by Ruth Knafo Setton
Counterpoint, 2000

Justine, a sexually ambiguous photographer from Paris, guides a young woman named Brit through the mellah, the Jewish quarter of a town in Morocco. They see a "shrunken door on which a spindly gold hand is painted," enter a hidden synagogue stripped of all decoration, and glimpse a woman in black as she turns her head at the end of a narrow archway. "A Chinese box world: door into door into door, no end," murmurs Justine. "I think I'll call this series: Land of the Door."

Land of the Door could serve as a title for this novel, too – filled as it is with doors, windows, and archways between cultures and realities. Justine and Brit are Jewish women who have broken away from the insular, fearful life of the mellah to enter a wider world. But Justine, though she loves Paris, is continually drawn back to Morocco, where she tries to rescue history by photographing "doors and windows and faces." Brit, who spent a dull grey childhood in Pennsylvania, her parents trying to pass themselves off as "Christians from Paris," has returned to Morocco for other reasons: to try to forget her mother's death, to visit the grave of a Jewish martyr at her mother's request, and most of all to see her uncle Gaby, with whom she fell in love as a little girl.

Gaby, a troubled, intense man of about thirty, works in a sardine factory but pours his creative energy into making ceramic art at a pottery where he is the only Jew among the Arabs. To Brit, her uncle is the real-life embodiment of her imaginary Blue Man, a "fearless gentle hero" who knows what it's like to be "different and alone." Crossing one of many forbidden boundaries, Brit finds her way past the always-locked blue door of Gaby's room to collect ingredients for a love spell: his shaving brush, an undershirt, a matchbox. Gaby meanwhile expresses his feelings by sculpting a barbed-wire wall with tiny openings through which Jew and Arab, Suleika and her forbidden lover, or he and his own dangerously attractive niece can see each other.

The legend of Suleika becomes more and more important as the story progresses, and is handled so ingeniously that it is nearly as intriguing as the present-day love story. In one version of the legend, Suleika, a beautiful Jewish girl, falls in love with an Arab boy, marries him and recites the formula of conversion to Islam. The boy is murdered by the brothers of the fiancée he jilted, and when Suleika tries to return to her people she is beheaded as a traitor in the city of Fez. The legend comes in many other versions, sometimes from members of Brit's family and sometimes in excerpts (apparently invented by the author) from interviews and memoirs and travel books. Each version is intended to make a different point, but in each of them Suleika, like Brit, is a beautiful and headstrong Jewish girl who courts danger by crossing boundaries.

While in Morocco, Brit hears a mysterious humming sound that seems to call her to Suleika. And when Gaby finally admits that he loves Brit as she does him, they leave at once for the city where Suleika was executed and buried. Their road trip is rendered as a series of sharp and sometimes sinister vignettes. When they arrive in Fez at last, a layered city of "minarets and mosques and mellah and medina and ville nouvelle," this novel, an intriguing blend of outsiders' and insiders' perspectives on Morocco, comes to a dramatic and unexpected end.

———

Turbaned and wrapped in a white apron, I dust the salon arabe in my grandparents' house, a stranglehold of memory – from the wall of old photos to Gaby's ceramic vessels: at least four feet high, red-stained sentinels from an ancient desert palace, guarding each corner. But the heart of the room is the long brass key that hangs in the center of a white wall. When I first saw the key, with a wall to itself, as if it held the answer to every mystery, I thought it was Gaby's key – miraculously out in the open, like Poe's purloined letter, where no one would think to look. But one night after dinner, when we all sauntered into this room for mint tea and sweets, Papa Naphtali told us a story about our old house in Toledo, with its orange trees and blue-tiled walls, and he pointed to the key and said: "One day we'll return home."

Later, Perla explained that he was talking about our family's house in Spain, when our ancestors fled the Inquisition by sailing across the Strait of Gibraltar to Morocco. But he had described the scent of orange blossoms and the courtyard where we drank wine and watched the moon, so vividly and fondly, it seemed as if we had just left Spain yesterday.

I stare at the brass key now, gleaming yet forlorn on its wall, and think of Gaby's key, and the key to the mellah gate: somehow all related, as if they are all the same key, but I can't find the link to unlock the door.

Mozambique

Voices Made Night by Mia Couto

Translated from the Portuguese by David Brookshaw

Heinemann, 1990

oices Made Night is the first collection of stories by the poet and
journalist Mia Couto. The titles of many of the stories, such
as "The Girl with a Twisted Future" and "Patanhoca, the Lovesick
Snake Catcher," have a whiff of magical realism that is borne out
by events that go a little beyond the realm of ordinary reality. But
underlying many of these stories is the hard historical kernel of the
suffering brought by terrorism and civil war.

Sometimes in these stories reality is distorted not by a supernatural
event but by the blind workings of bureaucracy. In "The Tale of the
Two Who Returned from the Dead," two men believed drowned
when a coastal village floods return unexpectedly. Because they have
been left off the list of flood-relief victims, and because the village
officials have allocated all the relief supplies (with a suitable rake-
off for themselves), it is no easy task for the two to reestablish their
existence.

"Suddenly, the ox exploded," begins one story. "It burst without so
much as a moo. In the surrounding grass a rain of chunks and slices fell,
as if the fruit and leaves of the ox. Its flesh turned into red butterflies.
Its bones were scattered coins." Though the explosion of the ox has a
conventional explanation, the cowherd responsible for it is sure it was
caused by *ndlati*, the bird of lightning. In another story, the arrival of
a submarine on the coast, carrying supplies to rebel forces, grows into
the legend of a whale that vomits food and supplies on request. As if
to prove that they are not naive, the villagers speculate on the political
meaning of the whale. "Who could be certain that the whale didn't
come from the socialist countries?"

Again and again in these concentrated tales, the intrusion of
"real life" causes an eruption of speculation and mythmaking on the
part of the Mozambican villagers. Yet the horrors of life in war-torn
Mozambique may be more unreal and fantastic than the traditional
legends the people use to explain them.

It happened right there, in the middle of the square, full of people queueing at the store. Zuzé Paraza, a retired painter, spat out bits of his two-a-penny cigarette. Then he coughed, shaking the gauntness of his body to its bones. Suddenly, so those who witnessed the event say, he vomited a live raven. The bird emerged whole from his belly. It had been so long inside him that it already knew how to talk. All covered in spittle, at first it didn't look like a bird. People gathered round Zuzé, peeping at the creature fallen from his cough. It shook itself free of its mucus covering, raised its beak, and to everyone's astonishment, uttered some words. With conviction, despite the bad pronunciation.

Mozambique

Dumba Nengue: Run for Your Life by Lina Magaia

Translated from the Portuguese by Michael Wolfers

Africa World Press, 1988

How do you write about the most extreme atrocities committed by one person against another? A journalistic voice can seem too cold and detached, but fancy literary techniques may come across as beside the point, or even obscene.

The stories in this collection are true. They have titles like "Their Heads Were Crushed like Peanuts" and "Pieces of Human Flesh Fell in Belinda's Yard." The shortest of them is only three paragraphs long.

Some of the episodes described were witnessed by the author, and some are reported secondhand. The author tells them in the plainest possible style, while leaving in the human and emotional details. The result reads like some of the cruelest of the Grimm brothers' fairy tales, but without the consolation of being imaginary.

In 1976, as the book's introduction explains, the Rhodesian security forces organized a group of armed bandits. It was called the MNR (for Mozambique National Resistance) or Renamo (its Portuguese abbreviation), and its purpose was to wreak havoc in Mozambique, which had just gained independence under a socialist government. Mozambique was harbouring guerrillas who were fighting the Ian Smith regime in Rhodesia. When these guerrillas succeeded in overthrowing Smith and creating the state of Zimbabwe, the apartheid government in South Africa became the new masters of Renamo. South Africa used the bandits not only to keep Mozambique impoverished and vulnerable but also to help thwart efforts by South Africa's neighbours to build economic cooperation.

Renamo's methods are starkly rendered. A group of bandits meets Bertana's husband (the author doesn't appear to know his name), who has returned home after working in Johannesburg. Seeing his boots, the bandits take him for a militiaman, but he tells them he knows nothing about the militia or where they are. The bandits hang him upside down from a tree and slit his throat as if he were a goat

being slaughtered. They forbid Bertana to take the body down, and after she buries her husband they return, break her jaw, and order her to dig up the body with her bare hands.

Villagers in these stories are shot, bayoneted, drowned in wells, hacked with axes, or beaten to death with pestles. Some fight back – one unarmed old man even grabs a gun from a bandit and drives him off – but retaliation comes swiftly. The bandits kidnap young boys and "baptize" them by forcing them to kill neighbours or relatives. Some of these recruits become addicted to killing as if to a drug. Kidnapped girls are gang-raped or taken as "wives" by bandit leaders. The return of one of these traumatized girls who has managed to escape is one of the most moving scenes in the book.

Though in one sense this collection is simply one atrocity story after another, a surprising amount of detail emerges about what normal life is like for these Mozambican villagers, and what it is they are fighting to protect. Wealth for them means a cement block house, a well, some cattle, a few cashew trees, and maybe a mafurra tree, which bears a tasty white fruit. In "The Lovely Newlyweds," the author describes a joyful wedding ceremony in which the whole community takes part, joking and singing and exchanging gifts – until the inevitable arrival of the men with guns. Though it's a short book that no one would wish longer, *Dumba Nengue* helps us understand the continuing human cost of conflict not only in Mozambique but also in places like Liberia and Sierra Leone.

———

The militiamen waited for the bandits to emerge from the cane field.

As the day got brighter, one of the militiamen suggested setting the cane on fire. Everyone agreed.

The bandits were inside the cane. The flames leapt high because the cane burned well.

One bandit ran out in flames. He was shot and fell forever. Others, unfortunately, managed to escape on a flank the militiamen could not cover.

They searched near the river. Five bodies were found, then another that was charred and bullet-ridden. The bodies were taken away.

Several days later, the river brought up the bodies of two other bandits with their knapsacks stuffed with stolen cigarettes, medicines, sugar and the exercise books of the children of Calanga school.

Someone said, "Let's leave these bodies in the river to feed the fish."

The bodies were still floating up and down, according to the tide.

Namibia

The Harmless People by Elizabeth Marshall Thomas
Alfred A. Knopf, 1959

"The harmless people," though it sounds like an anthropologist's slightly condescending description, is in fact the translation of *zhu twa si*, which is what the San of the Kalahari Desert call themselves. "*Twa* means 'just' or 'only'," says Thomas, "in the sense that you say: 'It was just the wind' or 'It is only me.'"

This charming humility seems characteristic of the San, a people who were known then as the Bushmen. Elizabeth Marshall Thomas lived with them for extended periods in the 1950s together with her anthropologist parents and other family members, and *The Harmless People* is her account of the last of these visits. The first part of her book describes her time among the Gikwe San of Botswana (then Bechuanaland), while a little over half of the book deals with the Kung San of north-eastern Namibia (then the territory of South-West Africa – a former colony of Germany turned over to South African trusteeship after World War I).

Except when setting the scene at the beginning of the book, Thomas avoids analysis and explanation to a remarkable degree. Most of this book, which is written in a simple and seemingly easy style, reads as if she simply followed the San around for a certain period of time and wrote down everything they did. The narrative is very much in the moment, and we experience both the mundane and the extraordinary events with little or no mediation by the author – not even an expression of surprise. Beginning writers are often directed to show, not tell, but few have followed this advice as thoroughly as the young woman whose first book this was. Yet the reader gradually realizes that her method is much more sophisticated than it seems, and that by telling seemingly unrelated episodes she is building up a coherent picture of an endangered culture.

That culture is particularly interesting because, as she notes, the San and the related Khoikhoi people are the "earliest human inhabitants still living in southern Africa." At the time she knew them, the San of the Kalahari dressed in scraps of leather, hunted with little bows and poisoned arrows, and carried their water in empty ostrich shells.

Though the Plains Indians of North America were celebrated for making use of every part of the bison, they had nothing on the San, who ate every part of the antelope, "even the mucous lining of the nostrils and the gristle inside the ears," then carved new arrowheads from the bones.

Though their existence seems "primitive" and the San themselves suffer from feelings of inferiority to bigger and more powerful peoples, subtle details reveal the tenacity and intelligence they bring to the task of surviving in the desert. They know which of the many insect grubs is highly poisonous, for instance, and at what stage of its life it should be harvested and applied to the arrow shaft (not to the actual point, to help prevent their children from accidentally pricking themselves).

One example illustrates their exact sense of geography and their scrupulous honesty regarding their few possessions. Thomas's family's party was travelling by truck over many miles of seemingly featureless desert, with a number of San as passengers, when the driver spotted a broken ostrich shell. Knowing how valued it might be for making jewellery, he offered to stop. Toma, the local San leader, told him to keep going. "The egg, he thought, belonged to a man named Crooked Kwi who had left it there one season and would return for it someday soon. ... It was just where Crooked Kwi had said it would be."

Despite her admiration for the San's abilities, and her obvious liking for many individuals, Thomas doesn't overlook their more unpleasant habits – such as eviscerating and cooking a tortoise while it is still alive. The San are as particular about manners and appearances as a society matron, and they consider Toma's wife to be a "model personality ... in spite of her extremely jealous and vindictive moods," because she is good-looking and keeps her hands and face clean.

Yet their stories, their sense of humour, the music they make with an instrument called a *guashi*, and their magic (Thomas witnesses a very successful rain dance) make the San seem a fascinating and endearing people. It is all the more heartbreaking, then, to read the final chapter of this book, which describes how the San of the 1980s, for many years used as slave labour on white-owned farms, were now being pressed into service as trackers to help the South Africans crush the movement for Namibian independence.

The little girl took after her mother, Gao Feet's ugly wife, but her two men, her husband and her stepson, were a family of great beauty. Both had wide, grave eyes and golden skins, and both were musicians, but the young father himself was an Orpheus. He owned a guashi, a stringed instrument which he had made, and he carried his guashi wherever he went. As he plucked the strings, playing chords with his long fingers, he would hum the notes of a song that were not the same notes that his fingers were playing; he wove two themes and made a web of music, the guashi playing an intricate accompaniment while he sang a melody.

The guashi was made of a hollowed log about a foot long with a wooden lid fixed over it, forming a sounding-chamber. At one end of the log, five wands were fixed which held five sinew strings that reached from the tips of the wands to the opposite end of the log. Anyone but a Bushman finds it hard to play a guashi, for the strings are always slipping out of tune and the position one plays it in is awkward. The guashi is set on the ground and the player squats before it, holding it steady with his feet or the edges of his hands; but the sound is beautiful, sometimes full, sometimes thin, and makes very deep and various music, for Bushmen, their music being by far their greatest art, are not given to whistles or clear, shrill sounds – all their instruments make blurred and vibrant music with a richness in every note. Their compositions, too, are never simple, not even the music of their musical games, but always mixed, always subtle, partly gay but partly sad.

Namibia

The Purple Violet of Oshaantu by Neshani Andreas
Heinemann, 2001

Gracefully told and deceptively simple, *The Purple Violet of Oshaantu* is the story of a disastrous marriage and a woman's struggle to reclaim her life. An African woman who marries the wrong man, the novel conveys, must face not only domestic violence but also a society that places a high value on appearances.

Shange, the husband of Mee Kauna, shames his wife by openly carrying on a series of affairs: the latest with a young woman who lives in a white blockhouse that Shange has built for her. He beats his wife as well. "We all remember how beautiful she was when she first arrived here as a new bride," says Mukwankala, a feisty old woman who is the only one to stand up to Shange. "She was so delicate and she came when these flowers were in bloom." Now Kauna's face is scarred.

When Shange dies suddenly (he is found sitting in the living room over a meal his wife has left for him), the villagers understandably see it as a very convenient development for Kauna. The widow's utter lack of sentiment – she will not cry, she will not wear black, she will not agree to speak at the funeral – only makes matters worse.

Behind her back, Kauna is accused of killing her husband through witchcraft or poison. At a hastily organized tribunal, a crowd of Shange's relatives question her about her husband's death and his property. "We need to know about his money, bank accounts, insurance policies, his cattle and all sorts of other things," one man insists.

"You knew how he treated me," Kauna responds. "Do you honestly think that he would entrust me with his money and the papers you are talking about?"

Mee Kauna's closest friend is Mee Ali, who narrates the story and works hard to save Kauna from herself. Ali keeps her company, cleans her rooms, deals with visitors, speaks up for Kauna at the tribunal, and agonizes over whether to stand up and speak on her behalf at the funeral.

What really happened to Kauna's husband? Though Ali has faith in her friend, the reader, like the villagers, may have doubts. But while we wonder, we also learn about the rituals and customs that govern life in a Namibian village – including the custom whereby a widow can be stripped by her husband's relatives of everything she owns.

———

I never understood why Shange and Kauna had ever married in the first place. They were like day and night. Two such different human beings. "I was the daughter of a pastor and a teacher, a high school girl and a virgin. I was perfect for him. It was more for his ego than anything else. I realised that later," Kauna told me one day. "He worked at the mine. You know how impressive mineworkers are. And before I knew it, I was married," she said, as if it was a joke.

I had heard it was a big wedding, bigger than the village had ever seen before, a fancy, flashy wedding. Her mother, Mee Maria, preened herself like a big bird. But as soon as Shange built their own homestead, he changed.

What I still did not understand was the way people in this community treated her. It was as if the failure of their marriage was her fault! They laughed at her and stigmatised her.

It was her fault that her husband looked at other women.

It was her fault that her husband beat her.

It was her fault that her husband did this or did that. Oh, it was just too much.

Kauna started to say, "Maybe if I had been a nurse, a teacher or any of those office workers, he would have treated me better. Maybe if, maybe if ..."

Niger

In Sorcery's Shadow
by Paul Stoller and Cheryl Olkes
University of Chicago Press, 1987

When the anthropologist Sir Edward Evans-Pritchard, doing research among the Azande of Central Africa in the 1920s, wanted to learn about witchcraft and sorcery, he sent his cook to learn and to report back to him. When Paul Stoller set out to investigate sorcery among the Songhay of Niger in the 1970s and 1980s, he became an apprentice sorcerer himself – a decision that changed his life.

Though he shares authorship with his wife Cheryl Olkes, *In Sorcery's Shadow* is Paul Stoller's story. As a Peace Corps volunteer in the westernmost tip of Niger, near the borders of Mali and Burkina Faso, Stoller taught school and became fluent in Songhay, the language of the shopkeepers and millet farmers who inherited the legacy of the once-powerful Songhay kingdom. When he returned to Songhay territory as an anthropologist, he came with an understandable confidence in his ability to understand the local culture.

One day while Stoller is living in the village of Mehanna, he is visited by a muscular young man named Djibo Mounmouni. Djibo is a *sorko*, "one of three kinds of Songhay magician-healers," and during his visit Djibo witnesses a minor accident that he takes as a sign that he should teach Stoller how to be a *sorko* as well. A friend of Stoller warns him against Djibo. "He's after your money. He lies. He rapes women." Yet despite Stoller's scepticism about the reality of sorcery, he is already sorely tempted. "I had arrived at a crossroads. I couldn't refuse an opportunity to learn magic from the inside. I couldn't deny my private desire to become a more powerful person."

Djibo sets Stoller to work learning magical herbs and roots and memorizing incantations. He prepares "sorko food" that swells in Stoller's belly, and that is meant to stay in his body permanently and prepare him to be a sorcerer. He tells Stoller tales of his own father, also a *sorko*, who visits the water spirits under the Niger River for

166

as long as three days at a time, emerging dry at the end of his visit. The village of Mehanna has a sinister reputation for witchcraft, and Djibo teaches him how to identify witches.

The real test of Stoller's belief in his new powers comes when a friend in Niamey, the capital, asks him to do something about a Frenchman who has been treating his employees cruelly. Stoller has been learning from another sorcerer, an older and seemingly more honourable man in the village of Tillaberi, who tells him, "In the case of a mean chief, the solution is simple." Stoller, taking no chances, censors the sorcerer's instructions for this book. "You take the ___ __ of a _____ chicken and bury it under the threshold of the mean chief's compound, a place he steps over every day. When you recite the incantation, no one must see you and no one must overhear you." Balanced between belief and disbelief, Stoller performs the rite, which produces a dramatic effect – though not the one intended.

As Stoller moves deeper into the world of Songhay sorcery, he faces the responsibility of his newfound powers and uncomfortable realizations about his own character, as well as the dangerous resentment of other sorcerers who sense his abilities. In the remote town of Wanzerbe, where he has gone to see a powerful woman named Kassey, he finally reaches the limits of his courage.

Djibo tapped my arm. He pointed to a woman who was walking toward us. Balanced on her head was a mountain of brightly decorated enameled metal pots. "Paul, you have the sorko food in your belly, do you not?"

"Yes, I do," I responded …

He waved his hand in the direction of the woman with the pots on her head. She had stopped to talk with another woman going toward the river. "Go up to that woman with the pots on her head. Look at her eyes even if she attempts to avoid your gaze. When your eyes meet, a tear will roll out of her left eye."

"Sure it will," I said sarcastically. Hoping to prove Djibo wrong, I approached the woman with the pots on her head: she was slowly walking away from the market. When she realized that I intended to intercept her, she quickened her

pace. She lost her balance and some of her pots thumped into the sand. Like a conqueror, I stood over this woman as she picked up two of her pots. For a second our eyes locked. A large tear dropped from the corner of her left eye and ran down her cheek. She stood up stiffly and ran away, somehow holding on to her pots. I returned to Djibo, stupefied.

"I don't believe it, Djibo. The woman would not look at me, and when she did, a tear dropped onto her cheek from her left eye."

"Did you smell her?"

"No, I didn't."

Djibo shook his head. "One day you will be able to smell them, but that lies ahead of you on your path."

"Smell what?"

"Witches, you fool."

Nigeria

Things Fall Apart by Chinua Achebe

Anchor Books, 1994 (first published 1959)

Things Fall Apart, possibly Africa's best-known novel, tells the story of Okonkwo, a strong man with a hot temper and a devotion to tradition. Relating his tale in a clean, authoritative, almost biblical prose, Chinua Achebe succeeds in making us sympathize with this violent, often intolerant man, and to feel the tragic dimensions of his inability to adapt to changing times.

Like the heroes of Greek tragedy, Okonkwo is monumental but not especially complex. Achebe makes no mystery about what motivates his hero: "Perhaps down in his heart Okonkwo was not a cruel man. But his whole life was dominated by fear, the fear of failure and of weakness." Okonkwo is determined to be nothing like his father, a charming but idle flute player who spends any money he has on palm wine, and dies owing debts to everyone. Okonkwo forges himself into a harsh and hard-working man of honour, a role that gains him prestige in the village but proves a fatal weakness in situations demanding more gentleness and subtlety.

Things Fall Apart illustrates traditional Ibo life in both word and action. "Among the Ibo the art of conversation is regarded very highly," says the narrator, "and proverbs are the palm-oil with which words are eaten." The novel is seasoned with dozens of proverbs, from "When mother-cow is chewing grass its young ones watch its mouth" to "When the moon is shining the cripple becomes hungry for a walk." So many ceremonies take place in this short novel that Ibo village life begins to resemble a pageant. There are consultations with the local oracle, the Week of Peace between harvest and planting, wrestling contests, wedding feasts, funerals marked by cannon fire, and perhaps most important, the frightening appearances of the *egwuwu* or masked spirits that represent the nine villages of Okonkwo's clan.

One might expect a man like Okonkwo to thrive in this world of ceremony, where everything must be done in the accepted way, but his rigidity causes him to run foul of tradition, as if he sabotages himself by trying too hard. When his youngest wife fails to cook the afternoon meal, he violates the Week of Peace by beating her – his

scandalized reaction to a woman's failure to fulfil her role making him forget a much more important custom. And when, to resolve a feud, a young man from another village is sent to live with him as a hostage, the conflict between Okonkwo's fatherly feelings toward the boy and what he sees as his obligation to the community is resolved in a way that is tragically wrong.

Though tradition is the lifeblood of the Ibo, Achebe subtly underlines that tradition is never cut and dried. Customs vary from one village to another, and though Okonkwo's people believe it is only right to throw away twin babies in the Evil Forest, they consider it foolish that men of title are forbidden to tap palm trees, and are forced to stand by while young men kill trees by doing it incorrectly. "All their customs are upside-down," says Okonkwo's friend Obierika about two neighbouring villages. "They do not decide bride-price as we do, with sticks. They haggle and bargain as if they were buying a goat or a cow in the market."

It is perfectly in character that when the first white missionaries come with their strange new religion, Okonkwo can find no way to accommodate himself to them. In the end, he attains a kind of grandeur by sacrificing himself in defence of traditions that mean everything to him, yet that he does not entirely understand.

———

Okonkwo spent the next few days preparing his seed-yams. He looked at each yam carefully to see whether it was good for sowing. Sometimes he decided that a yam was too big to be sown as one seed and he split it deftly along its length with his sharp knife. His eldest son, Nwoye, and Ikemefuna helped him by fetching the yams in long baskets from the barn and in counting the prepared seeds in groups of four hundred. Sometimes Okonkwo gave them a few yams each to prepare. But he always found fault with their effort, and he said so with much threatening.

"Do you think you are cutting up yams for cooking?" he asked Nwoye. "If you split another yam of this size, I shall break your jaw. You think you are still a child. I began to own a farm at your age. And you," he said to Ikemefuna, "do you not grow yams where you come from?"

Nigeria

The Slave Girl by Buchi Emecheta

George Braziller, 1977

Early in this evocative novel, a little girl and her older brother walk from the edge of their village into the forest. "The gray mist of dawn lay so heavily upon the horizon that it was impossible to see beyond a few yards. ... The night animals had gone into hiding and the day ones were still reluctant to come out into the open to start their early morning activities." The boy and girl walk in silence, awed by a power that they sense in the forest, and the girl tries to muffle the sound of the metal charms that she wears to ward off death. She is the first of her mother's daughters to survive infancy, and her parents have recently died from a new disease called "felenza."

They come to a pure stream, and Ojebeta, the girl, wonders aloud why the water is so clean. Haven't the spirits of the dead been washing themselves during the night?

"The people of the dead are not as dirty and noisy as we are," says Ojebeta's brother Okolie. "They don't go about disturbing the peace or stirring up mud. They float, almost like birds."

The closeness of the two orphaned children is beautifully rendered, but what makes the scene heartbreaking is that the reader knows – and the girl does not – that Okolie is taking her to be sold as a slave.

Students of slavery are aware that the institution existed in Africa long before the Europeans introduced "chattel slavery," the system under which Africans were torn from their homeland and carried on disease-ridden ships to the New World, where they lived in most cases without rights and without hope of freedom, worked without compensation, and knew that their children and their children's children would remain the personal property of the master. In Africa, a slave might be a prisoner of war, a poor relation, or a twin child rejected because twins were unlucky. The slave would often be treated like a member of the family – though perhaps a second-class member – and might marry into the family that owned him or her, or be granted freedom.

171

This milder form of slavery is the subject of *The Slave Girl*, and it makes the quiet point that the kindest forms of bondage are still bondage, and still take their toll.

Ojebeta's story is sadder because her bondage is so preventable. The novel takes place in the early twentieth century, when the trans-Atlantic slave trade has ended and the English colonizers are shutting down the slave markets in West Africa. Ojebeta's brother – not cruel or heartless but very self-centred as the young so often are – has decided to sell his little sister so that he can dress in style for his coming-out dance. On his way to sell her, he encounters Eze, an older man who questions him sharply. "The way you are holding her, one would think you were going to sell her or something. But no blood brother would think of doing such a thing."

Yet Okolie does not turn back, and sells his sister to the rich market woman Ma Palagada after a haggling session that shames him. Afterwards he is unable to suppress his remorse: "Who would encourage her to save her first earnings to buy herself a new European cloth? Who would call her by her pet names and tell her she was prettier than the queen of Idu, who would show her the farm that used to belong to their father, and tell her what he used to say and what he used to do?" But before long Okolie finds a way to rationalize what he has done, and to live with himself.

Is it a virtue to be adaptable? History tells us that the attempt to turn Native Americans into slaves failed because they quickly died under a regime of forced labour. Imported Africans were hardier and more adaptable. Is it better to remain oneself and die, or to change and survive? Ojebeta, festooned through her childhood with protective charms, is destined to be a survivor, but by the time she sees her native village again she has changed deeply.

—

He knew why they were laughing. It was not just because of Ojebeta's safety charms, the bells and cowrie shells that jingled and clanged when she made the slightest movement. It was because his sister also had a very interesting face. All over her features were traced intricate tattoos, the pattern of spinach leaves, with delicate branches running down the bridge of her nose, spreading out on her forehead and

ending up at the top of her ears. On each cheek was drawn the outline of a large spinach leaf looking ready to be picked. It was not that many Ibos did not have facial tribal marks of different kinds, rather that few would have put so many on the face of one little girl. But Ojebeta's mother Umeadi, when she realised that her daughter was going to live, had had a reason for going to the expense of engaging the services of the most costly face-marker in Ibuza. For, with such a riot of tribal spinach marks on her only daughter's face, no kidnapper would dream of selling her into slavery. What was more, if she got lost her people would always know her, for although the patterns on her face might seem madness here to these Ibos from the East who frequented Otu Onitsha market, among the Western Ibos called the Aniochas it was a distinctive and meaningful design.

Nigeria

The Palm-Wine Drinkard by Amos Tutuola

Grove Press, 1994 (first published 1952)

The hero of this "brief, thronged, grisley and bewitching story," as the poet Dylan Thomas called it, is a devoted drinker of palm-wine – so devoted that drinking palm-wine is his only occupation. His father hires an expert tapster to supply his son with drink, and before long he is drinking (with some help from his friends) a total of 225 kegs of palm-wine a day.

One day disaster strikes. The tapster dies in a fall from a palm tree, and our hero is unable to find a suitable replacement. "When I saw that there was no palm-wine for me again, and nobody could tap it for me, then I thought within myself that old people were saying that the whole people who had died in this world, did not go to heaven directly, but they were living in one place somewhere in this world. So that I said that I would find out where my palm-wine tapster who had died was."

So begins this unusual small epic, written by a civil service messenger with six years of elementary education. Steeped in Yoruba storytelling traditions but peppered with modern-day references, crowded with strange monsters and improbable events told with perfect sincerity, and enlivened with psychologically charged imagery that would make even a non-Freudian sit up and take notice, this tale violates dozens of grammatical rules and novelistic conventions yet provides in abundance the one indispensable quality of literature: it is alive.

The palm-wine drinkard, armed with a supply of juju, sets out from village to village in search of his tapster. After seven months he meets an old man who is actually a god, and who promises to tell him where his tapster is if he will find the house of Death and bring him back in a net. "When I reached his (Death's) house, he was not at home by that time, he was in his yam garden which was very close to his house, and I met a small rolling drum in his verandah, then I beat it to Death as a sign of salutation." Annoyed to be visited by a living man, Death commands the drum strings to tighten around the drinkard, but the drinkard retaliates with his juju by making the

174

"ropes of the yams in his garden" tighten around Death. They release each other, and Death, seeming to relent, shows the drinkard around his property and gives him a bed for the night.

After surviving another attempt to kill him, the drinkard succeeds in capturing Death and hauls him back to the village of the old man, who had hoped to get rid of the drinkard and is shocked to see him still alive. Death escapes, and as a result "has no permanent place to dwell or stay, and we are hearing his name about in the world."

More adventures follow. The drinkard rescues a beautiful young woman from a Skull who has equipped himself as a "complete gentleman" by renting body parts from various other creatures. The drinkard marries the young woman, and before they reach the Deads' Town they face dangers and challenges on Wraith-Island, in Unreturnable-Heaven's town, and with the Red-people of Red-town. They are helped by Faithful-Mother and by the benevolent creatures Drum, Dance, and Song, and threatened by the Invisible-Pawn, the hungry-creature, and by the eerie sight of four hundred dead babies marching down a road with sticks in their hands. What does it all mean? It would be too bold to say for sure, but this odd and fascinating story sends the imagination in unexpected directions.

—

We met about 400 dead babies on that road who were singing the song of mourning and marching to Deads' Town at about two o'clock in the mid-night and marching towards the town like soldiers, but these dead babies did not branch into the bush as the adult-deads were doing if they met us, all of them held sticks in their hands. But when we saw that these dead babies did not care to branch for us then we stopped at the side for them to pass peacefully, but instead of that, they started to beat us with the sticks in their hands, then we began to run away inside the bush from these babies, although we did not care about any risk of that bush which might happen to us at night, because these dead babies were the most fearful creatures for us.

Nigeria

Aké: The Years of Childhood by Wole Soyinka

Random House, 1982

The theme of many African novels and memoirs is the clash between traditional village life and the "modern" world of Western culture, education, and technology. This clash is often presented as loss or even tragedy, but in this luminous memoir of childhood, Wole Soyinka paints a picture of a world in which the encounter can be fruitful, and in which the saints and the forest spirits are equally alive and powerful.

Soyinka grew up in the self-contained world of a parsonage compound. His father, headmaster of the local school, was known to his friends as S. A., a name his son understands as Essay, "one of those careful stylistic exercises in prose which follow set rules of composition, are products of fastidiousness and elegance, set down in beautiful calligraphy that would be the envy of most copyists of any age." Fond of debate, Essay would argue for hours with his friend the bookseller. His mock threats alarmed the young Soyinka, who felt he should warn the bookseller's wife that "her husband was about to be sold into slavery, banished from Abeokuta, hurled from the church tower, tied to a tree in the dead of night alone with evil spirits ..." But although Essay never followed through on his physical threats, he was verbally formidable. In one memorable scene, he reduces a man who has picked one of his roses to utter humiliation while never departing from perfect politeness.

Soyinka's mother, known as Wild Christian, has all the turbulent emotionality her husband lacks. Her Christian faith doesn't prevent her from telling hair-raising tales of the supernatural. In telling how her uncle repelled a forest spirit with his Bible and some well-chosen words, her aim is not to deny the existence of the traditional gods and spirits but to prove the ability of Christianity to contend with them.

Soyinka never condescends to his childhood self, and for the most part he avoids hindsight, describing long-ago events with the freshness, immediacy, and partial understanding of a child. He portrays himself as given to daydreaming and capable when

abstracted of unconsciously shredding a houseplant or even blowing a hole in the ceiling with his father's rifle. But at the same time he is not overly self-absorbed: the book teems with miniature portraits of neighbours and friends, from the deranged old man who guards the village against Hitler to the eternal houseguest known to everyone as Mayself.

Sheltered for years in his own compound, Soyinka doesn't really experience the world of his own village until the day he hears a police band pass by and slips out the gate to follow the musicians. What follows is a miniature epic, a long day's adventure in which the boy, entranced by the red fezzes of the musicians and the vibration of the bass drum in his own stomach, passes a familiar bookshop and into terra incognita: a photographer's studio, a bicycle repair shop, a maternity clinic, a "sewing academy," and a market where skulls and dried snakes are sold as well as crayfish, roots, and slabs of meat. In a few pages, the author allows us to experience the town as freshly and directly as his boyhood self once did.

In its sensual immediacy, its cast of memorable characters, the vividness of its language, and the subtlety of its insight into the mind of a young boy, *Aké: The Years of Childhood* is one of the greatest achievements of African literature.

———

When Essay dissected a piece of yam, weighed it carefully, transferred to his plate, paused, turned it around, sliced off a piece and returned it to the dish, then commenced the same ritual with the meat and stew, she would shake her head and ask,

"Does that extra piece really matter?"

Essay merely smiled, proceeded to chew methodically, slicing off each piece of meat, yam, like a geometric exercise, lifting a scoop of stew with the edge of his knife and plastering the slice of yam like a master mason. He never drank between mouthfuls, not even a sip. At debate time however, he soon grew as excitable as the bookseller, the shrillest of them all with his tiny twinkling eyes. He appeared to have the sun permanently beamed in his eyes. The bookseller brought into the house that aura of guinea-fowl, turkeys, sheep and

goats all of which he raised in his abundant compound. The sheep were always being rounded up; either the gates had been left carelessly open by a visitor or the stubborn animals had found yet another gap in the stone-and-mud walls. Thin and peppery, leather-taut cheekbones thrust out restlessly, he punctuated his discourse with bird-like gestures. Even at his most aggressive his shoulders slouched, his fingers refused to release the cloth-cap which, outside, never left his head, perhaps because he was completely bald. We could tell his laughter apart, shrill and raspy, revealing gapped teeth which imparted to his face, finally, the look of an old wicker-chair.

Nigeria

Efuru by Flora Nwapa

Heinemann, 1987 (first published 1966)

Everyone agrees that Efuru is a remarkable young woman –
beautiful, intelligent, hardworking, and goodhearted. People in
her Niger River village don't understand why she has chosen Adizua,
a poor and rather ordinary man, to be her husband. But although the
villagers accept the newlyweds, two things bother them: a year after
the marriage, Adizua has not yet paid a dowry to Efuru's family, and
Efuru has not yet had a child.

When the dowry is eventually paid, the villagers are left with only
one problem to fret over. Though everyone recognizes Efuru's fine
qualities, these are outweighed by her one basic failure. "They did
not see the reason why Adizua should not marry another woman
since, according to them, two men do not live together. To them
Efuru was a man since she could not reproduce."

Efuru is written by Flora Nwapa, the first African woman to
found a publishing company. The author recounts Efuru's story in
a leisurely, assured storytelling style that presents scenes both plain
and dramatic without straining after effect. No rhetoric is needed to
make plain how difficult life is for a Nigerian woman.

As we watch Efuru cope with the problems of life, we gradually
absorb a wealth of cultural detail as well. Customs are rarely
explained, and even a number of unfamiliar terms are left undefined,
but the story is told so clearly that the reader gets the essentials
from the context, and has the intimate sensation of looking on as
an invisible observer. We hear lullabies and stories and rhymes for
children (some of which make no sense even to those who repeat
them), and we notice the recurrence of certain customs: the breaking
of a kola nut for a guest, or a saying like "Your ears are not for
hearing, but for decoration." A five-day-old baby is given alligator
pepper to chew "so that her tongue will be free." We are shown how
a house is decorated with white clay, red mud, and charcoal, and we
learn the secret of the "mud wardrobe," a room within a room where
valuables and homemade gin are hidden.

Other details, dropped in passing, hint at strange or even supernatural dimensions of life that are calmly accepted by the villagers. "You know, I was looking for uziza the other day," Efuru said, "and I only asked a woman from whom I had bought some pears and she told me at once where to get it. I went straight there and got it. Another day, I was looking for akpukpo akabo and the fat of a python. I asked somebody and he took me to where I got them. But what puzzles me is the cheapness of the things in that market." What did Efuru need with the fat of a python? She doesn't say, and her friends, who presumably know, don't ask. As for "uziza" and "akpukpo akabo," we are left to wonder.

Efuru goes to her father one day to ask him about a series of dreams she has had, in which she dives to the bottom of a lake and meets a beautiful woman who combs her long black hair with a golden comb and uses fish as firewood. Her father realizes at once that Efuru has been chosen to worship Umahiri, the woman of the lake. Yet even though the villagers believe that Efuru's unsought connection with this divine being is the reason for her troubles with motherhood, the stigma still remains.

The various characters of the novel are never passive victims. We see them constantly taking action to better their situations, helping one another, and changing in the process. One of the most touching relationships develops between Efuru and Ajanupu, the sister of her mother-in-law. Ajanupu is loud and opinionated, yet perceptive. She is the first to notice when Efuru becomes pregnant, and is quick with advice on what to eat (no snails, no okra, no ogbono soup) and how to behave. Despite Ajanupu's brashness, the two women become increasingly close as the years pass. Like Ajanupu, this novel is full of feeling but also tough and thoroughly unsentimental.

Efuru was very worried in the second year of her marriage. "My mother had only me," she said one night to herself. "My father told me so and also that she found it difficult to become pregnant. Am I going to be like my mother? But if I am going to be like her, then I too will have a daughter like her. But what if that is denied me? What if that also is denied me? What will I do, Oh, what will I do?" she wept.

Efuru did not sleep that night. Early in the morning before the cock crew she got up, dressed and went to her father. She opened her heart to her father. "Something must be done, my daughter. It is not in our blood. Our women are productive. There must be a reason for this. We shall see a dibia."

Efuru and her old father went to see a dibia. He was a very old and dirty man. He was almost blind and was unable to walk. His two grand-daughters lived with him and ran errands for him. They were sent to the bush to collect some leaves or roots, to the market to buy things required for medicines and they cooked for him. It was understood that they would not live with him when they were over fourteen.

When Efuru and her father entered the compound, the dibia shouted, "Nwashike Ogene, I am happy you are coming today with your daughter. But I won't see you today because your daughter is menstruating. My medicines will be ineffective if she comes nearer. When she finishes bring her to me." Efuru was spellbound.

"How did he know?" she asked her father.

"He is a dibia," was the old man's reply.

Nigeria

Jagua Nana by Cyprian Ekwensi

Heinemann, 1987 (first published 1961)

Jagua Nana is one of the first novels of urban African life, and still one of the best. This raucous, rambunctious, sometimes satirical tale is said to be one of the most popular African novels among Africans themselves. It tells the story of Jagua Nana, a young woman from Iboland who answers the call of Lagos and becomes, if not the proverbial hooker with a heart of gold, at any rate a hooker who at least has a heart.

When we first meet Jagua Nana she has just washed her hair and is gazing into a mirror gripped between her knees. A habitué of the Lagos nightclub Tropicana, she is the lover of Freddie Namme, a young man with prospects who intends to study in the UK. At the age of forty-five, she is well aware that her appeal may not last much longer, but she uses all that remains of her considerable natural beauty, her sense of style, and a battery of alluring walks and gestures to hang onto her young man, whom she genuinely cares for. If she also spends time with the businessmen, politicians, and well-to-do expatriates that she meets at the Tropicana, she is only being realistic. Freddie can't afford to keep her in the style to which she's accustomed.

Trouble looms, however. Freddie will leave soon for the UK, and so will Nancy, a fresh young woman of nineteen who has recently caught his eye. Both Jagua and Nancy conceive the idea of visiting Freddie's family in Bagana, but Nancy gets there first. In a melodramatic development, Jagua swims after her rival while they are bathing in the river, chasing her to the border of a hostile chief's territory where Nancy is captured by the chief's followers, and seems likely to be executed. Contrite at what she's done, Jagua uses all her feminine wiles to gain Nancy's release, and wins the heart of the chief.

Many more events fill out this short novel, one of the first to capture the allure of the big city for rural Africans, and of the alienation and disillusionment that wait there for many. Though for the most part it is a comic novel, peppered with many examples of

the racy Nigerian patois, it also has a number of graceful and moving passages that are easy to miss because they are tossed off so casually. The plot is constructed ingeniously, so that scenes from Jagua's early life, giving clues to her personality, are saved until almost the end of the story, where they add retrospective depth. Jagua Nana is not a complex character, but her feelings are conveyed with honesty, and the thugs, thieves, politicians, prostitutes, and chiefs she meets in her career convey a range of modern Nigerian types.

One day when he went to his filling station, leaving the house to her, she dressed up and walked into the streets. She was passing by the Railway Station and on a sudden impulse she went in and asked for the time table. A young man smilingly told her when the next train would be leaving for L-A-G-O-S. Lagos! The magic name. She had heard of Lagos where the girls were glossy, worked in offices like the men, danced, smoked, wore high-heeled shoes and narrow slacks, and were "free" and "fast" with their favours. She heard that the people in Lagos did not have to go to bed at eight o'clock. Anyone who cared could go roaming the streets or wandering from one night spot to the other right up until morning. The night spots never shut, and they were open all night and every night; not like "here" where at 8 p.m. (latest) everywhere was shut down and the streets deserted, so that it looked odd to be wandering about.

When she came away from the railway counter, Jagua felt a sudden uneasiness. There was something sinful in her act, and from that moment on, she began to look at her man with a detached air. To her, he was good as dead. Dead and buried in her heart though he did not know it. She gave him her body, and thought instead of the slim young men in the dark bow-ties and elegantly cut lounge suits.

Nigeria

Stars of the New Curfew by Ben Okri
Viking, 1989

B en Okri, like his compatriot Amos Tutuola, is a leading
proponent of magical realism, Nigerian-style. Though Okri is
best known for his vast, perplexing novel *The Famished Road* – the
winner of England's Booker Prize – this collection of six stories is a
more various and accessible introduction to his work. Several of the
stories take place on the shifting boundary between life and death,
and many paint a picture of the city of Lagos as a pulsating termite's
nest of ambition, greed, corruption, guilt, violence, and supernatural
eruptions. The shadow of the Nigerian civil war, in which the Ibos
broke away to form the new country of Biafra, only to be brutally
crushed, hangs over these stories. Police and soldiers crop up as
sinister presences.

The title story, "Stars of the New Curfew," the longest and perhaps
the best in the collection, tells of a young man named Arthur, his
parents killed during the war, who leaves his town for the capital in
search of a living. He finds a job with an insurance company, which
quickly fails, and after he is thrown out of his room and spends
six weeks living under a bridge, he turns to selling "rather dubious
locally made medicines at various markets and on the molue buses
that career all over Lagos."

Hard-working and inventive, Arthur throws himself into his
work and develops a variety of effective selling techniques. Hawking
medicines for children's diseases, malaria, yellow fever, dysentery, and
ringworm, he is brought face to face with the sufferings of the poor.
Worse than that, he realizes that he has become part of the machinery
that exploits and destroys them. The accomplices he hires to mingle
with the crowds and buy his wares turn out to be pickpockets. Then
he discovers that the ringworm medicine he sells actually worsens
the ailment. "The children were covered in welts so big and red, so
obscene, that I couldn't possibly believe it was ringworm. It seemed
more like ringsnake." He leaves his company to work for another,
only to find himself selling new medicines with new varieties of
bizarre side-effects.

Soon Arthur takes a job with yet another new employer, an energetic toad-faced man with a large operation and great enthusiasm for his own drugs, which he insists that his salesmen use themselves. Suffering from persistent nightmares, Arthur has been staying awake at night and falling asleep on the job. The new drugs revive him during the day but leave him exposed to his visions after dark. "I would become lost in a labyrinth: I would come to a crossroad, take a turning, and would see children clutching my bottles of medicines, dying on the roads. The smell of burning tar, and charred flesh, came from them, as if the medicines were acids that dissolved their insides."

His tortured conscience reveals itself in nightmares of predatory capitalism, conveyed in images of war and violence. Night after night he dreams of a "lunar landscape" where an auctioneer sells the stars in the sky to the highest bidder, in exchange for "huge sums of money, a special part of the human anatomy, or the decapitated heads of newly-dead children." Then one day his boss offers him three yellow boxes containing his latest creation: POWER-DRUG, which claims to cure every known illness and affliction of the poor ...

In this and his other stories, Ben Okri shows himself to be a master of the surreal, of the bizarre distortions wrought by the aftermath of war, grotesque political corruption, and hunger that can lead to hallucination. His powerful images are cryptic but don't seem arbitrary; they follow a dream logic that is forever just out of reach.

In the village everything had a voice and everything spoke at me. Sounds and voices assaulted me and my ears began to ache. Then slowly my sight returned. At first it was like seeing through milk. When my vision cleared, the voices stopped. Then I saw the village as I had not seen it before.

I went out of the place I was staying and walked around in bewilderment. Some of the people of the village had their feet facing backwards. I was amazed that they could walk. Some people came out of tree-trunks. Some had wings, but they couldn't fly. After a while I got used to the strangeness of the people. I ceased to really notice their three legs and elongated necks. What I couldn't get used to were the huts

and houses that were walled round with mirrors on the outside. I didn't see myself reflected in them as I went past. Some people walked into the mirrors and disappeared. I couldn't walk into them.

After some time of moving around, I couldn't find my way back to where I stayed. I went about the village listening for the voice of the women who had been taking care of me. I stopped at a communal water-pump and a woman came up to me and said:

"What are you doing here?"

"I'm lost."

Nigeria

GraceLand by Chris Abani

Farrar, Straus and Giroux, 2004

At the centre of *GraceLand*, a novel set in the turmoil and repression of modern Nigeria, is a young man named Elvis Oke.

Named by his late mother for her favourite musician, young Elvis is not only a fan himself but also an Elvis Presley imitator on a small scale. With pancake makeup, a jumpsuit, and a boom box, he performs for tourists on the beach and hopes for tips – just one of many schemes, some more illegal and dangerous than others, with which he tries to survive.

GraceLand is set in Lagos, with flashbacks to other locations, and Abani presents all the filth and violence and energy of the city, from the smell of the lagoons to the shantytowns that spring up under the highway flyovers. So fatalistic are the inhabitants of Lagos that they cross the highways by flinging themselves into traffic. The many pedestrian bridges go unused.

GraceLand is packed with incident and observation: sometimes a little too packed. But when the observations are as sharp as most of Abani's, it's forgivable. It might not have been necessary, for instance, to have one character explain how the World Bank and IMF rip off developing countries – but the explanation is one of the most clear and concise I've ever seen.

The novel features scenes of intense violence that are hard to read, but both books are redeemed by scathing honesty and a good dose of dark humour. Toward the end of the book, Elvis observes a starving man who is dancing and talking to himself. "The man laughed, and as his diaphragm shook, Elvis thought he heard the man's ribs knocking together, producing a sweet, haunting melody like the wooden xylophones of his small-town childhood."

—

Elvis stood by the open window. Outside: heavy rain. He jammed the wooden shutter open with an old radio battery, against the wind. The storm drowned the tinny sound of the portable radio on the table. He felt claustrophobic, fingers gripping the iron of the rusty metal protector. It was cool on his lips, chin and forehead as he pressed his face against it.

Across the street stood the foundations of a building; the floor and pillars wore green mold from repeated rains. Between the pillars, a woman had erected a bukka, no more than a rickety lean-to made of sheets of corrugated iron roofing and plastic held together by hope. On dry evenings, the smell of fried yam and dodo wafted from it into his room, teasing his hunger. But today the fire grate was wet and all the soot had been washed away.

Nigeria

Waiting for an Angel by Helon Habila
W. W. Norton, 2004

Waiting for an Angel is one of the high points of a recent wave of excellent fiction by young Nigerian writers. Though the stories in this volume are not knit together closely enough to constitute a novel, they reflect each other in a way that makes the whole greater than the sum of its parts.

The stories take place in and around Lagos in the 1990s, when Nigeria was in the grip of the military rulers Ibrahim Babangida and Sani Abacha. Each story touches on the life of a young man named Lomba, but in very different ways. Some take place in Lomba's mind, some follow him from an omniscient point of view, and in some of them Lomba is a secondary character in someone else's drama. The author shifts from first person to third person within the same story, and even dips into the seldom-used second person: "You accept the inescapability of your fate; and with that, you learn the craft of cunning." Late in the book we even see an unflattering glimpse of the author himself, as a young man who rushes out of a literary party and vomits over a balcony railing.

The technical skill of this collection, though, is not the most impressive thing about it. In Lomba's journey, and in what we see of the lives of those around him, we get a picture of a time when hope is all but crushed. The stories move backwards in time, with occasional flashbacks and flash-forwards. In the first, Lomba is in prison. We read the diary entries he writes when, after one and a half years, he manages to get paper and pencil. In the stories that come later, we see the many influences that brought him here: a crackdown on students by the government's "khaki boys," a friend who goes mad, three years spent writing a novel that cannot be published, the beginnings of a career as a journalist, the impact of seeing the iron gags and shackles in a slavery museum, and his slowly evolving political consciousness. On the last page of the book he decides to cover a demonstration. "Suddenly a vision of handcuffs and stone walls flashes in his mind, like a presentiment; he shivers."

Waiting for an Angel excels in dramatic scenes of violence as well as in quieter, more emotionally telling episodes. The grief of Lomba's friend, and the clumsy, yet tender support of his family, are note-perfect. And Habila does not make the arc of Lomba's life quite as merciless as he might have. Though Lomba's incarceration seems fated, the possibility of hope remains. Somehow, muses the anonymous voice, "it is hard to imagine that Lomba died." But we never get to see Lomba leaving prison, except in a kind of allegory, half comforting and half ridiculous, in which Liberty herself arrives to release him.

"Eeao!" Michael exclaimed and bolted for the road. I started after him, but Ade grabbed my shirt and pointed up to the leafy darkness of the mango tree. In a single, adrenaline-charged leap I grabbed a branch and hauled myself up. I did not stop going till there was nowhere to go. I fixed myself in the crook between branch and branch, panting, looking for Ade. He was to my right, clinging with both hands to a branch. But before we could congratulate ourselves on our narrow escape, the tear gas reached us. I closed my eyes, I felt trapped. Now I realized how small animals feel in a bush fire. The air below us was filled with scared wails and shrieks; women screaming the names of their children. But the dominant sounds were of batons on flesh, and boots on flesh, and tear gas popping out of projectiles. Suddenly the wind altered direction, blowing the noxious fumes towards the Secretariat building, and I was able to open my eyes. My eyes and mouth ran with fluid, my sweaty skin was pepperish with dissolved tear gas. But I could see through the mango leaves. The people, scared witless, hemmed in on all sides, stupefied by the choking tear gas, ran out in all directions, like quails beaten out of their hiding places, coughing and falling.

Rwanda

Gorillas in the Mist by Dian Fossey

Houghton Mifflin, 2000 (first published 1983)

In 1967 Dian Fossey set up a research camp in the saddle between two volcanoes in Rwanda's Parc des Volcans and began studying the endangered mountain gorillas who lived there. *Gorillas in the Mist*, her own account of her years at the Varisoke Research Station, was published in 1983. Two years later Dian Fossey was murdered in her cabin at Varisoke by an attacker wielding a machete.

Because her story was not yet finished when *Gorillas in the Mist* was written, the book throws only a certain amount of light on the question of who killed her. (Though an American graduate student was convicted in absentia for the murder, many believe the killer was one of the poachers Fossey had struggled against for years.) In writing about herself, Fossey shows a self-deprecating humour that one wouldn't expect from other accounts of her, yet she chooses to omit many details that are discussed in Farley Mowat's biography *Woman in the Mists* and Alex Shoumatoff's essay in *African Madness*. Fossey doesn't mention the engagement she broke off when she first went to Africa, or her later involvement with a photographer from *National Geographic*, whom she describes simply as a helpful friend and handyman. She doesn't mention long periods during which she reportedly drank heavily and lived as a recluse, ignoring both people and gorillas, though the leapfrogging chronology of her book raises questions about what is skipped over. Nor does she admit to some of the more extreme actions she was accused of taking against poachers: staging mock hangings and whipping them with nettles.

On the other hand, *Gorillas in the Mist* provides a valuable inside look at the mind of what Shoumatoff terms the Thoreauvian strain of animal lover: those whose reverence for wildlife is coupled with a low opinion of mankind. She battles with all three major ethnic groups of Rwanda – the Hutu, Tutsi, and Twa (Pygmies) – though without taking much interest in their language or culture and without seeming to recognize that the Pygmies were arguably as endangered as the gorillas themselves. Like Mark and Delia Owens, whose memoir of Zambia is reviewed in this book, she practises "active conservation"

by taking the battle to the poachers: tracking them, destroying their traps, and having them arrested (but without the diplomatic initiatives that the Owenses also practised). Like the Owenses, she buys uniforms, tents, and equipment for the park guards, and like them she discovers that the guards are poorly motivated to do their job, and often in cahoots with the poachers. And just as the Owenses were nearly assassinated by the poachers they opposed, Dian Fossey may have met the same fate.

The focus of Fossey's book is on the gorillas, so much so that their personalities are more vivid than those of the people she encounters. She works to habituate several gorilla families to humans so that they can be observed, but strives not to interfere with them and avoids touching them (except when she discovers how much they like to be tickled). Though she doesn't make the mistake of regarding them as people – she is remarkably cool in her reaction to dung-eating and other less than endearing behaviour – she discusses their motivations, facial expressions, and parenting skills without apology. Her compassionate yet unsentimental attitude toward the gorillas lends additional power to the scenes in which she describes the death of individuals from disease, infanticide, or poachers, or the plight of baby gorillas captured by slaughtering their families.

One of the quietest, yet most moving, moments in the book comes when the four-month-old female gorilla Muraha approaches her on her own. Muraha is retrieved by her mother Pantsy, who looks at Fossey with "an almost apologetic facial expression," but returns a short time later and climbs onto Fossey's legs before being retrieved once again. "My thrill of that remarkable display of trust," she writes, "has never diminished."

—◆—

Puck, up to a point, was content in the company of Effie and two younger sisters, Tuck and Poppy, but was often among the first to show boredom during the tedious day-resting hours. He indicated his mood by tapping a forefinger up and down on an arm or by yawningly looking around for something to entertain himself. Buzzing flies were one

attraction. Intent, he would sit up, grab at the insect, and if quick enough trap it within his palms. Because of being walleyed like Effie and his siblings, his eyes almost crossed as they tried to focus on the fly held several inches from his face. He then usually pinched the victim between his forefinger and thumb before tearing it into small fragments, yet closely examined each piece before discarding it. The longer the dissection process, the more rapt Puck's facial expression, until his lower lip hung down in a manner more typical of a chimpanzee than a gorilla. Once the fly was no more, Puck's lips puckered with discontent as he looked around for other sources of entertainment.

At these times Puck's substitutes were usually the contents of my knapsack – camera, lenses, and binoculars – all of which the inventive Puck used to look through and to reflect his image as well. He looked through the binoculars from the wrong side because that was the only side that could span the distance between his eyes. I felt certain he was actually looking through them rather than simply copying human behavior because of his prolonged reactions to far-distant images of vegetation or to his fingers. He would wiggle the fingers of one hand directly in front of the binoculars before swiftly lowering the glasses to regard his fingertips inquisitively, as if verifying their attachment to his hand. His perplexity about distortion of surrounding objects was as fascinating as it was comical to watch.

Rwanda

We Wish to Inform You That Tomorrow We Will Be Killed with Our Families by Philip Gourevitch

Farrar, Straus and Giroux, 1998

Beginning in April of 1994, killers belonging to the Hutu majority of Rwanda massacred roughly a million of their Tutsi countrymen. Though the killers had no gas chambers or ovens for the quick disposal of their victims, they managed to kill the Tutsi at a rate even faster than the killing of the Jews of Europe by the Nazis. When it was all over and some of those responsible were brought to justice, they were charged under UN auspices for the crime of genocide – the first time in history that this charge had been made.

For several years, beginning in 1995, Philip Gourevitch travelled through Rwanda and its neighbouring countries, observing the scenes of the massacre and interviewing both survivors and killers in an attempt to understand what had happened. *We Wish to Inform You That Tomorrow We Will Be Killed with Our Families* – the title comes from a letter that went unheeded – is an unusual and compelling blend of passion and analysis. It succeeds not only in conveying some of the horror of the bloodbath in Rwanda but also in revealing the factors that made it possible and exploding many of the myths that have sprung up about it.

Gourevitch notes that apart from the victim of a car crash, he never saw anyone recently killed in Rwanda. His sense of the killings came indirectly. At the church in Nyarubuye in eastern Rwanda, where the bodies of Tutsi victims had been left where they died as a kind of memorial, he feels a flash of anger when a Canadian colonel accidentally steps on one of the "stray skulls" in the tall grass – only to step on a skull himself a moment later. At a refugee camp in Zaire (now the DRC), he watches a Hutu refugee, perhaps one of the killers, butchering a cow. "It took many hacks – two, three, four, five hard hacks – to chop through the cow's leg. How many hacks to dismember a person?"

Most of all, however, he seeks understanding through the stories the survivors tell him. "I had eighteen people killed at my house," says

a man named Etienne Niyonzima. "Everything was totally destroyed – a place of fifty-five meters by fifty meters. In my neighborhood they killed six hundred and forty-seven people. They tortured them, too. You had to see how they killed them. They had the number of everyone's house, and they went through with red paint and marked the homes of all the Tutsis and of the Hutu moderates. My wife was at a friend's, shot with two bullets. She is still alive, only ... she has no arms."

In the face of the sudden and seemingly irrational eruption of cruelty, it was easy for many Westerners to believe this was an unplanned outbreak of what the *New York Times* called "the age-old animosity between the Tutsi and Hutu ethnic groups." This "age-old animosity," however, dates back no further than 1959, when the first incident of political violence between the two groups occurred. Even to refer to the Tutsi and Hutu as "ethnic groups" is problematic, as Gourevitch points out. Although legend has it that the Hutu were an agrarian Bantu people while the Tutsi were taller and lighter-skinned cattle herders from the region of Ethiopia, the two groups had lived together and intermarried for so many generations that they were often indistinguishable even to other Rwandans. One of the most destructive legacies of the Belgian colonists in Rwanda was to introduce identity cards that made "Tutsi" and "Hutu" into rigid and inescapable categories.

Perhaps the most important insight of *We Wish to Inform You* is that mass violence must be organized. Gourevitch demonstrates that although the killing had no single obvious great villain behind it – no Hitler or Pol Pot – it was meticulously prepared and carried out in the interest of a political ideology. The killings were the work of a political movement bluntly called Hutu Power, whose supporters were bent on reversing the social and economic dominance of the Tutsi minority, whom they called "cockroaches." A climate of violence was nurtured by Hutu Power demonstrations, unrelenting anti-Tutsi radio propaganda on the radio, and even by Hutu Power pop singers.

The massacre of 1994 began less than an hour after the event that triggered it: the death of President Habyarimana, a Hutu, in a plane crash while returning from negotiations with an exiled rebel force that included many Tutsis. Many believe that Hutu Power was responsible for the crash as well as for the deaths of Hutu moderates who opposed the bloodbath.

In investigating the causes and consequences of what happened, Gourevitch doesn't stop at the borders of Rwanda. He is harshly critical of US Secretary of State Madeleine Albright, UN official Kofi Annan (not yet Secretary General), and other political figures for their failure to heed unambiguous warnings of the killings, and to send more than a token force of UN soldiers to Rwanda. (Though their orders prevented them from firing on the murderers, the soldiers killed hundreds of dogs that were feeding on Tutsi corpses.)

Gourevitch also provides one of the clearest explanations available of how the agony of Rwanda spilled over into its neighbouring countries. When the Rwandese Patriotic Front, a rebel army led by Tutsi exiles, invaded the country and ended the genocide, thousands of Hutus fled from Rwanda. Humanitarian organizations fed and sheltered the Hutu refugees, many of them what the Tutsi termed the *génocidaires*, and allowed them to militarize the camps. The result was that the conflict spilled over into Rwanda's neighbouring countries in a way that Gourevitch says, had it happened in Europe, would have been termed a world war.

———

"You cockroaches must know you are made flesh," a broadcaster gloated over RTLM. "We won't let you kill. We will kill you."

With the encouragement of such messages and of leaders at every level of society, the slaughter of Tutsis and the assassination of Hutu oppositionists spread from region to region. Following the militias' example, Hutus young and old rose to the task. Neighbors hacked neighbors to death in their homes, and colleagues hacked colleagues to death in their workplaces. Doctors killed their patients, and schoolteachers killed their pupils. Within days, the Tutsi populations of many villages were all but eliminated, and in Kigali prisoners were released in work gangs to collect the corpses that lined the roadsides. Throughout Rwanda, mass rape and looting accompanied the slaughter. Drunken militia bands, fortified with assorted drugs from ransacked pharmacies, were bused from massacre to massacre. Radio announcers reminded listeners not to take pity on women and children. As an added

incentive to the killers, Tutsis' belongings were parceled out in advance – the radio, the couch, the goat, the opportunity to rape a young girl. A councilwoman in one Kigali neighborhood was reported to have offered fifty Rwandan francs apiece (about thirty cents at the time) for severed Tutsi heads, a practice known as "selling cabbages."

São Tomé and Príncipe

The Heinemann Book of African Women's Poetry
edited by Stella and Frank Chipasula
Heinemann, 1995

São Tomé and Príncipe is the smallest country in Africa, consisting of two small islands off the coast of Gabon, with an area of 371 square miles and a total population of about 150 000. Like Cape Verde, São Tomé had no permanent inhabitants before it was colonized by the Portuguese. And as in Cape Verde, Portugal made little effort to promote literacy or culture. Originally exploited for sugar cane, São Tomé later became a way station for the Atlantic slave trade. Later still, coffee and cocoa were grown there. The country gained its independence in 1975.

With such a history, it is not surprising that São Tomé has produced little literature. A few collections of poetry and a couple of novels have been published in Portuguese but are not yet available in English.

The Heinemann Book of African Women's Poetry shows, however, that what little is available is worth seeking out. The editors draw particular attention to Alda do Espirito Santo, whose verses "were once considered subversive and dangerous by the Portuguese colonial authorities" and who was imprisoned and tortured after protesting against a massacre in 1953. Though her work is included in other anthologies, her life is so little known that she appears in three of them with a misspelled name (Aldo rather than Alda) that transforms her into a man.

Maria Manuela Margarido, the other São Tomé poet included here, shares Espirito Santo's militant spirit in poems like "You Who Occupy our Land," addressed to the "barely empty ghosts of men" who have brought a smell of "guando fruit and death" to her country. In that poem and others included here, she conveys dramatic scenes with memorable and unexpected imagery.

'Landscape'
by Maria Manuela Margarido
Translated from the Portuguese by Julia Kirst

Nightfall ... grass on the back
of the gleaming black man
on his way to the yard.
Grey parrots
explode in the palm trees' comb
and cross each other in my childhood dream,
in the blue porcelain of oysters.
High dream, high
like the coconut tree along the ocean
with its golden and firm fruits
like obstructed stones
oscillating in a tornado's womb
ploughing the sky with its mad
plumes.
In the sky the severe anguish
of revolt passes by
with its claws its anxieties its uncertainties.
And an image of rustic lines
takes over the time and the word.

Senegal

God's Bits of Wood by Sembène Ousmane

Translated from the French by Francis Price

Heinemann, 1989 (first published 1960)

Though better known in recent years as a film director, Sembène Ousmane staked an early claim as one of Africa's finest novelists. *God's Bits of Wood*, aside from being one of the best novels to have come out of Africa, is also one of the best political novels of the twentieth century. A highly dramatic account of a revolutionary struggle, it carries a clear message but avoids descending into propaganda.

God's Bits of Wood describes the epic strike of 1947–48, in which workers on the railroad line from Dakar in Senegal to Bamako on the Niger River walked off the job, demanding higher wages, pensions, family allowances, and the recognition of their union. Ousmane took part in this struggle as a young man, but his novel is not just a thinly disguised memoir and he does not limit himself to a single point of view. As one might expect from a future film director, the novel's scenes are visually striking and each one has a dramatic point that carries the plot forward. Even more impressive are the dozens of memorable characters the author creates, and the imagination and authority with which he reveals their motivations.

God's Bits of Wood begins in Bamako, in what is now Mali, with the family of Bakayoko, the leader of the strike, who has disappeared some time before. Though unsure of themselves without Bakayoko's guidance, the local people reach the decision to join the strike and later grapple with the question of how to deal with strike-breakers.

Scenes in Dakar introduce characters who are more sophisticated and morally ambiguous, such as Beaugosse, a good-looking young man whose dedication to the cause is compromised by a love of comfort and his condescension toward the common people. The Islamic priests or imams of Dakar are portrayed as supporters of the French colonial regime. One of the most memorable scenes of the novel occurs when the prize ram of a sanctimonious district chief is unceremoniously butchered by his sister when it eats her family's

rice, touching off a conflict between local women and the police that escalates to a firestorm.

Almost half the book, however, takes place in the Senegalese town of Thiès. The town is characterized by "rickety shacks, some upturned tombs, walls of bamboo or millet stalks, iron barbs, and rotting fences" – yet it proves to be the heart of the railway strike. Here live some of the stalwarts of the struggle: Samba N'Doulougou, a "curious little man" who serves the community as a "walking newspaper," Maïmouna, a blind "goddess of the night" who sings the legends of her people, and Penda, a feisty young woman said to be a prostitute, who plays a key role in the women's march on Dakar with which the novel culminates.

Although the characters spend much of the book wishing for the return of their leader Bakayoko, it's noteworthy that the hard work of the struggle continues without him. The author may have realized that Bakayoko is more intriguing as an absent ideal than a real man, because when he does appear he is a bit of a revolutionary cliché: self-sacrificing, humourless, totally dedicated to his work. The most interesting characters in the novel, and the author's greatest achievement, are the women who overcome their fears, superstitions, and petty animosities to take part in a protest march from Thiès to Dakar. The march brings to a head a struggle that has lasted over four months and caused immense suffering and the loss of lives. An important reason for its success is that, more than Bakayoko and the other men, the women understand that the goal is to struggle without giving way to hate.

———

"Do you have any news from Doudou, at Thiès? Or from Bakayoko?"

"Bakayoko, Bakayoko!" Beaugosse repeated. "That man is beginning to get on my nerves."

"You don't even know him, so how can he get on your nerves?"

It was not so much the question as the mocking tone of N'Deye's voice that made Beaugosse lose his temper. "You've never told me what there is between you and him," he said harshly.

N'Deye Touti brushed the foulard scarf back from her hair and drew her feet up to the parapet. Crossing her arms around her knees, she stared absently at the scene around her, as if seeking an answer. At the end of the avenue El-Hadji-Malic-Sy the sky was propped against an uneven wall of rooftops. The clouds were gathering into a long, ash-gray pool, ringed with little islands, shadowed in purple, and being pushed into the pool by the wind. On the highway, two cows were coming back from the fields, followed by a man waving a stick. Then a bus went by, sounding its horn, and the noise brought N'Deye Touti back to reality.

Senegal

Ambiguous Adventure by Cheikh Hamidou Kane

Translated from the French by Katherine Woods

Heinemann, 1963

It is tempting to say that *Ambiguous Adventure* is not really a novel but a prose poem or extended meditation. The actions of the characters are barely sufficient to move the narrative from one dialogue to another, and the dialogue itself is relentlessly high-minded and philosophical, unlike anything ever spoken by a real person. Yet anyone about to decide that this is not a "real" novel must acknowledge that it contains a number of expertly drawn characters and landscapes, that its language is exceptionally beautiful and sometimes highly original, and that the experience of reading it is oddly moving.

We first meet Samba Diallo as a young boy studying the Koran. His teacher beats him for making the slightest mistake in his recitation, or jabs his earlobe with a sharp thumbnail. Yet we gradually realize that things are not exactly as they seem. The teacher is not just a sadist: he punishes Samba in order to drive him to even greater excellence, believing that the boy has a divine gift and might reach "the most exalted levels of human grandeur." Samba himself is devoted to the teacher, and responds to what he is learning on the level of faith as well as language. "The Word of God flowed pure and limpid from his fervent lips."

Samba's people, the Diallobé, are demoralized and slowly dying out. The French have conquered their country, bringing a new day "spangled over with smiles, with cannon shots, with shining glass beads." Samba's older cousin, an imperious woman known as the Most Royal Lady, calls a meeting of the community and proposes that Samba be sent to one of the new Western schools. She hates these schools, but believes that the children of the elite must go there in order to learn "the art of conquering without being in the right." Samba, a gifted student and the son of a high-born father, is a prime candidate.

Samba excels at his Western school just as he did in his Koranic studies. Years later he muses that he was conquered by the letters of the French alphabet. "When I learned to fit them together to form

words, to fit the words together to give birth to speech, my happiness knew no further limit." Yet Samba's Western education leaves him with a sense of unease that he spends much of the book attempting to define.

Ambiguous Adventure is an indispensable book for anyone wishing to delve into the psychology of colonialism. Samba breaks off his Koranic studies just at the point, he believes, when he is about to attain "rational understanding of what up to then I had done no more than recite." At his Western school he enters what he believes at first is a world of "marvellous comprehension and total communion," only to be gradually disillusioned. Living in Paris, Samba feels a spiritual loss and a sense of disconnection from his land and people – even from his understanding of death. He comes to hate the people who have colonized his mind, but understands that his hatred is the product of frustrated love. "I loved them too soon, unwisely, without knowing them well enough. Do you understand? They are of a strange nature. They do not inspire simple sentiments. No one should ally himself with them without having observed them well beforehand."

———

"It is difficult," Samba Diallo began at last. "It might be said that I see less fully here than in the country of the Diallobé. I no longer feel anything directly. You know, on reflection all this seems ridiculous to me. It may be, after all, that what I regret is not my country so much as my childhood."

"Go on trying. Tell us the form that your nostalgia takes."

"It seems to me, for example, that in the country of the Diallobé man is closer to death. He lives on more familiar terms with it. His existence acquires from it something like an aftermath of authenticity. Down there, there existed between death and myself an intimacy, made up at the same time of my terror and my expectation. Whereas here death has become a stranger to me. Everything combats it, drives it back from men's bodies and minds. I forget about it. When I search for it in my thought, I see only a dried-up sentiment, an abstract eventuality, scarcely more disagreeable for me than for my insurance company."

"In sum," said Marc, laughing, "you are complaining of no longer living your death."

Senegal

So Long a Letter by Mariama Bâ

Translated from the French by Modupé Bodé-Thomas

Heinemann, 2000 (first published 1981)

Ramatoulaye and her friend Aissatou are educated women, part of the first generation of "new African women" in the newly independent Senegal. Admitted after a competitive examination to an elite school, they are inspired by a headmistress who strives to "lift us out of the bog of tradition, superstition and custom, to make us appreciate a multitude of civilizations without renouncing our own, to raise our vision of the world, cultivate our personalities, strengthen our qualities."

Still, as they begin their careers and enjoy the pleasures of Dakar, the two women must find ways to reconcile their way of life with the older traditions of their culture. Aissatou, the daughter of a goldsmith, marries a doctor whom some people think is too good for her. When her husband takes a second, younger wife, Aissatou decides to leave him.

Ramatoulaye marries a trade union organizer, a handsome olive-skinned man whom her mother disapproves of. Ramatoulaye's husband also takes a young second wife, but unlike her friend, Ramatoulaye chooses to remain and make the best of the situation.

Which of the women has made the right decision? The question is too simple. Aissatou rents her own house, pursues her studies, and ends up with a successful though somewhat solitary career at the Senegalese embassy in the US. Her husband is shaken and embittered by his wife's desertion, but nonetheless gives his second wife one child after another. Ramatoulaye, though she reconciles herself to sharing her husband, finds herself just as alone as her friend. Her husband spends all his time with his new wife, and she is left to take care of the household, learn to drive, and distract herself at the movies.

The epistolary novel is a very old genre, but it generally takes the form of an exchange of letters. This one consists of a single letter, written by Ramatoulaye to Aissatou. Ramatoulaye begins it after the death of her husband, and doesn't finish until forty days later, when the initial period of mourning is over.

In its shifts from joy to regret to anger to nostalgia, the book is an extended meditation on what it is to live as a woman through the emergence of modern Africa. Though it is not particularly dramatic – most of what happens is told rather than shown – it is wonderfully atmospheric, written with restrained lyricism and full of memories of old loves, painful episodes, and a "sharp green mango" eaten long ago. There may be no other novel that lets the reader linger so long and so intimately in the mind and emotions of an African woman.

�longer⟩

I conjure you up. The past is reborn, along with its procession of emotions. I close my eyes. Ebb and tide of feeling: heat and dazzlement, the woodfires, the sharp green mango, bitten into in turns, a delicacy in our greedy mouths. I close my eyes. Ebb and tide of images: drops of sweat beading your mother's ochre-coloured face as she emerges from the kitchen, the procession of young wet girls chattering on their way back from the springs.

We walked the same paths from adolescence to maturity, where the past begets the present.

My friend, my friend, my friend. I call on you three times.

Yesterday you were divorced. Today I am a widow.

Senegal

I Get on the Bus by Reginald McKnight
Rager Media, 2006 (first published 1990)

Strange things are happening to Evan Norris. He feels as if an ice pick is being driven into his head, and he hears a high-pitched squeal as if air is leaking out. Someone has been leaving dead lizards in his room. He hears a person or creature pacing all night outside his window. He dreams of whirlpools and dust devils. Sometimes he finds himself inside other people's bodies. And sometimes he is on a bus to an unknown destination, with a boy whose scalp is scabby and who has cryptic and sinister things to say.

What's going on here? Evan may have malaria, because he hasn't been taking his quinine pills. Someone – perhaps the old *marabou* with whom he lives – may have put a spell on him. He may be turning into a *demm*, a soul-eater. Or he may just be going crazy. "You don't look too good, my man," someone tells him, and it's no wonder.

Evan Norris, the hero of this taut, eerie first novel, is a black American who has come to Senegal from Denver. He has joined the Peace Corps, in part to escape Wanda Wright, his therapist turned lover, and her plans to organize, motivate, and marry him. Wanda wants to get Evan away from the group of ageing white hippies he hangs out with and to instill in him a stronger sense of black identity. Evan loves Wanda, and he admires her clarity and honesty, but he is not ready to let himself be moulded by her. "She, herself, is finished, complete with or without me. But I need something of my own. Life is not as she and my mother would have it. It is not a gift. Life is hard. It is stupid. One must earn it."

Evan is not the ideal Peace Corps volunteer. His French is sketchy, his Wolof nonexistent. He smokes a lot of marijuana, and exerts more energy killing flies than preparing his classes. He finds the Peace Corps too easy, too meaningless. Before long he has dropped out and gone to the capital, Dakar, where in a hallucinatory state reminiscent of Camus's *The Stranger*, he kills – or believes he has killed – a legless beggar.

Shaken and disoriented, he goes to the village of N'Gor, and after a medical crisis ends up in the home of the one-eyed M. Gueye and his beautiful daughter Aminata. M. Gueye is a *marabou*, which Evan

understands to be a kind of Koranic scholar crossed with a voodoo priest. Evan fears Gueye, and believes that Gueye hates him, but he is fascinated by Aminata, who seems to offer him a deeper understanding of Senegal, and of his own identity, than he could find anywhere else.

Once Evan has become a drifter, he is at the mercy of people who are far more skilled at manipulating and deceiving him than anyone he had known back home. M. Gueye with his silence and his one-eyed gaze, Aminata with her cool seductiveness, and her brother Philippe with his scattershot monologues, hinting at secret knowledge of Evan's problems, may be weaving a web that Evan cannot yet see.

The chapters of *I Get on the Bus* are labelled, starkly, "I quit," "I find a chicken," "I write a letter," and so on. Like these headings, much of the novel's prose is laconic, first person, present tense. The pared-down prose perfectly expresses the desperate concentration of a man who fears he is losing his mind, and who must examine every perception to disentangle the real from the hallucinated. The other characters use language as a kind of magic, spinning strange tales that may or may not be true, and that intrigue and baffle the reader as they do Evan. In the end, Evan's life depends on which stories he chooses to believe.

—

I am embarrassed as I realize that I miss being around white people. I miss their impassiveness, their arrogant blindness. They leave one alone.

It is so strange for a black person to leave America where one is looked through, yet feels conspicuous, then come to Africa where one is most assuredly conspicuous and feels seen through. Africans are skilled in the way of people. They do not spend hours a day watching television, hiding from even their own family members in their own rooms, or compartmentalized in their cars, blasting down highways at invisible speeds, or eating TV dinners prepared by strangers. Most Africans have nothing to do in their "leisure" hours but spend time with one another. They are more literate in the tao of humans than any people I have ever seen. This angers me, frightens me.

Seychelles

Beyond the Reefs by William Travis

Calusa Bay Publications, 1997 (first published 1959)

This edition of *Beyond the Reefs* contains two books: the original *Beyond the Reefs*, first published in 1959, and *Shark for Sale*, published in 1961. Together, they make up an absorbing volume of tropical adventure.

William Travis, a pilot for the RAF and afterwards for commercial airlines, escaped to the Seychelles in the 1950s, seeking a "radical and immediate" change from his clock-bound routine. For several years he had spent his spare time pursuing scuba diving and underwater photography, and he planned to join a friend who was a schooner captain to search for specimens of the coelacanth – the "fossil fish," long believed extinct, that had recently been rediscovered in the Indian Ocean.

The coelacanth plan fell through, but before long another opportunity presented itself: hunting for the Green Snail, whose shell with its mother-of-pearl lining was in demand. Travis knew little about the Green Snail, but it appeared that no one else did either. Undaunted, he quit his airline job, bought diving gear, and headed for the Seychelles to recruit a team of Creole divers.

Beyond the Reefs recounts the author's quest for the Green Snail among the outer islands of the Seychelles archipelago. Though snail-hunting soon turns out to be a much more difficult way to make a living than flying planes, Travis never hints that he is tempted to go back to his previous life. Every step of this quixotic quest is recounted with straight-faced detail, as if it all makes perfect sense. The local fishermen know where some Green Snail colonies can be found, but Travis quickly discovers that their knowledge is mostly limited to the shallow waters where they ordinarily fish. When he begins to hire skin-divers he finds that many of the supposedly expert young Creole divers can barely swim. Travis sets up a demanding course of diving and scuba lessons, eliminating most of the candidates and subjecting the rest to extreme tests. To train them to recognize the signs of oxygen deprivation or carbon dioxide poisoning, he sends them down to fifteen feet and leaves them there until their tanks are exhausted. "Then they were rapidly hauled up, the salt-water they

had swallowed pumped out of their lungs, and left to vomit in peace. … It was cruel and dangerous, but it had to be done."

With a team of eight trained divers, Travis sets out on a vessel christened the *Louis Alfred* but known as the *L. Fred* after part of its nameplate was lost in an accident. Most of *Beyond the Reefs* recounts the journeys of the *L. Fred* among the outer islands of the Seychelles, brought alive by the author's leisurely, detailed descriptions of deserted islands, coral reefs, dramatic rescues, and underwater wrecks. On the island of Aldabra, Travis rides a giant tortoise and carries a smaller one into the water to see if it will float (it does). He and his men are threatened by violent storms and menaced by barracuda and a variety of sharks, including hammerheads and tiger sharks. They return to port only after several months – not only because Travis recognizes that they are worn out from hard work, continual danger, and short rations, but because, at least for now, the pleasure has gone out of the work. "I found myself looking out across the sea at Astove and suddenly I realized that I had not really *seen* the island at all until that moment."

Shark for Sale tells of Travis's next money-making scheme: a plan to profit from the demand for high-quality dried and salted shark. Once again, this plan is more complicated than it seems at first. Travis develops new fishing techniques to enable him to bring in bigger sharks, and he obtains the use of a small island where the shark meat can be dried and processed in the open without the risk of theft. Darker and more dramatic than *Beyond the Reefs*, *Shark for Sale* is packed with lore about this fast, powerful, deadly fish, which compensates for low intelligence with lightning reflexes and an almost unbelievable life force. "Ton Milot showed me how sharks, hauled on board alive, gutted completely and then thrown into the sea devoid of all entrails, liver and heart, would swim steadily off again as though nothing had happened." Suffering injuries and risking death, sleeping at night on the bodies of dead sharks, and telling stories about sinister spirits and the skull abandoned on an isolated sandbar, Travis and his crew struggle to make a living from the awesome beast that he likens to Job's Leviathan.

It was my habit each morning to get up before daylight and watch the sunrise. There was a reason for this. I knew that during the night many large sharks came close to the beaches in search of turtles and I wanted to ascertain the exact hour of their return across the reef out to the depths. Every day as soon as there was sufficient light I would spend an hour or more watching the sea-bed from a vantage point on the bowsprit. Eight fathoms down, the beginning of each day came far later than it did on the surface, and not until the sun was well above the horizon would any fishy activity begin in the coral jungle that lay below our keel. But the night prowlers returned to the safety and darkness of the abyss before this. As soon as the pale lead light of the pre-dawn lay upon the sea you might see their shadowy silhouettes pass, slinking like giant alley-cats, furtively and silent, back over the reef, to curve down in a last smooth arc and disappear from sight.

Sierra Leone

The Last Harmattan of Alusine Dunbar
by Syl Cheney-Coker
Heinemann, 1990

Like his Congolese contemporary Sony Labou Tansi, Syl Cheney-Coker was inspired and influenced by the pioneering magical realism of Gabriel García Márquez. But whereas *The Seven Solitudes of Lorsa Lopez* owes something to García Márquez's novella *Chronicle of a Death Foretold*, *The Last Harmattan of Alusine Dunbar* is even more ambitious. In a sense, it is a West African version of *One Hundred Years of Solitude*.

The Last Harmattan has a long timeline – the events unfold over three centuries, not just one – but a narrow focus. The mythic history told here centres around the town of Malagueta. Malagueta (which is also the name of a hot pepper) is never mentioned as belonging to any larger colony or country, though late in the book we are told that neighbouring towns have been included under its name. Still, in a dreamlike way Malagueta stands in for Sierra Leone. It is situated on the coast of West Africa, and the Fulani people of the Fouta Djallon mountains are said to be only a three days' journey away. (The quickest way to the Fouta Djallon from the coast is through Sierra Leone.)

Like the country of Sierra Leone, the town of Malagueta is founded by freed slaves who first arrive in the years after the American Revolution and struggle to accommodate themselves to the African community they find there. But while the returned slaves of Sierra Leone are brought there by British merchants and philanthropists, the returnees of Malagueta are bold pioneers who have made it there on their own. Sebastian Cromantine, a leader of the newcomers, offers the local king "a trunk full of silver spoons and ceramic jars," and promises that his people will "obey the laws and keep their hands off the women."

The settlers build a collection of "neat log cabins" facing the sea, with separate kitchens, outhouses, and vegetable plots. Sebastian Cromantine sets up a trading post and rum shop, and one day his wife

Jeanette walks to the nearby town of Kasila and begins teaching some of the local women how to make dolls and sew dresses. Sebastian's promise to keep his men away from these women doesn't last long: Gustavius Martins, the other leader of the settlers, sees a beautiful young woman bathing in a stream and is "held by the brilliant gold of the woman's skin with its polish of an onyx, with her long and graceful neck."

In time Malagueta becomes a full-fledged town where twelve streets named after the months of the year cross twelve others named after Jesus' disciples. Struggles develop between the religious fanatics and the freethinkers among the Malaguetans, and later between the Malaguetans and the forces of Captain Hammerstone, a British officer who establishes a garrison in the town and gradually tries to control and exploit it. The narrative moves forward and backward in time, stories grow organically from other stories in a way that defies summary, and what seem at first like mere digressions become fully developed plot lines. The sprawling story is held together not only by Cheney-Coker's richly sensual style and use of twenty-dollar words ("she felt the chrysanthemum of his love which sprang about her in a brilliant flabellum of colours") but also by the unusually long life of certain characters, who provide a connecting thread through the generations.

Antonio the Mulatto was just opening his shop when the black woman with the lustrous eyes of a gazelle walked in. The shop was a mud-brick structure with a cast-iron door which had come from a disused mine, built on a plot of land near where the sea was noisy and treacherous. By assiduously working day and night, he had built a prosperous trade in rum, tobacco, smoked herrings, cod fish and cheap Indian cotton which he bought wholesale from the pirates who frequented the Man-of-Wharf Bay on the unruly and rocky coast. Behind the shop was an old stone house of red laterite, thatched with palm fronds and protected by a fence of liana and guava stalks. No one knew where he had come from but he had about him the warm and inviting air of trust, the piercing concentration of an

honest man, and was allowed to stay among the people of the town. He was dark and quiet, solitary like a crab and about forty. On the bridge of a slightly crooked nose he had a small mark which he said was the result of having been bitten by a shark while swimming in Portugal, and when he walked there was a pronounced limp which, with the touch of grey on his temple, made him a rather distinguished figure. When he came to the village he had left behind him the byways of the past: the veneration of the Black Virgin of Saragossa; the women in perennial black; the hot dusty roads where the men walked beside their donkeys laden with fruits; the village taverns in the small Portuguese town where his drunken father had returned to die, bitter from his experience in Lourenço Marques where he had failed as a coffee planter, bringing up the son whom he had forced upon the beautiful Mozambican woman who had died in childbirth.

Sierra Leone

The Devil That Danced on the Water
by Aminatta Forna
Atlantic Monthly Press, 2002

"I had spent twenty-five years in ignorance," writes Aminatta Forna toward the end of this memoir, "and one year gradually uncovering the truth, and yet now I could barely recall what it felt like not to know."

Forna is too hard on herself. As a child she knew the essentials: that her father was an ambitious, sometimes arrogant man, an African doctor turned government minister, that the marriage between her father and her free-spirited Scottish mother was tempestuous, and that some time after breaking from the leaders of Sierra Leone, he was taken away and never returned. What she learns twenty-five years later merely confirms the details of what she knew already. "It was as though this terrible knowledge: of the lies and the manipulation, the greed and the corruption, the fear and violence had been with me for ever."

As a third-year medical student in Aberdeen, Scotland, Mohamed Forna had a confidence that made him seem tall and attractive, though he was four inches short of six feet tall, with a face pitted by smallpox scars. A photograph, his daughter relates, reveals an expression "amused and utterly self-possessed." An unobservant Muslim, he acquired a taste for "sweet alcoholic drinks" and developed cavities. When his country, Sierra Leone, became independent in 1961, he threw a party, got "flamboyantly drunk," and smoked six cigarettes at once, holding three in each hand. "I'm smoking the smoke of freedom," he explained.

Back in Sierra Leone, young Dr Forna opened a clinic in the town of Koidu. One of the author's earliest memories, though, is not of her father treating a regular patient but of his reaching down the throat of their English sheepdog to try to remove a chicken bone stuck there – then putting down the dog with a dose of anaesthetic when it proves impossible.

While running a military hospital, Dr Forna refused a demand by the head of the army, who wanted the hospital to provide a certain young woman with an abortion. The doctor's backbone attracted the attention of the APC, an opposition party that was organizing to prevent the attempts of the ruling SLPP to turn the country into a one-party state. Dr Forna lent his support to Siaka Stevens, the opposition leader, and the party chose him to run for his local seat in parliament. When the election was held, Dr Forna won his seat "by the greatest margin and the greatest number of votes cast in favour of any one candidate during the entire elections." The APC swept the elections, and Stevens was being sworn in as prime minister when the army carried out a military coup.

Dr Forna joined the APC government in exile, and a few years later – when the so-called Privates' Revolt overthrew the regime – Siaka Stevens was appointed prime minister once more, with the 32-year-old Dr Mohamed Forna as his minister of finance. Dr Forna threw himself into his new profession, and attempted to chart a course for Sierra Leone that would lead to real economic prosperity, without the crippling dependency on Western loans and aid that had weakened other African countries while enriching their elites. Soon, though, when Siaka Stevens began to put the country on the path to a one-party state, Dr Forna resigned his position and became a member of the opposition once more.

The personal and the political intertwine in this memoir, and the author does an extraordinary job of weaving together past and present, memories and reportage, to create a coherent and dramatic story. *The Devil That Danced on the Water* is the story of Dr Forna, but it is also the story of a small girl growing up in wrenching circumstances. She loves her father but resents his absences and infidelities. She loves her mother, but recognizes that her mother has instilled in her some prejudices that will make it hard to accept herself. The book circles around the childhood memory that begins it: the day that a man appeared at her father's clinic with wounded hands, hours before two men with the improbable names of Prince Ba and Newlove came to take her father away. Aminatta Forna reconstructs that day in detail, but even more impressive, she returns to Sierra Leone twenty-five years later to conduct the interviews and elicit the confessions that make clear the meaning of that day: who betrayed her father and who was faithful to him.

A man sat almost motionless on one of the hard-backed chairs. His face was damp, great globes of sweat hung on his forehead, his head and eyes rolled slightly backward. Our father, balanced on the arm of an old black plastic easy-chair, was bent towards him.

I pushed in past them all and eased myself in next to my father. I smelled stagnant sweat and alcohol rising from the man, who must have been in his twenties. His skin was dusty grey. It reminded me of something I once saw on a trip we made up-country. We were driving back to Freetown, late at night; everyone around me in the car was asleep. Our driver swung the car around a bend and we came suddenly upon a dark figure walking at the side of the road, miles from any village, petrol station or even crossroads. The walker turned abruptly and the headlights lit up his face. I gasped and so did Sullay, the driver. The man's black face was smeared with pale ashes. His robes were dark, their colour obscured by the darkness. He came like an apparition out of the night. Seconds later the car had left him far behind. That, and the time a boy I knew was stung by a scorpion, were the only occasions on which I had ever seen someone turn that colour.

Somalia

First Footsteps in East Africa by Richard F. Burton

Dover, 1987 (first published 1856)

Sir Richard Francis Burton was one of the boldest explorers, most erudite scholars, and most difficult individuals of the nineteenth century. Long fascinated with Eastern cultures, in 1853 he disguised himself as an Afghan pilgrim and succeeded in reaching Mecca and Medina, the holiest cities in the Muslim world. In 1854 he set out on a journey to another forbidden city: Harar, the capital of Somaliland in East Africa, which no European had ever reached and returned from alive.

Although the city of Harar is inside the borders of Ethiopia, Burton's journey took him through what would become the country of Somalia. Disguised as an Arab merchant, Burton travelled with a small caravan from the Somalian coastal city of Zayla (now Saylac) to Harar, where he met with the "Amir," remained ten days, then returned through the desert to the coast, supplied with only "five biscuits, a few limes, a few lumps of sugar, and a single skin of water."

Burton's descriptions of the people he travelled among are punctuated with outbursts of scathing contempt. The Habr Girhajis (his own servants' people) and the Ísa Musa are "treacherous races," he says, and the Gudabirsi are "such inveterate liars that I could fix them no number between 3 000 and 10 000." The Badawin (or Bedouin) present "a spectacle of savageness. Their huge heads of shock hair, dyed red and dripping with butter, are garnished with a Firin, or long three-pronged comb ... and sometimes with the ominous ostrich feather, showing that the wearer has 'killed his man.'"

The reader quickly realizes that Burton's contempt is combined with a deep curiosity about alien cultures. The language of the people of Harar, he notes, is "harsh and unpleasant," and "contains no literature except songs and tales, which are written in the modern Naskhi character." Yet in the same breath he says, "I would willingly have studied it deeply." Lengthy footnotes correct the mistakes of other scholars and detail the customs of the Somalis and the geology, flora, and fauna of their land. Burton describes the diet of the Ísa, the

218

games their children play, and how they treat a variety of diseases: "Dysentery is cured by rice and sour milk, patients also drink clarified cow's butter; and in bad cases the stomach is cauterised, fire and disease, according to the Somal, never coexisting."

There are even hints that Burton feels more comfortable in East Africa than he would at home. "In the mining counties of civilized England," he writes, "where the 'genial brick-bat' is thrown at the passing stranger, or in enlightened Scotland, where hair a few inches too long or a pair of mustachioes justifies 'mobbing,' it would have been impossible for me to have mingled as I did with these wild people."

Burton seems to have relished the experience of adventuring in a country where his flamboyance and machismo, as well as his learning, could be a positive asset. In East Africa, he explains, "English phlegm, shyness, or pride, will bar every heart and raise every hand against you," whereas "a certain *rondeur* of manner" is essential. "You should walk up to your man, clasp his fist, pat his back, speak some unintelligible words to him – if, as is the plan of prudence, you ignore the language – laugh a loud guffaw, sit by his side, and begin pipes and coffee." He ensites wonder and admiration by shooting vultures and other wildlife, and at the end of the book, back on the coast at Berberah, his courage and fighting abilities are called upon in earnest during a deadly attack on his camp.

First Footsteps in East Africa is dedicated to Burton's friend James Grant Lumsden, and the two volumes are studded with references to "dear L.," as if they were one very long letter. Addressing himself to an intimate friend may have made it easier for Burton to maintain his outrageously opinionated and unbuttoned approach to his subject. In at least one place, he may have been more unbuttoned than English society could tolerate.

An appendix to the first edition was to have included a "brief description of certain peculiar customs ... under the name of fibulation." Never one to shy from controversy, Burton might have been among the first to reveal the details of the extreme form of female genital mutilation practised in the Horn of Africa – but according to a footnote, his editors "found it necessary to omit" this material. The subject survives in the book only in Burton's remark that Somali women are generally "of cold temperament, the result of artificial as well as natural causes."

—

The present city of Harar is about one mile long by half that breadth. An irregular wall, lately repaired, but ignorant of cannon, is pierced with five large gates, and supported by oval towers of artless construction. The material of the houses and defences is rough stones, the granites and sandstones of the hills, cemented, like the ancient Galla cities, with clay. The only large building is the Jami or Cathedral, a long barn of poverty-stricken appearance, with broken-down gates, and two white-washed minarets of truncated conoid shape. They were built by Turkish architects from Mocha and Hodaydah: one of them lately fell, and has been replaced by an inferior effort of Harari art. There are a few trees in the city, but it contains none of those gardens which give to Eastern settlements that pleasant view of town and country combined. The streets are narrow lanes, up hill and down dale, strewed with gigantic rubbish heaps, upon which repose packs of mangy or one-eyed dogs, and even the best are encumbered with rocks and stones. The habitations are mostly long, flat-roofed sheds, double storied, with doors composed of a single plank, and holes for windows pierced high above the ground, and decorated with miserable wood-work: the principal houses have separate apartments for the women, and stand at the bottom of large court-yards closed by gates of Holcus stalks. ... The city abounds in mosques, plain buildings without minarets, and in graveyards stuffed with tombs – oblong troughs formed by long slabs planted edgeways in the ground. I need scarcely say that Harar is proud of her learning, sanctity, and holy dead.

Somalia

Secrets by Nuruddin Farah

Arcade Publishing, 1998

Secrets, set in Somalia in the tense period just before the dissolution of Mohamed Siad Barre's regime into the chaos of clan warfare, is a big philosophical novel told in alternating voices, and replete with a bewildering system of symbols, a variety of secrets, sexual and otherwise, and some of the most peculiar yet engaging language in modern literature. Though *Secrets* is the third novel in the Blood in the Sun trilogy (the others are *Maps* and *Gifts*), it stands as a self-contained novel.

As the book begins, Kalaman, a Somali man with a successful computing business, has been visited by Sholoongo, a childhood playmate who has just returned from the US, where she is married to a man referred to as a Moroccan fire-eater. As a ten-year-old boy, Kalaman played sexual games with the fourteen-year-old Sholoongo, who (we later learn) had also made advances to Kalaman's grandfather Nonno.

Sholoongo is the tumultuous, sexually insatiable centre of many of the secrets that swirl around this novel. In addition to Kalaman and Nonno, she is suspected of having had relations with her own brother (though he has since become a gay activist in San Francisco) and of an entanglement with Kalaman's father. Sholoongo is said to be a shape-shifter, and when an elephant kills a hunter who was Kalaman's childhood friend, goring him in his hut and then carrying away a pile of ivory, some suspect her of having transformed herself into the elephant. Her purpose now, which she states straightforwardly but does not explain, is to have a child by Kalaman.

In counterpoint to Sholoongo is the novel's other major character: Kalaman's grandfather Miftaax, known as Nonno after the Italian for "grandfather." A chain-smoking, nonobservant Muslim, sexually vigorous in his eighties, Nonno is an endlessly philosophical ruminator, the source of many cryptic monologues on the subject of his turbulent family and the growing political crisis in Somalia. "I cannot imagine a world without taboos, a culture without its notion of right and wrong," he tells his grandson. "Honors are maintained, pledges kept,

gods worshipped. It is anathema to imagine a world in which there are no secrets. Secrets have a life energy, they keep us alive." A man of special powers as well as intellect, he can summon birds and speak to them in their language. If Sholoongo is an uncontrollable force of anarchy, Nonno in his cloud of cigarette smoke is a still point and a comforting anchor for those around him, even when they (and we) may not understand him.

Farah has a creative way with similes, which the reader may find either irritating or intriguing. "My neck, with which the palm of my hand came into contact, felt rough as a giraffe's coat of stretchy skin." "Nonno's voice had in it a touch of humidity, which affected his delivery, making his words emerge curled up like the pages a fax machine spits out." Farah sometimes turns familiar clichés inside out, making them yield fresh new meanings. Like the early novels of Saul Bellow, *Secrets* gives the impression of a new literary style being formed, strange yet powerful, and giving promise for the future.

—

Now Kalaman had the shivers. An instant later he was so hot the sheet covering him seemed to curl up at the edges, like a piece of paper close to a tongue of flame. His reflection in the mirror startled him. He had difficulty acknowledging his own face. So much change in such a short time, and such a loss of weight. Could a day's stubble be that preponderous? He felt alien to himself when he looked in the mirror, as though he were face-to-face with his nightmares, of which he had so far had several.

In one of them, Kalaman had come in on his mother chewing away at the soft ends of a human skull. Disturbed, he asked her who the skull had belonged to, when alive. His mother explained that it once belonged to the head of a person from an "enemy clan." Would he like a bite of it? In another nightmare, he was a newt in the vast belly of a whale, at whose intestine it pulled in an effort to get out. The whale was branded with the identity of his mother's clan on one flank, on the other his father's. He was a prisoner in the whale's all-inclusiveness, a newt-man with no recognizable identity. His wish to reclaim his deracinated, not-clan-based

222

identity was denied. He was given the choice of dying at the hands of a nonmember of his mother's clan or his father's, or to roam in the belly of the whale as a newt. He chose to be a newt, preferring this to allying himself with the murderers.

South Africa

Long Walk to Freedom by Nelson Mandela

Little, Brown, 1995

Nelson Mandela began writing *Long Walk to Freedom* in 1975, shortly after he celebrated his fifty-seventh birthday on Robben Island as a prisoner of the apartheid government. After days spent in the island's lime quarry, Mandela worked secretly through the night on the manuscript. His fellow prisoners helped edit it, recopied it in a minuscule shorthand, and smuggled it out of the prison. A typescript was prepared and presented to Oliver Tambo, Mandela's former law partner and the leader of the ANC during Mandela's imprisonment – but the book never appeared. "I heard nothing from Lusaka about the manuscript," Mandela writes, "and still do not know precisely what Oliver did with it." That is the last comment he makes on the subject.

Did Mandela never press his old friend Tambo about what happened to his book – either through intermediaries or years later after he was released? Apparently not. It is just one example of Mandela's extraordinary patience, and his ability to put aside his own needs and preferences in favour of preserving relationships and advancing the larger cause. Fortunately, however, Mandela returned to his story years later and completed this extraordinary memoir.

Long Walk to Freedom begins with Mandela's childhood in the Transkei region of the Eastern Cape in South Africa, where he grew up in a village of beehive-shaped mud huts. Born into a royal family, he was expected one day to become an adviser to the rulers of his people. Early in life he was impressed by the African tradition of making decisions by consensus, and by the importance of allowing an opponent to save face. "I learned that to humiliate another person is to make him suffer an unnecessarily cruel fate."

Not a brilliant student but a diligent one, Mandela pursued his studies, evaded an arranged marriage, and found himself the only African studying law at the prestigious University of the Witwatersrand. Having lived for a time in the violent, dynamic, melting-pot community of Alexandra, he began to understand that tribalism could be overcome. "Urban life tended to abrade tribal

and ethnic distinctions, and instead of being Xhosas, or Sothos, or Zulus, or Shangaans, we were Alexandrians." Mandela helped to create the ANC Youth League, "as a way of lighting a fire under the leadership of the ANC," coordinated strikes and other protests, and soon became a prominent ANC leader, his importance confirmed when the government placed him under a banning order that barred him from attending meetings of any kind.

The years that followed were a whirlwind of protest and repression, related here with clarity and balance: the forced evacuation of Sophiatown, the writing of the Freedom Charter, the enormous Treason Trial, the women's protest against passes, the creation of artificial "homelands" for Africans, the massacre at Sharpeville, and the banning of the ANC. Though acquitted along with his fellow defendants at the end of the lengthy Treason Trial, Mandela had the forethought to go underground at once.

Having failed to crush its opponents through the legal system, the regime turned to harsher methods. "During the Treason Trial," Mandela writes, "there were no examples of individuals being isolated, beaten, and tortured in order to elicit information. All of those things became commonplace shortly thereafter." In response, Mandela argued that the ANC must "fight fire with fire." Many of the ANC's leaders believed in nonviolence as an unshakeable principle. Mandela believed in nonviolence as a tactic, to be used whenever possible but set aside when it ceases to be effective. Mandela's impassioned arguments led to the formation of Umkhonto we Sizwe, the "spear of the nation," which carried out a series of sabotage attacks – intended to minimize loss of life – until Mandela was captured, convicted, and sent to Robben Island to serve out the first of his twenty-seven years of captivity.

The outlines of Mandela's life – especially his imprisonment, his triumphal return, and his election as the first president of a free South Africa – are well known. This unselfish memoir presents that life in the context of the times and of an extraordinary cast of characters, and presents the details that make the story come alive. Mandela describes how his taste for sour milk nearly betrayed him, how he smuggled messages in matchboxes while on Robben Island, and how he tried to promote understanding between his ANC colleagues in prison and the followers of the more militant PAC. He tells us of his love for gardening and tennis, and for setting out on road trips at 3 a.m.,

when "the roads are empty and quiet, and one can be alone with one's thoughts." Mandela is a man who looks for the core of decency within everyone he meets, even his jailers. Strength, dignity, and a generous spirit are the hallmark of this book.

———

Prison and the authorities conspire to rob each man of his dignity. In and of itself, that assured that I would survive, for any man or institution that tries to rob me of my dignity will lose because I will not part with it at any price or under any pressure. I never seriously considered the possibility that I would not emerge from prison one day. I never thought that a life sentence truly meant life and that I would die behind bars. Perhaps I was denying this prospect because it was too unpleasant to contemplate. But I always knew that someday I would once again feel the grass under my feet and walk in the sunshine as a free man.

I am fundamentally an optimist. Whether that comes from nature or nurture, I cannot say. Part of being optimistic is keeping one's head pointed toward the sun, one's feet moving forward. There were many dark moments when my faith in humanity was sorely tested, but I would not and could not give myself up to despair. That way lay defeat and death.

South Africa

July's People by Nadine Gordimer
Penguin, 1982

Nadine Gordimer, winner of the Nobel Prize for literature, is the author of over a dozen novels and several collections of short stories. Where to begin?

July's People is a short novel with a unique place in Gordimer's work. It falls between the books of the apartheid era, like *Burger's Daughter*, and those that chart the ambiguities of post-apartheid South Africa, like *The House Gun*. *July's People* imagines a future time when that regime is under serious attack and perhaps crumbling, a period of transition when – as the author quotes Antonio Gramsci – "the old is dying and the new cannot be born." Ironically, at the time *July's People* was published, the end of apartheid was only a decade away, yet even dedicated opponents of the system could not imagine that it would end in their lifetime.

Maureen Smales, the daughter of a gold-mining family, and her husband Bamford (known as Bam), a successful architect, have fled Johannesburg with their three children. The novel begins as the Smaleses' long-time servant July arrives at daybreak to bring their morning tea. It is a familiar ritual in a world turned upside down. Instead of taking their tea in their comfortable home in the city, they are taking it in a thatched hut in the rural compound that July comes from but the Smales have never seen. The couple and their servant seem determined to act as if nothing much has changed, but it is impossible to keep up the pretence for long.

How did they get there? The situation in the outside world is sketched in with quick strokes. "Riots, arson, occupation of the headquarters of international corporations, bombs in public buildings – the censorship of newspapers, radio and television left rumour and word-of-mouth as the only sources of information about this chronic state of uprising all over the country." Some time before, hearing from a bank accountant that the banks might shut down, Bam has withdrawn a large sum of money. Though he feels foolish when nothing happens, the accountant, like "the legendary warning hornbill of African folk-tales," proves to be an accurate prophet of

227

doom. When things get worse, the white family load up their bright-yellow bakkie, a small truck that Bam had bought for hunting trips, and flee "the gunned shopping malls and the blazing, unsold houses of a depressed market." July, the servant they have taken pride in treating well – for the Smaleses consider themselves kind and progressive people – has agreed to help them.

One of the greatest successes of the apartheid system was in dividing whites and blacks so thoroughly that the average white South African had no idea how his cooks and servants lived. (The cooks and servants, naturally, had a much better idea of how the whites lived.) Some of the most striking passages in this novel convey the awkwardness with which the guest family adjust to an utterly alien way of life. Maureen discovers the smell of her own body and her husband's body, and the way that the insects hidden in a thatched roof are "activated by the moisture" when it rains. The children adapt faster, making friends while they learn to mould toy cattle out of clay and to wipe themselves with a stone instead of toilet paper.

While the radio reports power struggles from the outside world, local power struggles revolve around the control of the keys to the yellow bakkie, and the question of whether the Smaleses will be allowed to stay. These struggles develop in unpredictable ways. When Bam and Maureen are taken to see the chief, they expect that as white oppressors they might be told to leave. Instead they find that the chief has swallowed the government's anti-Communist line of propaganda and is looking for allies against the Cubans and Russians and "those people from Soweto."

"You're not going to take guns and help the white government kill blacks, are you?" pleads Bam, repeating the liberal rhetoric that he and his wife have lived by, and that no longer seems to work. "For this – this village and this empty bush?"

It was the first time the Smaleses had had to come home to: the iron bed, the Primus, the pink glass cups and saucers in the enamel basin with its sores of rust, the tin of milk powder and the general-store packet of sugar covered with a newspaper. Living within the hut they had lost sense of it. But now it was waiting for them. Coming from the stare of the

sun into the dim enclosure smelled rather than seen – old, smoky grass and earth damp with what spilled from vessels and human bodies instead of dew and rain – they scarcely made each other out. In a tin-bright angle of sunlight drawn by the slide-rule of the doorway a fowl with a bald neck was sitting on the suitcase of their possessions. Maureen read the labels to herself as if she had never seen them before. Statler-Hilton Buenos Aires Albergo San Lorenzo Mantua Heerengracht Hotel Cape Town. Bam chased the fowl.

South Africa

Age of Iron by J. M. Coetzee

Random House, 1990

Anger is an underrated force in contemporary literature. Literary works are expected to end on a note of reconciliation, if not harmony. Yet some of the earliest and greatest works of Western literature are driven and concentrated and purified by anger: the smouldering anger of Achilles in his tent, or the vengeful fury of Medea. J. M. Coetzee draws on this tradition in the classical purity and intense anger of *Age of Iron*, and it is perfectly appropriate that the old white woman who is his protagonist should be a classical scholar.

J. M. Coetzee, a professional scholar himself, began his career as a novelist with a series of brooding Kafkaesque tales set in timeless, almost allegorical lands. *Age of Iron* is the first of his novels to be set in a recognizable South Africa. Begun in 1986 and set in that year, it takes place in the waning era of apartheid, when the militant "comrades" have succeeded in their aim of making the townships ungovernable, when "the worm-ridden ship is so clearly sinking," and yet when the outlines of a new society cannot yet be seen.

Age of Iron is an epistolary novel: "so long a letter," as the narrator calls it in an apparent nod to the Senegalese novel of that name. Mrs Curren, the author of the letter and the book's narrator, lives alone and is dying of cancer. She is writing to her daughter, who lives in North America and has sworn that she will never return to her homeland while the apartheid regime is in power. Day by day, writes Mrs Curren, "I render myself into words and pack the words into the page like sweets ... drops of myself, for her to unpack in her own time, to suck, to absorb."

Hearing her daughter's "brisk American voice" on the phone, Mrs Curren wants to call her back to South Africa, but she never does. And because she plans to have her letter mailed after her death, Mrs Curren ensures that there will be no reply. With no one else to ask, Mrs Curren extracts a promise from Mr Vercueil, an African derelict and drunk whom she first meets camped in the alleyway beside her home, to mail the package to her daughter once she passes on. It is a

small favour she is asking – the package will be stamped and ready to go – but she still feels some doubt as to whether it will be done.

Mrs Curren's letter is as emotionally unsparing as one might expect from a woman with little to lose, and as sharp and concentrated as one might expect from a woman with a training in Latin and Greek. She is angry at the officials of the apartheid regime whose speeches she hears on television: "the slow, truculent Afrikaans rhythms with their deadening closes, like a hammer beating a post into the ground." She is furious at her own weakness and mortality, writing that in certain moods "I am capable of putting a hand on the breadboard and chopping it off without a second thought." She is afraid of the roving gangs of black and mixed-race youths, "sullen-mouthed boys, rapacious as sharks," and she is afraid in a somewhat different way of the oblivious white children, "their innocence the innocence of bee grubs, plump and white, drenched in honey, absorbing sweetness through their soft skins."

Mrs Curren wants, understandably, to preserve her peaceful life as long as possible, but at the same time she is not ready to disengage herself from what is going on around her. Despite her diagnosis she stays away from hospitals and stops taking her drugs when she finds they are blurring her thoughts. Mrs Curren's desire to protect herself from the suffering around her battles continually against her compassion. She has no wish to turn into the nightmare figure she imagines herself becoming: a hollow doll with a crab inside.

Mrs Curren's relationship with the derelict in her alleyway is one of the chinks through which the world comes flooding in. Though she orders him away at first, she soon allows him to stay, then offers him food, then pays him for work around the house. Her respectable housekeeper Florence wants to get rid of Mr Vercueil, and Florence's son Bheki teams up with a friend – one of the young comrades – to torment the man. In a wrenching conversation, Florence explains she is proud of the courage and revolutionary zeal of the township children. She argues that their parents have little to teach them, and excuses their cruelty as the fruit of white oppression. Mrs Curren argues that these children of iron still need parents to teach them compassion and respect for their elders, even when those elders, like Mr Vercueil, are aimless drunks.

Mrs Curren's relationship with Mr Vercueil deepens throughout the book, but it never becomes cosy or sentimental. For a while Mrs

Curren imagines redeeming herself through a dramatic act of self-sacrifice – an act that Mr Vercueil is strangely eager to help with. Though the letter Mrs Curren leaves behind is an indictment of the society made by apartheid, it is also a warning of how hard it will be to leave the age of iron when apartheid is over. Mrs Curren has few illusions about Mr Vercueil, but by entrusting her letter to him she is doing her best to have faith in the possibility of a better South Africa than the one she has known.

Since life in this country is so much like life aboard a sinking ship, one of those old-time liners with a lugubrious, drunken captain and a surly crew and leaky lifeboats, I keep the shortwave radio at my bedside. Most of the time there is only talk to be heard; but if one persists into the unlikely hours of the night there are stations that relent and play music. Fading in, fading out, I heard last night – from where? Helsinki? the Cook Islands? – anthems of all the nations, celestial music, music that left us years ago and now comes back from the stars transfigured, gentle, as evidence that all that is given forth will at length return. A closed universe, curved like an egg, enclosing us.

South Africa

Mother to Mother by Sindiwe Magona

Beacon Press, 1999

The murder of Amy Biehl was one of the last and most-publicized tragedies of the apartheid era in South Africa. A 26-year-old Fulbright scholar from the United States, Amy Biehl went to South Africa to research voter education and women's rights as the country was preparing for its first free election. In August 1993, shortly before she was due to return to the US, she agreed to drive three South African friends to their homes in the township of Guguletu near Cape Town. When they reached the township the car was stoned by a group of African students chanting "one settler, one bullet." Amy Biehl was beaten and stabbed to death while attempting to flee.

Amy Biehl's death prompted a number of difficult questions. Why was she killed – at a time when apartheid was all but defeated? Were her attackers fully responsible for the crime, or were the militant leaders of the country and the township to blame? Should Amy Biehl have known that it was dangerous for a white woman to travel to Guguletu? Was her death part of the last throes of apartheid, or was it a prediction of continued racial tension and violence? Was it right for the international press to focus so much attention on the death of one white American when thousands of black South Africans had died anonymously at the hands of the security forces?

Sindiwe Magona, according to her publisher, "raised her children just steps away from the site of Amy's death." In *Mother to Mother*, she takes the risky step of applying her imagination to this very recent and very raw event, and addressing the questions that swirl around it through fiction.

In *Mother to Mother*, the author follows the reported details of the Amy Biehl case closely, though without using the victim's name. She sharpens and simplifies the moral questions involved, however, by implying that although the victim was attacked by a mob, one young man was primarily responsible for her death. The novel begins by stating the situation as starkly as possible: "My son killed your daughter."

Mxolisi, the narrator's son, has shown no sign of being a killer. Like many township children, he has had a difficult upbringing. His father disappears when he is very young, and not much later he suffers a terrible trauma. Two older boys, his friends, seek refuge in his house, and when the police come looking for them he innocently gives away their hiding place. Moments later he witnesses their murder, and for two years after that he is mute.

Mxolisi grows up to be a young man with principles – he saves a woman from rape, and he refuses to take part in the killing of suspected government collaborators. But he is emotionally unstable and spends his time roaming the streets with the volatile young "comrades" who have become the de facto rulers of the community.

Tout comprendre est tout pardonner, goes the French saying. To understand everything is to forgive everything. But can any amount of information about a killer's troubled life really make a murder pardonable? Rather than make the guilt go away, in the end *Mother to Mother* places it more widely: not on the killer alone but on the apartheid system that brutalized him, the reckless radicals with their quick judgements and easy slogans, and with parents who are too quick to let their children, the "young lions," fight the system in their own way.

It was getting late. Very late. Still, of the three men in the house, only Lunga was home. Not my husband, Dwadwa, Father-of-Siziwe. But about him, I was not that worried. He works in the Docks in Cape Town and it is not unusual for him to be late. But where was Mxolisi? Not for the first time, I asked myself what it was that made him so different from the other two children. How many times had I not spoken to him about his gadding about? About his being the eldest and therefore the one who had to set a good example for the others? Why was he so consistent in being disobedient?

Siziwe had a pot of *mngqusho* (samp) simmering when I came. I was rested now. As rested as I could get with all that had happened to me earlier that evening. I waited, hoping that Mxolisi and Dwadwa would come so we could all eat together. Hoping, though, that Mxolisi would be the

first to make an appearance. I was sick and tired of hearing Dwadwa's mouth on the subject of Mxolisi's long foot that wrote itself on all the streets and corners of Guguletu ... day and night. What had made Mxolisi stop confiding in me? And when had that wall of silence sprung between us? I couldn't remember. He used to tell me everything ... and then, one day I woke up to find I knew almost nothing about his activities or his friends.

South Africa

The Heart of Redness by Zakes Mda

Farrar, Straus and Giroux, 2000

The great cattle killing of 1856 is one of the strangest and most tragic episodes in South African history. Prompted by the vision of a young girl named Nongqawuse, the Xhosa people stopped farming and began to slaughter their own cattle and destroy their grain supplies. By doing so, they believed, they would help bring on the resurrection of their ancestors, the arrival of new people from the sea and new cattle from the earth, and the elimination of the British who had conquered and colonized them. The Crimean war was going on, and some hoped that the Russians would beat the British and come to free them. The Russians, they believed, were actually black men – the resurrected ancestors of the Xhosa. Before it was all over, thousands of Xhosas had starved to death, and the Xhosa nation had suffered a crippling blow.

The cattle killing provides the background for this sometimes comic, sometimes moving novel of life in the coastal town of Qolorha. The action shuttles between the time of the cattle killing and the present day, in post-apartheid South Africa. Characters in one time have their namesakes and counterparts in the other, and the repercussions of past decisions can be seen in the present. In between the two times are the Middle Generations, a time of suffering that everyone agrees it is better not to dwell on.

Did all the Xhosa believe the words of Nongqawuse and slaughter their cattle? *The Heart of Redness* supposes that they didn't, and imagines two twin brothers (known as Twin and Twin-Twin) who reach opposite conclusions. Both have suffered from the British – their father was killed in battle and his head boiled so a British officer could keep the skull as a souvenir. But Twin is a Believer and Twin-Twin an Unbeliever, and when Twin kills not only his own cattle but also his brother's, the rift between them becomes permanent. Modern-day Qolorha reflects the same rift, with Twin's descendant Zim and the other Believers set against Twin-Twin's descendant Bhonco and the Unbelievers. The Unbelievers, who favour education, "progress," and rationality, welcome a proposed development that would bring

236

a casino, motorboats, and (they hope) jobs to the unspoiled town of Qolorha. The Believers, more traditionalist in outlook, would like things as they are.

Redness, for the people of Qolorha, is associated with the red ochre that traditional Xhosa women use to colour their bodies and their skirts. A constant simmering debate – carried on with anger, wit, and ingenuity – concerns the nature and value of redness.

A short review cannot convey the liveliness and unexpected twists of this irreverent tale. Though the author has clear sympathies with tradition, he is more than willing to expose the fools and knaves on either side of the schism. Along the way we meet Africans who playact their culture for profit, a white man who speaks better Xhosa than the Xhosas, professional hecklers and ululators, and people who get ahead by using their "struggle credentials." There are lovely descriptions of rural South Africa, taboos and rituals, and an unusual love story between a middle-aged exile and a young girl, part Xhosa and part Khoikhoi, who is more than feisty enough to take care of herself.

In a clearing in front of the pink rondavel, women's upper bodies are vibrating in the *umngqungqo* dance. Bhonco is joking with the men under the umsintsi tree. He sees Camagu walking away and calls him back.

"Hey, teacher, are you just going to disappear like a fart in the wind, without even saying good-bye?" shouts Bhonco.

"Oh, Tat'uBhonco, I am sorry. I did not see you," says Camagu.

"Did those children expel you so early? The feast is still young."

"I have enjoyed myself, thank you. They entertained me enough."

"With fights? A woman came wailing that the teachers were fighting. I told her to leave us alone to enjoy our beer in peace. The learned ones always fight when they are drunk. What was it all about?"

"I do not know. It started with the discussion about the developers."

237

"The developers are still going to cause more fights in this village!"

He is passionate about development. His wrath is directed at the Believers who are bent on opposing everything that is meant to improve the lives of the people of Qolorha.

"They want us to remain in our wildness!" says the elder. "To remain red all our lives! To stay in the darkness of redness!"

Sudan

Season of Migration to the North by Tayeb Salih

Translated from the Arabic by Denys Johnson-Davies

Heinemann, 1969

Despite its somewhat ponderous title, this is a brief, graceful, and powerful novel about the collision of cultures, and the destructive potential of cultural fantasies and stereotypes. Edward Said, the eminent Palestinian writer and academic, has called it "among the six finest novels to be written in modern Arabic literature." Among other things, it is an investigation of Said's concept of Orientalism, the fascination of the "mysterious East" for Westerners of a certain kind – in this case impressionable young English women.

The tale begins as if told out loud to a group of listeners. "It was, gentlemen, after a long absence – seven years to be exact, during which I was studying in Europe – that I returned to my people." The narrator has been drawn by a "great yearning" to return to his village in the northern Sudan, at a place where the Nile bends to the east. As he settles into village life, he is surprised to meet Mustafa Sa'eed, an educated man who is mysterious about his past, though he admits that he comes from the outskirts of Khartoum and claims to be a businessman who has turned to agriculture. After drinking too much with friends one night, he recites an English poem from World War I, and the narrator realizes there is more to Mustafa than he has let on.

Eventually Mustafa tells the narrator the story of his life. Like him, Mustafa had been a young man of promise: intellectual, and inclined to think himself superior to ordinary Sudanese. He goes to Oxford to study economics and falls in with a bohemian crowd. Mustafa cultivates the image of the exotic African, furnishing his room with pink curtains, mirrors, swansdown cushions, sandalwood and incense, and a variety of "pungent Eastern perfumes, lotions, unguents, powders, and pills." Essentially a cold man, Mustafa seduces and abandons a series of idealistic young women, driving several of them to suicide, until he meets Jean Morris, a woman whose sexual allure and urge to self-destruction react with Mustafa's own obsessions to culminate in a different kind of tragedy.

When Mustafa disappears from the village, the narrator draws closer to Mustafa's wife, an educated Sudanese woman, and gains access to a locked room that contains more of the man's secrets. In grappling with the meaning of Mustafa's life, the narrator is forced to consider the meaning of his own. What has he gained from his years in Europe, and what has he lost? Is Sudan his true home any longer, or is he an alien in his own country? Did Mustafa begin to believe in the part he played while in Europe, and has the narrator fallen into the same trap? Is it too late to turn his life in a more productive direction than Mustafa has done? Along with a nostalgic and closely observed account of life in a Sudanese village, the author conveys the heartache of a man caught between two worlds.

<p align="center">——</p>

I breathe in that smell peculiar to my grandfather's house, a discordant mixture of onions and chillies and dates and wheat and horse-beans and fenugreek, in addition to the aroma of the incense which is always floating up from the large earthenware censer. The aroma of incense puts me in mind of my grandfather's ascetic manner of life and the luxury of his accessories for prayers: the rug on which he prays, made up of three leopard skins stitched together, and which he would use as a coverlet when it turned excessively cold; the brass ewer with its decorations and inscriptions, which he used for his ablutions, and the matching brass basin. He was especially proud of his sandalwood prayer-beads, which he would run through his fingers and rub against his face, breathing in their aroma; when he got angry with one of his grandchildren he would strike him across the head with them, saying that this would chase away the devil that had got into him.

Sudan

African Calliope by Edward Hoagland
Lyons and Burford, 1995 (first published 1979)

The Sudan is the biggest country in Africa. Stretching from Egypt to Uganda, from the DRC to the Red Sea, it contains most of the Nile, large tracts of the Libyan and Nubian deserts, and the largest swamp in Africa. One survey found that its people belonged to fifty-six ethnic groups and spoke one hundred and fifteen languages. How can a writer hope to describe it in a single book?

The response of most writers might be to limit the scope: to stay in a single town or region, or to write an in-search-of book, in which the quest for a person, place, or thing provides the organizing principle. Edward Hoagland, however, one of the best and most under-appreciated American writers, is anything but conventional. Like the long, looping essays for which he is best known, *African Calliope* is structured by theme rather than chronology and packed with fresh perceptions and unexpected associations. In his travels to Khartoum, Kosti, and Juba – even in a daring cross-border dash to visit the rebels of Eritrea – Hoagland is open to whatever surrounds him. His journey breaks off not when he has reached any particular goal, but only when he is "weary of the whole African calliope – that nagging, pulsing musical din that has been reverberating strongly without letup for thousands of years before you arrive and will be continuing without any respite for sickness or fatigue long after you have left the earth."

Somewhat older, at forty-four, than many African adventurers, Hoagland is less self-absorbed and more interested in the cast of unusual characters he encounters. *African Calliope* includes dozens of vivid thumbnail sketches of Arabs and Africans, missionaries, herdsmen, hippies, reporters, and priests. Costa, a hotel owner in Juba, is a "squat, dynamic cynic," half Cypriot and half Sudanese, pressured by local blacks who "would have preferred that he sold his business to an 'African.'" A photographer for the London *Telegraph* is "a square-set bloke with a bad back, older, raunchier than the others, a man who knew Morse Code from having been a merchant seaman." Even President Nimeiri isn't spared: his "puffy,

light-skinned face," Hoagland writes, "makes him resemble one of that procession of inoffensive prizefighters whom Muhammad Ali in America regularly eclipsed at weighing-in ceremonies ..."

Hoagland seems to have been a cautious supporter of Nimeiri, at least when *African Calliope* first appeared in 1979. He visited the Sudan during a pause in what now seems an endless civil war, about halfway through Nimeiri's sixteen-year rule. Caught between the rebellious tribes in the south and his "Saudi bankers," who saw the Sudan as "an arrowhead of the one true religion penetrating Central Africa," the Sudanese president adroitly balanced one set of forces against another. "The very unity of Africa seemed to require that an adjustment be found in this mercurial country, which – Arab in the north and black in the South – was a miniature of the continent." In a series of moves Hoagland calls "brilliant," Nimeiri released twelve hundred political prisoners, recalled Sadiq al-Mahdi from exile (the great-grandson of the Mahdi who defeated General Gordon), and opened negotiations with leftist leaders. It was not until several years later that Nimeiri imposed Islamic law on the entire country, the civil war flared up again, and he finally lost his hold on the presidency.

Hoagland seems most at home, if not exactly comfortable, in the less developed south of the country: African rather than Arab Sudan. He spends much of his time in the town of Juba, the capital of the Southern Region. "Set on a grassland with thorn trees and mangoes and palms, Juba is located at just about the inmost crux of the great war-club shape which on the map represents Africa." Here the Dinka herdsmen compose songs about their cattle, and each boy inherits a "personality ox" whose colour and pattern are chosen according to his position in the family. A lion-coloured ox is called "Ambusher of the Animals," and one with a dark body and white spots is called "The Shining Stars." It is this region that has been most devastated by the continuing war, and in an afterword to the 1995 edition of *African Calliope*, Hoagland describes what he saw on a return visit there, and how deeply it shook him.

A healing, miracle-working savior who would be locked in a cage within an hour if he appeared in Los Angeles or London could resurrect himself in Juba and see the populace catch fire, believe the evidence of their eyes, and make the sand streets resound once again.

Maybe for all this to happen, it is necessary that there be lepers sitting beside the road, lazy, high-horned, biblical kine, a blind albino girl with stumps for arms, a man bustling about on all fours with his thin buttocks canted as high as a baboon's because of a spinal injury that had never been treated when he was a child, and a hunter arriving on foot, carrying gazelle meat on a shoulder frame, with five spears in his hands, a brown bush hat, mud smeared on his neck and forehead to ward away the flies, and a calabash full of milk hanging from a thong around his neck. Another man stumped along on a eucalyptus stick strapped with a strip of goathide to his left hip, followed by his wife with an enormous fold of flesh which had gradually swallowed one ear and now was enveloping the whole side of her head. Miracles that wouldn't happen in New York or Jerusalem might occur in a place where the Son of God, if he were arrested, might still be killed, not entrusted to the care of social workers and psychologists.

Swaziland

Sangoma by James Hall
Putnam, 1994

An African knows that he or she is called to serve the ancestors when things begin to go wrong. The prospective healer may suffer accidents, sickness, or bad luck until he or she realizes what is going on, and decides it is useless to try to resist fate.

James Hall is a writer from a conservative Catholic background in the American Midwest, the coauthor of a book about the life of the South African singer Miriam Makeba. To write that book, Hall interviewed Makeba at her home in Guinea. Makeba's mother was a sangoma or traditional healer, and when Hall unconsciously filled in blanks in Makeba's story, the singer began to suspect that he had the same gift. "You can see, I think," she said.

But it is not until the streetlights begin going out that Hall takes this idea seriously. Again and again, especially when he is feeling agitated, streetlights turn off unexpectedly as he walks or drives near them. Then one day as he is "concentrating with particular intensity," he hears a "sudden and noisy crackle of electricity" and smells ozone, as if after a lightning strike. He thinks at first that his chandelier has shorted out, but the lamp is fine. In fact, his hair has caught on fire.

When he meets Makeba again, she suggests that her niece, who lives in Swaziland, should take Hall to a sangoma and get to the bottom of the problem. And so in 1988 he finds himself on a plane to a "tiny, pineapple-shaped country, slightly larger than Connecticut."

The bulk of this book recounts Hall's experience as the first white person in Swaziland ever to undergo *kutfwasa*, the lengthy training and initiation required of a sangoma. He undergoes sweat treatments and vomiting purges, and learns how to prepare and administer herbal treatments. He hones his psychic ability to find hidden objects, and learns to throw and interpret the divination bones that are an essential part of a sangoma's equipment.

Hall also becomes a medium for a growing number of ancestral spirits who appear in his dreams or take over his body during periods of trance. These come to include, in his words, a Scottish farmer, a Spanish settler from colonial California, a Native American medicine

man, an ancient African zebra hunter, his own Italian-American grandmother – and a cigarette-smoking American ad executive called Harry. It is Harry who reveals to Hall the very secret of life. Life, he tells him, is a "series of moral choices," adding, "If you pass, then one day you'll find your peace."

Hall sympathizes with readers who may find this hard to swallow. Though his dreams and visions of the spirits are compelling to him, and although the Swazis accept his spirits as genuine, Hall keeps looking unsuccessfully for hard facts that will prove they are real – a name he can check, or a language his spirits speak that he doesn't know himself. (Hall has himself recorded when in trance, but the spirits speak only languages such as English, Spanish, and Italian that he himself is familiar with.)

Whether or not one chooses to believe what the author believes, *Sangoma* is an absorbing account of an experience few if any non-Africans have undergone. In the end, it is also the story of a man who finds a new home and a new purpose, and changes his life utterly from what it was.

—

MaZu placed each of the animal bones, seashells, dominoes, and coins that comprised her set of divination bones on the mat between us. She swept her hand over them, said something to me in her native tongue, then sat back expectantly, waiting for me to do something. The people of her neighboring Zulu tribe spoke a language similar to SiSwati. Know one and you know both. My problem: I knew neither. While I sat blank-faced, La Shonge tried to be helpful by repeating, "*Khetsa! Khetsa!*" I opened the SiSwati-English dictionary I carried around with me, and found the word: "Choose."

I smiled, reached forward and took a large, polished sea shell. MaZu gave an exclamation of amazed delight, and several adolescent girls who had come in to see what I was up to cheered happily. Sam lived elsewhere, and I was told that Prince Vovo was rarely here at this the smallest of his homesteads. I seemed to be the only male who now lived at this place. But it was the idea of a white kutfwasa student that fascinated the women. Every time they saw me, they

welcomed me with smiles and gestures of greeting as if determined to make me feel at home. They were succeeding; I was feeling less awkward and more at ease.

MaZu placed the shell I had chosen before me, and again waved her hand over the pile of bones, commanding me to choose. I spotted a polished stone and took it. MaZu and La Shonge exclaimed in wonder, and the girls squealed with delight. I had no idea why.

Tanzania

Paradise by Abdulrazak Gurnah

The New Press, 1994

As the story of *Paradise* begins, a Swahili boy named Yusuf is twelve years old. He lives with his parents, an impoverished hotel keeper and his wife, in a town in the interior of what was then known as German East Africa. The book starts at the railway station, with the boy's first glimpse of Europeans: a woman in a frilled white blouse and a man who appears to be "carved out of a single piece of wood" and who bares his teeth at Yusuf when he notices the boy staring at him.

Yusuf's Uncle Aziz comes to visit – a rich merchant who arrives with a train of porters, drummers, and hangers-on, and who gives off "a strange and unusual odour, a mixture of hide and perfume, and gums and spices, and another less definable smell which made Yusuf think of danger." This visit is different from those that have come before, because when Uncle Aziz is about to leave, Yusuf is told he will accompany him to Aziz's home on the coast. Without asking or even wondering why he is leaving or when he will return, Yusuf boards the train with his bundle of possessions: "two pairs of shorts, a kanzu which was still new from last Idd, a shirt, a copy of the Koran, and his mother's old rosary."

Yusuf settles into life with Uncle Aziz, working and sleeping in his shop, before he discovers that Aziz is not his uncle at all. Yusuf has become a "rehani," pawned by his parents as security for their debt to Aziz. Like the Joseph of the Old Testament, he has been sold into bondage by his own family. And like the biblical Joseph, Yusuf proves clever enough to make the best of his situation.

Yusuf's story is told in a transparent, seemingly timeless storyteller's style, with only an occasional clue – the Germans at the railway station, and rumours of conflict between the Germans and the English to the north – to indicate that it takes place around the time of World War I. Yet the novel is subtler than it seems at first, and events continually slip away from the reader's expectations. We might expect Yusuf to try to rejoin his family, but he does not. He accompanies his "uncle" on a hazardous trading journey into the interior, but neither the perils

(which include the lecherous foreman of the trading column) nor the attractions (a young girl who visits him when the party is temporarily captured) culminate in any dramatic development. Meanwhile, we move through a richly described world that includes the Arab merchants of the Swahili coast, only recently retired from the slave trade, the isolated and sometimes hostile settlements of the interior, and the first incursion of Europeans bringing their prisons, churches, railways, and deadly methods of warfare.

Yusuf is an attractive boy, sometimes described as "an angel," who grows into a good-looking and charming young man. Like the biblical Joseph, he suffers vivid dreams, but he cannot interpret them, except when he dreams of his own cowardice "glimmering in moonlight, covered in the slime of its afterbirth." Though he gains the trust of Uncle Aziz (once referred to as Pharaoh), he gains little more from this trust than the chance to spend his afternoons in Aziz's garden, a fallen Paradise where four water channels radiate from the centre like the rivers of Eden. Yusuf's resourcefulness, the author seems to suggest, is not entirely admirable. The charm and adaptability that help Yusuf to avoid conflict, and that make him sympathetic to the reader, may have their roots in cowardice, and instead of charting his own course he may be destined to serve a succession of masters, slipping from one form of captivity to another.

The lakeside town lay in soft impossible light, violet with an edge of crimson from the great cliffs and hills which formed the banks. Boats were pulled up along the water's edge and a row of small brown houses lined the bank. The lake stretched away in all directions, making the men lower their voices with the feeling the sight stirred in them. The travellers waited outside the town as was their custom, until permission was granted for entry. A shrine stood nearby, surrounded by snakes and pythons and wild animals. Only if the spirit allowed it could a person reach the shrine safely and leave in peace. Mohammed Abdalla told them this as they waited, pointing to a grove not far from their resting place. "That's where their God lives. Savages believe

anything if it's crazy enough," he said. "It's no good saying to them that this or that is childish. You can't argue with them. They only tell you endless stories about their superstitions."

Tanzania

The Gunny Sack by M. G. Vassanji
Heinemann, 1989

Henry James, reacting to the profusion of characters in Tolstoy's *War and Peace*, its sometimes wild coincidences, and the way it sprawls over geography and generations, once referred to it as a "loose baggy monster." *The Gunny Sack*, a crowded and rambunctious tale of East Indians in East Africa, has similar characteristics, but it is also baggy in the most literal sense: the memories and events it recounts all come out of an enormous burlap bag.

This bag, the gunny sack of the title, is a bequest to the novel's hero and narrator, a young man named Salim Juma, from his grand-aunt Ji Bai. Ji Bai, who grew up in a village of the Shamsi sect in India, was engaged at the age of thirteen and packed off to the coastal town of Matamu in the German colony of Tanganyika, where she began to make a new life. The gunny sack she leaves behind when she dies contains "a bead necklace shorn of its polish; a rolled-up torn photograph; a cowrie shell; a brass incense holder; a Swahili cap so softened by age that it folded neatly into a small square; a broken rosary tied up crudely to save the remaining beads; a bloodstained muslin shirt" – and three padlocked books handwritten in Arabic. These objects help Salim to reconstruct the stories that make up the past. In his mind the sack itself becomes a storyteller, a kind of parody version of Sheherezade that he calls Shehrbanoo, "telling stories that have no beginning or end."

The stories that spill from the gunny sack defy summary, and a bewildering number of characters compete for the reader's attention, especially in the early chapters. But as the narrative moves forward in time and Salim begins to tell his own story, the narrative comes into focus and gains an unexpected emotional power.

Indians in Africa suffer from a poor reputation, and not many books like this one have emerged to celebrate their lives and express their point of view. As shopkeepers and traders, they have been vilified as miserly and standoffish, willing to profit from the business of Africans but not to let their sons and daughters associate with them.

Salim breaks from this stereotype in a couple of ways. First, he

is one-eighth African himself, descended from the first Indian of his family to settle in Africa, and a slave woman "discarded" on the coast after the slave trade came to an end. Second, his military service forces him to leave the insular Shamsi community of Dar es Salaam and lands him in a remote camp near Lake Victoria, where he lives among the other young soldiers of a newly independent and militantly nationalistic country. There he meets Amina, a pretty and intelligent young African woman also doing her national service. The two circle each other warily, discussing poetry and trading political barbs as they become more intimate.

In the end, *The Gunny Sack* is about crossing over and making connections. Set in the ancient crossroads of the East African coast, it celebrates the cultural stew created by Africans, Arabs, and Indians. The Shamsi sect to which Salim belongs is an odd hybrid of Hinduism and Islam. Its members have emotional ties both to Africa and to India, and their trade partners and relatives straddle the border between German and British East Africa. In a continent often portrayed as torn by ethnic divisions, this novel is an appealing vision of how adaptable people can be in their efforts to find love and happiness.

Ji Bai opened a small window into that dark past for me. She took me past the overgrowth into the other jungle. And a whole world flew in, a world of my great-grandfather who left India and my great-grandmother who was African, the world of Matamu where India and Africa met and the mixture exploded in the person of my half-caste grandfather Huseni who disappeared into the forest one day and never returned, the world of a changing Africa where Europe and Africa also met and the result was even more explosive, not only in the lives of men but also in the life of the continent.

I remember my first view of Shehrbanoo ... a dumpy gunny sack enclosing a broken world, the debris of lives lived ... slumped in the inner room beside Ji Bai's bed, her mouth closed with a sisal twine. Ji Bai untied the loose knot, instantly a smile appeared on the gunny where there was a grimace before, and that laughing mouth was never shut again. Eh, Shehru, but for me in my grey shorts and flip-flop chappals where would you be now?

Togo

The Village of Waiting by George Packer
Vintage Departures, 1988

"I arrived in Lavié already sick of Togo, sick of Africa, wanting out." This is the inauspicious first line of *The Village of Waiting*, George Packer's book about his Peace Corps experience in Togo. A bureaucratic dispute has kept him in Lomé, the Togolese capital, for six weeks, and Lomé, he finds, in addition to being hot and humid, lacks the virtues of other West African nation capitals – the urbanity of Abidjan or the bustle and energy of Lagos. At the end of the book, the author, taking a Christmas vacation in Spain after a year and a half in Africa, realizes he cannot face another five months there, and bolts for home. Have things been better in the meantime? Not really.

What makes Packer something of a malcontent is also what makes this a good book: empathy, a restless nature, and an unwillingness to settle for the easy answer. The problem of how to be a white person in Africa perplexes and irritates him. He dislikes being pointed at and referred to as "yovo" but also hates the privileges that are handed to him as a matter of course. He wants the villagers of Lavié to accept him, but once they are calling him Fo Georgie – Brother Georgie – he finds himself in a false position, looked to for more help than he can give them. As an English teacher he is locked into a rigid and antiquated educational system, a relic of French colonialism that demands that pupils be force-fed scraps of European history and culture, and that leaves the few pupils who excel in it unable to find jobs suitable to their education and distrusted by the quietly repressive regime. He is uncomfortable with Western tourists who see Africa from lavish hotels in game parks, but also with those fellow Peace Corps volunteers who "go native" and deny the value of any and all Western influence.

Packer likes to get to the bottom of things, a trait best illustrated by his extreme and finally successful efforts to catch a thief who has been stealing from his room. Just as he unintentionally hurts the old chief of the village when the thief turns out to be his nephew, so

Packer's other investigations into the culture and politics of Togo turn up disheartening results.

Packer takes the trouble to draw out the Togolese he meets, and his vignettes of them are revealing, particularly those in the chapter "Cicada Philosophy" of three men who have been seduced and abandoned by the dream of "development." Like Edward Hoagland's *African Calliope*, *The Village of Waiting* sets itself apart from most travel books on Africa by its complex descriptions of people and its organization by theme rather than by chronology. Chapters are devoted to teaching, the roles of men and women, agriculture, sickness, and other matters. This is a sensitive account both of a small African country faced with the promises and hazards of development, and of the country's effect on a young American posted to a remote village.

—

Palm wine flowed, the color of soapy dishwater. We all drank. It was a sweet, heavy batch. Flies buzzed around the lip of the gourd and floated in the surface foam. A flick of the full calabash got rid of the fly bodies and gave the ancestors their portion of wine in the same motion. I'd heard that the puddle's configuration in the dirt could be read like tea leaves to divine the future. When I asked him to read mine, Faustus stared at me and didn't answer.

We drank another calabash, and another. A glass jug was produced. Distilled palm wine is as close to grain alcohol as anything you can legally buy in the West – sickly sweet on the tongue, fire going down. With each swallow my throat rose. I chased gin with palm wine to clear the taste, and sat back against the palm trunk, looking up in the gathering dusk at the cacao trees, which slowly revolved against the sky.

Tunisia

The Scorpion by Albert Memmi
Translated from the French by Eleanor Levieux

Grossman Publishers, 1971

A scorpion, it is said, when surrounded by a ring of embers and unable to escape, will sting itself to death out of rage and frustration. Or will it? Perhaps this is an old wives' tale. Perhaps the scorpion stings itself, but accidentally. Perhaps it stings itself and appears to be dead, but recovers after all the onlookers are gone.

This ambiguous image frames *The Scorpion*, an ingeniously constructed existential novel set in Tunisia's first years of independence from France. Presented as a collage of texts commenting upon one another, the book paints a picture of a country and people struggling to discover their own identity.

Emile, a well-known and politically engaged Tunisian writer, has disappeared, leaving a desk drawer stuffed with seemingly disconnected writings and clippings. Emile's brother Marcel, an ophthalmologist and surgeon, sets out to make sense of this mass of documents: some evidently fictional, some apparently excerpts from a journal (but with artistic liberties taken), and others quotations from unidentified sources. *The Scorpion*, which includes all this in addition to a few photographs and the comments of Marcel, is the result of this labour. The documents are distinguished by different colours of ink corresponding to their nature. Albert Memmi (the real-life author) regrets in an introductory note that his publisher was unable to print the novel in various colours as well, making do with contrasting typefaces.

Memmi, it turns out, is also the family name of Emile and Marcel: just one of the many identity games played by the author. The brothers belong to the Jewish branch of a family that divided between Judaism and Islam at some point in the past. Early in the book, Emile traces the roots of the Memmis with the help of various clues, including an ancient medal, but cannot decide whether his people came from North Africa, from Italy, or from both places. Emile describes his childhood in a ramshackle castle on the coast, not far from the capital, where he explores the disused staircases and breaks into the closed-off rooms,

and where the oppressive humidity finally forces his asthmatic father to move the family to the city.

The subject matter of *The Scorpion* darkens and expands as the book proceeds, moving from harmless childhood memories, to a family tragedy presented in varying fictional disguises, to the violent, unsettled period of Tunisian independence, and finally to the questions that face both brothers under the new regime.

Marcel's attitude to his brother's writings changes, too. The doctor is scornful of his brother's flights of fancy in the early passages, though he himself waxes poetic when he describes the wonders of the human eye, and the courage and self-control required to perform eye surgery. Gradually he recognizes the truths in what Emile has written about their family and about their country. In a section called "The Four Thursdays," he presents (almost without commentary) an extraordinary series of conversations in which a former student of Emile's returns to confront his teacher with his own ideas about identity and loyalty. In a sense, immersing himself in his brother's mind and struggling with his ideas may be the way that the doctor prepares himself for a decision that he reaches only at the end of the book.

I was born at La Goulette, a little Berber port near the capital, only a few hundred paces from the Walls and the Fort of Charles V, which are still standing. From the time I was born until I was four years old, so that I still remember it – like remembering a shadow that has been wrapped around all the houses I have lived in since – my parents, along with two other families, lived in a kind of small palace full of cupolas and terraces, verandas and corners that jutted out onto the beach and that were periodically linked and ringed by the sea. This meant that although the house was delightful in the summer, the humidity had made much of it unfit for habitation. In one of the bedrooms which, oddly enough, had not a single window and was constantly battered by waves during the severest part of the winter, the humidity was so dense that the room was filled with a heavy mist. Although we were frightened by the almost total darkness of the place, we had chosen it as our *hamman* and, in the light of little oiled paper torches, we played at taking the ritual bath.

Uganda

The Last King of Scotland by Giles Foden
Alfred A. Knopf, 1998

Writing a novel about a historical character is difficult, because the reader comes to the book with a store of knowledge, opinions, and preconceptions that restrict the author's ability to present the character in a fresh way. If the character is a notorious dictator like Idi Amin, the challenge is even greater.

In *The Last King of Scotland*, his first novel, Giles Foden meets this challenge boldly and shrewdly. The novel, if not entirely successful in conveying the inner life of Amin and the secret of his rise to power, does present a believable picture of the dictator as he would have been seen by a member of his entourage, and something of the charisma that made this repellent person strangely attractive to those who knew him.

Nicholas Garrigan is a young, somewhat standoffish Scottish doctor who accepts a government contract to practise in Uganda, a country he knows little about. He arrives around the time that the dictator Milton Obote is overthrown in a coup led by a young army officer named Idi Amin. (Obote, whose brutality rivalled Amin's, returned to power years later after Amin's departure.) After a short stay in Kampala, where a British embassy official asks Dr Garrigan to keep him posted on his impressions of the political situation, he travels in a battered *matatu* or bush taxi to a rural hospital, where he begins treating Ugandans for parasites, machete wounds, snakebite, tuberculosis, and sleeping sickness.

Driving through the countryside in a red Maserati, Idi Amin collides with a cow, and some soldiers fetch Dr Garrigan to bind up his sprained wrist. Amin, who identifies with the Scottish as fellow rebels against British imperialism, is impressed by the doctor and plies him with money and alcohol. Garrigan is intrigued by Amin's ebullience, his cryptic proverbs, and something "half-fascinating, half-frightening" in his eyes. Garrigan has an affair with a fellow doctor, a woman from Israel, but Amin's rantings about a secret Zionist army prompt her to leave the country. Garrigan misses her but overlooks the sinister implications. Eager for a change of scene, he accepts Amin's invitation to become his personal physician.

Garrigan is an intelligent man, well able to understand what is going on around him, and yet he stays with Amin until the very end, when the dictator is driven out by Tanzanian troops. Why? In part because he is afraid to leave (though he has more than one opportunity to slip out of the country). In part because Amin's patronage makes him an important person with a comfortable lifestyle. In part because he is hypnotized by the contradictions of Amin's personality: a volatile compound of high intelligence, charm, cunning, and ruthlessness. And in part because Garrigan, on some level, genuinely likes the man.

For much of the book, trapped in the point of view of the increasingly corrupt Dr Garrigan, the reader may have the queasy feeling of being invited to admire Amin for his vitality and humour. Atrocities occur, but they happen offstage, and it is possible to imagine that they happen without the knowledge of the dictator. Eventually Garrigan is brought so close to the horror that he can no longer deny it, but even when no possible doubt remains, he fails to leave.

Packed with convincing details on life in Uganda, from the elaborate wire toys made by children to the practice of tropical medicine, *The Last King of Scotland* is also a shrewd portrait of a modern day monster and of the self deceptions and moral compromises that can draw a well-meaning man into his orbit.

—

We drank more waragi, just the two of us sitting at the long mahogany table in the banqueting room at State House, with the loathsome masks and the paintings of the colonial governor-generals looking down on us. I looked up at them, at the white-polled one that parroted my father especially, and Idi Amin's voice echoed in the big, gloomy space.

"It is good of you to speak with me," he said. "I cannot tell you how tired I am getting, from all this work. Leading Uganda. It is very difficult."

"You should delegate more," I said. "Get other people to do things."

"You do not understand. I cannot trust. There are many who are my friends today, who would betray me tomorrow. The one that is famous in the sea is the shark, but there are many others."

"What do you mean?"

"I have to be on my guard always."

I sipped my waragi thoughtfully. "Have you ever thought of retiring?"

He gave me a strange, benevolent smile, his cheeks gleaming under the dim light of the lamps suspended over the table.

"I will be in charge here for the full distance. As a man of destiny, I cannot go to a shamba and raise chickens. Yes, I must run for the distance. And, as you know, Doctor Nicholas, there is no distance that has no end. That is my tragedy."

Uganda

Abyssinian Chronicles by Moses Isegawa
Alfred A. Knopf, 2000

Abyssinian Chronicles, the much-praised first novel by the Ugandan writer Moses Isegawa, is a vast, sprawling, ambitious tale that covers the history of Uganda from the 1950s to the present day, including the regime of Idi Amin, the two dictatorships of Milton Obote, the expulsion and return of the country's East Indians, and the periods of chaos in between. Isegawa has been compared to writers such as Salman Rushdie and Gabriel García Márquez, but his book may have more in common with another groundbreaking first novel: Günter Grass's *The Tin Drum*. Like *The Tin Drum*, this is an episodic novel with a vast range of characters that focuses on a child growing up in the most dysfunctional of societies. The heroes of both books are moulded by their experience in ways that may make them unsympathetic to the reader, and both books convey bitter messages about the moral compromises made by ordinary people in times of political turmoil.

Abyssinian Chronicles is told by its main character Mugezi, meaning "clever" – a boy when the story begins. Everything Mugezi says is touched by his rebellious and sometimes cruel and self-centred character, and his preoccupation with sex, violence, and excrement. As a child, he admires Idi Amin for his overweening pride – a pride he feels he needs himself in order to resist the crushing authority of his mother (nicknamed Padlock) and the priests at the oppressive Catholic school he attends. Like others around him, he finds the expulsion of the Indians a time of opportunity, and he uses the chaos of war as a chance to prosper as a smuggler and to find sexual conquests among the shell-shocked survivors. If Mugezi develops as a human being in the course of the novel, it doesn't appear to be in the direction of compassion. Even at the novel's end, in exile in the Netherlands, he expresses contempt for his fellow Ugandan exiles and their menial jobs, for the Dutch aid workers who have brought him there, and for the prostitutes he sometimes frequents.

Mugezi's family provides a gallery of unusual and sometimes grotesque characters. His father, traumatized as a boy by the death

of his own mother, earns the name Serenity by withdrawing from life. Mugezi's mother Padlock, a fanatic Catholic, looms over Mugezi's childhood like a terrifying idol. Other relatives offer glimpses of the outside world. Mugezi's Uncle Kawayida, a meter reader, appears periodically on his motorcycle, the "blue-bellied eagle," to tell tales of the lust and violence he witnesses on his rounds. Padlock's sister Lwandeka joins a resistance movement after being tortured by some thugs of the Amin regime, only to be gang-raped by the country's Tanzanian liberators when Amin falls.

Why are these "Abyssinian" chronicles? In part, because Mugezi's uncle believes that the "Abyssinia" of antiquity was not Ethiopia, as is generally thought, but Uganda. But more importantly, Mugezi considers Uganda to be "Abyssinian" because it is the country of the abyss.

Though it is often uncomfortable to read, the novel's knotty, tactile style puts the agony of Uganda in front of you, from the smell of bodies to the rumble of tanks. With its unexpected images (the Pope is a "holy armadillo … washed in the blood of imperial power") and sometimes unpalatable scenes, *Abyssinian Chronicles* immerses the reader in a nightmare of recent history. The book has a sexual frankness unusual in African fiction – and it is one of the few African novels so far to deal head-on with the ravages of Aids.

I sometimes felt the urge to go out and wander through the streets, dark lanes and piss-sodden alleyways, or negotiate my way to the taxi park and watch its midnight emptiness. I wanted to gauge its actual size, walk its length and breadth alone and fill it with my imagination, but it was unsafe. The caverns of darkness crawled with robbers. The mysterious depths of the night hid wrongdoers on the prowl. The length and breadth were alive with soldiers on patrol, in search of nocturnal excitement and illicit adventure. The sky was alive with ghosts of people killed in the coup, killed before the coup, killed during the state of emergency, killed at the dawn of independence as politics wore hideous masks and

became bloodier all the time. The night was full of ghosts redolent with earthly smells, ghosts in search of the next world, ghosts saying endless, faceless goodbyes, ghosts flying about for one last glimpse of their beloved, ghosts marking their loved ones with bat-like claws. Grandma was one of those ghosts. It was better to spend the night in the same place, in case she located me, in case she smelled me, in case she chose this particular night to reveal herself to me.

Western Sahara

Smara: The Forbidden City by Michel Vieuchange

Translated from the French by Fletcher Allen

Ecco Press, 1987 (first published 1932)

In 1930 Michel Vieuchange, a 26-year-old Frenchman and aspiring writer, attempted to become the first European to see the ancient desert town of Smara, in what was then the Spanish Sahara. It was a dangerous goal not only because of the desert's scarce water, poisonous snakes, and extremes of temperature, but also because the region was controlled by independent and hostile tribes. French pilots forced down in the area had been held as hostages, or sometimes killed.

For his first "raid" on the city, Vieuchange disguised himself in the stifling robes and veils of a Berber woman. With the help of a "trader in tirza wood" named Ahmed ben Hamou el Mahboul, he set out on camelback with a group of other North Africans, including two sheikhs. A month later, after many hardships, the group was forced to go back when one of the sheikhs hurt his foot on a thorn and refused to continue.

Only about two weeks later, Vieuchange tried again. This time he dressed as an Arab man, but when strangers appeared his companions stuffed him into a pannier on the side of a camel until it was safe to come out. Vieuchange and his companions reached the city of Smara, long deserted and used as temporary lodging by the nomadic tribes, but Vieuchange had only three hours to look around, measuring and photographing as quickly as possible, before the arrival of a large band of strangers forced him to leave. "I have seen your two kasbahs and your ruined mosque," he wrote after his departure. "I have seen you completely, seated on your plinth, face to the desert, deserted in the silence, under the glowing sun. I have seen your palms, to-day half withered." On the journey back he fell seriously ill, and by the end of November he was dead of dysentery.

Smara: The Forbidden City comprises two months of journal entries as transcribed and edited by Vieuchange's brother Jean, a

doctor who helped organize the expedition to Smara. These pages were never intended to be published as is, but perhaps for that reason they have an honesty and immediacy that are gripping. After describing a fit of anger against El Mahboul, during which he threw a pair of slippers at him, Vieuchange writes, "I put all this down because, here, I intend to enter everything, absolutely sincerely. My sincerity in the book will not be the same." Hungry, with bleeding feet, knowing only a few words of Arabic and Berber and in constant fear of discovery as a European or of attack by marauders (at one point bullets fly over the heads of his party), Vieuchange is always in the moment, with little leisure for reflection. Reading his entries gives the impression of being inside his head as he struggles to keep going, and to understand what is going on around him.

Two days before his journal breaks off, he wakes in a sweat from a weird dream: On his way to Smara he has met Rene Caillié, the "discoverer" of Timbuktu – like him, a poorly prepared, desert-obsessed young Frenchman – and he enters the city with him, though Caillié is none too pleased at this. But the Smara in his dream is a sinister trap: "It was a sort of quarry, cut off from the sky by a peculiar network of threads, like spiders' webs, which admitted only a little light." He finds a "repulsive little pygmy" living in one of a number of small excavations, and the air fills with "uncanny life" that obscures his sight. Then Caillié becomes Rimbaud, the great poet who gave up his art and disappeared into East Africa. Clearly and forcefully he speaks "the most abstruse words," which Vieuchange understands for the first time, but although he wakes up a moment later, the words and their meaning evaporate before he can write them down.

＊

On camel-back throughout the night, until daybreak. Plain with some small hillocks. The camel, which refused to go farther, lay down, and swung his long neck round, threatening my legs with his teeth.

We reached a lake. Country where delays are dangerous. Many tents, and no friends of the sheikhs. I took two photographs. The camels drank. We refilled the water-skins. I drank.

On camel-back. Tomb of a marabout (large pile of stones). Many tombs.

We travelled at speed to the right, towards the djebel Ouargziz. Dismounted and began to ascend. Climb which lasted perhaps an hour and a half. Long clothes which hampered the feet. El Mahboul was all in; so was I. The two camels jibbed, showing fright. Three photographs of me and one of the plain seen from mid-ascent. A camel, absolutely refusing to move, was led by the nose, by hand.

Stop for half an hour. Hidden under an overhanging rock, I wrote the beginning of this. Then someone called me.

Zambia

The Eye of the Elephant by Delia and Mark Owens
Mariner Books, 1993

On 15 May 1985, the American couple Delia and Mark Owens were thrown out of Botswana, where they had lived in tents for seven years, studying the lions and hyenas of the Kalahari Desert. Cattlemen had built miles of fences along the Central Kalahari Game Reserve, blocking wildebeest and other antelopes from reaching water during drought, and killing thousands. The Owenses' protests rendered them (temporarily) personae non gratae.

The Owenses cast about for another African wilderness where they could live and study animals. Eventually they found one: a tract of remote land along the Muchinga Mountains, east of Mpika in Zambia. The area was already part of a national park, but despite this nominal protection the couple soon found that poachers operated with impunity inside the park boundaries. A half-dozen major ivory poachers, based in the village of Mwamfushi, led assault teams armed with AK-47s into the park. Ordinary villagers, driven by hunger, poached elephants and other wildlife for food. And as it turned out, the game scouts assigned by the government to protect the park and its wildlife did some poaching of their own. "Since 1973," writes Mark Owens (whose chapters alternate with his wife's), "between seventy-five thousand and one hundred thousand elephants have been poached in the Luangwa Valley as a whole; *that's roughly one for every word in this book.*" The emphasis is his own.

Conservationists of the past, often more comfortable with animals than people, have fuelled the conflict between the needs of Africans and of African wildlife. The Owenses, to their credit, recognize that successful conservation efforts must provide something for everyone. "Perhaps if local people who live near national parks could benefit directly from them, for example through tourism, they would recognize the economic value of wild animals and work to conserve them." With creativity and tireless energy, the Owenses visit the surrounding settlements, offering sewing machines, grain mills, soccer balls, and jobs in exchange for promises to stop poaching and

information on the worst of the bandits. They reinforce their gifts with a heavy dose of pro-wildlife speeches and puppet shows.

The Owenses do all they can to prod the local game scouts into going on patrol: spotting the poachers from a small plane and even carrying the scouts to the vicinity. But because the scouts are woefully under-armed and under-equipped, and because some are in cahoots with the poachers, circling vultures continue to mark the mutilated bodies of more dead elephants. Mark Owens, an experienced bush pilot, eventually goes on a series of risky solo raids against the poachers, buzzing them from the air and firing noisy but harmless cherry bombs at them. The major poachers retaliate, shooting up the homes of the Owenses' assistants, poisoning villagers who cooperate with them, and coming very close to assassinating the Owenses themselves.

The Owenses have little to say about Zambian culture, but they describe the personalities of their beloved elephants with great sensitivity, and provide a vivid picture of one of the last extensive African wildernesses: "an area the size of Delaware with no roads, no buildings, and no people." They are scathing in their contempt for certain useless game scouts, brutal poachers, and corrupt officials, but they take care to dig into the reasons for some of this behaviour, and they are warmly appreciative (if a little patronizing) of the loyalty and courage of the men who work with them at their camp. Though for most of the book it appears that they may be killed at any moment, or driven out of Zambia as they were driven out of Botswana, unexpected developments conclude the book on an improbably hopeful note.

Elephants can move through the bush as quietly as kittens, but when they feed, they make a noisy racket as they strip leaves from a branch or topple small trees. Whether I'm working at the solar-powered computer, building the fire, or reading, I know where Survivor is by his loud slurps. At night he drifts through the sleeping camp like a large moon shadow. Lying in bed, I am lulled to sleep by the stirring wind, his soft footfalls, and the rustling leaves – the song of Survivor.

One night as he forages in front of the cottage, I cannot sleep, or perhaps do not want to. I get up and ease the door open. The half-moon winks through the marula leaves as Survivor feeds beneath the tree ten yards from where I stand. Inching forward, watching his every move, I step onto the stone verandah and slowly sit on the doorstep. Gracefully he turns to face me, lifting his trunk to take in my scent. He immediately relaxes, lowering his trunk and sniffing loudly for another fruit.

Ten yards from an elephant. Sitting down and looking up at an elephant. He covers the world. Even in this soft light I can see the deep wrinkles and folds in his skin. They look like the craters and valleys of the moon.

Zambia

A Cowrie of Hope by Binwell Sinyangwe
Heinemann, 2000

P arents across Africa struggle to pay their children's school fees, but that struggle has rarely if ever been the focus of a novel. Maybe the subject seemed too mundane to write about. *A Cowrie of Hope* dramatizes how critically important school fees are for a young girl's future, and the extremities of sacrifice and ingenuity that her mother will subject herself to to get them.

The novel plunges us at once into the mind of Nasula, a young widow who is desperate to give her daughter Sula a chance to attend boarding school. (Though Nasula has another given name, she is addressed by convention as the mother of her firstborn child.) "The whirlwind of desperation inside her was carrying, pushing her like a blade of grass toward the unthinkable." The "unthinkable," for her, is the idea of asking her brother-in-law Isaki to pay her daughter's school fees. She has every right to ask, since her in-laws, disregarding her late husband's wishes, stripped her of all her possessions after his death. But Nasula is reluctant to approach Isaki not only because he is a thief but also because he is a much-married lecher who would like the attractive Nasula for himself.

A Cowrie of Hope is written in an urgent, forceful style, and the author has a way with metaphor and authorial omniscience that is almost biblical. One example is when Nasula travels to Isaki's farm and finds him near death from the strange wasting disease that has spread throughout Zambia. "The world is fire. It can burn a life to nothing. This was Isaki Chiswebe, finished, shrunk to a stick in a lifeless, wrinkled skin, ridden with sores and pimples." Isaki's second and third wives are already dead, and Nasula realizes this would have been her fate if she had weakened and married him. It is clearly implied that Nasula's daughter, without an education, might be forced to depend on a man like this or even to "put her flesh on the street" and come to the same end. Nasula's in-laws cannot prevent this now even if they were inclined to do so. They are penniless, having taken out an agricultural loan they could not repay when drought devastated their crops.

Despite the "timeless" associations of his Old Testament language, the narrator insists that he is writing about a specific time and place: Zambia in the 1990s, when a new government offers signs of hope but when drought and the wasting disease have intensified the country's poverty, and the heartlessness of the powerful. "These are bad years, Nasula," says her friend Nalukwi. "There is bitterness in the taste of life everywhere and in everything in the land. In the city and in the village alike, the sun seems to be shining on nothing. It's a curse on us and on the land. You bring new people in government and hope the sky will open up and spill honey upon the earth; instead a dryness and a stubborn disease clothe it in harshness and blood."

Yet this is still a country where the spirit of cooperation has not died out, where people greet each other by saying, "We are well if you are well also." Nalukwi herself suggests another way Nasula could raise her daughter's school fees: by travelling to Lusaka and selling a 90-kg bag of the yellow and white beans grown in her district, which bring a good price in the capital.

A Cowrie of Hope tells a harsh story, but not so harsh as to rule out a happy ending. Though Nasula's happy ending might seem too good to be true, it cannot be said that it is unearned. Before she leaves Lusaka, where she finds generosity as well as thievery and corruption, her courage and stamina are tested to the limit.

———

Darkness, a deathly stink and stuffiness swallowed her as she entered the room. Then the pungent smell of freshly boiled, burnt and crushed herbs and roots; of rotting solutions of concoctions prepared a long time ago but not used; of medicines from the hospital; of stale human breath and excretion; and of burning charcoal. She halted and stood in silence until her eyes became used to the darkness in the room and she could see properly.

She had imagined finding Isaki Chiswebe lying huge and long on a high bed of metal and wood. There was neither a bed nor a corpulent figure in the room. A thin, torn, filthy, foam mattress was what she saw instead, spread sadly along the eastern wall. On it lay a dark blanket gathered around what looked like a narrow log beaten flat, at the southern

end of which a pale human head, dark and shrivelled, lay on a mound of old, torn clothes wrapped in a shredded *citenge*. Blood ran to her head in waves of horror. Could this be Isaki Chiswebe?

Zimbabwe

African Laughter: Four Visits to Zimbabwe
by Doris Lessing
HarperCollins, 1992

Doris Lessing was born in Persia and spent her youth in Southern Rhodesia – two countries whose names have disappeared from the maps. Her opposition to the racial oppression practised by the white Rhodesian government caused her to be made a Prohibited Immigrant, and she was unable to return to the country until it gained its independence in 1980. *African Laughter* describes four visits taken between 1982 and 1992.

African Laughter contains beautiful descriptive writing, particularly when Lessing tells of her wary conversations with her long-estranged brother and her return to the hill where she lived as a child. When, after years of misgivings and false starts, she goes to see the place, she finds the hilltop levelled and a "graceless greyish bungalow" standing where the house she grew up in once stood. The bush around the house, where once you could hardly take a step without starting a bird or an antelope, is gone. An African family is living there, and the house is full of children who look at her through the windows and don't respond to her smiles and gestures.

The bush, as she describes it, is a kind of paradise, and her descriptions of the heaped-up granite boulders of the kopples, the "dry, teasing, spicy" scent of the highveld flowers, and the call of an emerald spotted dove are meticulous and moving. "We lived in Eden and didn't know it," she tells her brother. "It's gone for ever," he replies.

By centring her book on the theme of paradise lost, and hazing over all the social and political turbulence that liberation has brought, Lessing could have produced a shapelier, more "artistic" account. Instead she has written one that is challengingly honest, inclusive, and contradictory. *African Laughter* is a baggy monster, teaming with facts, opinions, rumours, jokes, and news clippings. The headings of the book's bite-size sections give some sense of its scope: Witchcraft, Television, Talk on the Verandahs, Giving Lifts, A Betrayed Lover, The Aesthetic Approach to Revolution.

How does Lessing make sense of all this? In part, by listening for what "everyone" is saying. *African Laughter* has its representative figures: types she refers to as the Passionate Protagonists, the Third World Groupies, the Extension Workers, the Chefs (members of the new black elite), and the Povos. "Povo," which like "chef" is borrowed from Portuguese, is a common term for ordinary people, the masses – or, as the joke goes, People of Various Opinions. Before long the reactions of each type become predictable. When Lessing tells a Passionate Protagonist – a woman who "cannot bear the slightest criticism of Zimbabwe" – how she was relieved of a large sum of money by a couple of agile tsotsis in Harare Gardens, the woman is taken aback, but only for a moment. "You say it was a clever operation?" she asks. "Oh yes, brilliant," Lessing replies, "I can't imagine pickpockets in London with such charm, such persuasiveness." At which the Protagonist sits back "with a satisfied smile, like a proud mother."

Lessing has the insight that comes from having grown up in Rhodesia, as well as the credibility that comes from having been an exile during the liberation war. Whites talk to her freely because she was once one of them, and blacks because she bears no responsibility for the bloodshed under Ian Smith. "Swooping from the verandahs to the grass-roots and back again," Lessing is able to study the blinkered outlook of both white and black people, and to notice when their views come closer together than either side would acknowledge. "Do you realize who would understand you best in this country?" she asks her brother. "About the bush, I mean. The Africans, that's who, and you won't talk to them."

A Sunday morning mbira party. The mbira is a base of wood with metal strips of varying lengths and widths set on it, in tiers. It can be held between two hands and played while walking. When I was growing up the gentle sprightly tinkling of the mbira could be heard as you walked through the bush, and then the player came into sight, usually a young man with a hoe slung over a shoulder, his fingers conversing with the hand piano (which is what we called it) while his eyes searched the bush for game.

When played seated, the instrument is held inside a calabash, for resonance, and metal beer tops are used to add depth and tone. …

Pupils of a school some way out of Harare sat in tidy rows, wearing their dancing costumes, consuming soft drinks and peanuts. They are well known and entertain visiting Chefs, at parties and banquets. Now they are playing for fun. The meal was sadza, with relishes of peanut sauce and green leaves; rice and curry; stewed chicken, bread, and Mutare's famous mangoes. Ice-cream. Oceans of Coca-Cola.

Zimbabwe

The Stone Virgins by Yvonne Vera

Farrar, Straus and Giroux, 2003

Violence is harsh and ugly, we are told. Yet when carried out by a hardened warrior, a soldier who kills with no hesitation, it may be as graceful as ballet.

A strange man appears, "like an eagle gliding," at the hut of Nonceba and her sister Thenjiwe. As Nonceba looks up, the man beheads her sister so swiftly and cleanly that he seems to take her place, "replacing each of her moments, taking her position in the azure of the sky." Before he leaves he cuts Nonceba's face, a gesture she feels as a "fleeting touch" but that leaves her badly wounded.

The sisters live in the rural settlement of Kezi, not far from the city of Bulawayo. Near their home are the Kwakhe River and the hills of the Matopos, like enormous mounds of potato-shaped boulders. Thenjiwe, the murdered sister, has recently found love with a man she met at the one-room shop that is the social centre of Kezi.

Facts like these emerge only gradually from a sensual, poetic narrative voice that renders sights and sounds and smells but offers few explanations. It is even some time before any character begins to emerge. We follow Selborne Avenue out of Bulawayo, smelling the eucalyptus trees that border it and noting the purple blooms of the jacaranda. We observe the cobra-skin belts, "Slim Jim" ties, and nervously tapping fingers of the men who have returned from working in the gold mines of Johannesburg. We see the soldiers returning to their homes: the women more confident than before, "spitting onto the ground, rubbing the smoke of fires from their eyes," while the men "wear lonely and lost looks but have a touch mild as honey." Independence has come, and new mothers give their children names like Ceasefire and Freedom.

But if independence has come, the war is not really over. During the first years of Zimbabwe's independence, Robert Mugabe (mentioned here in passing only as "the prime minister") terrorized the people of the Matabeleland province in an effort to crush the power of his rival, Joshua Nkomo. Government soldiers, some of them belonging to a notorious North Korean-trained brigade, burned crops, destroyed villages, and committed mass murder and other atrocities.

The author never spells this out, and to those who don't know the history, what happens to Thenjiwe and Nonceba may seem like a random horror. All we have to explain it is accounts of the sisters' attacker camped in a sacred cave, eating the legs of spiders, then returning to his home in a township where each house has a stencilled number and finding his father gone. We are privy to his thoughts, but they are too cryptic to be much help. "A spider," he thinks, "knows the true agony of ecstasy, that violence is part of the play of opposites."

For all its frustrating indirection, though, *The Stone Virgins* is a brave book that offers a searing picture of a little-known episode in Zimbabwean history, and its human cost. It is even, in its way, a love story, and it ends with hopelessness but with the tender movements of Cephas, Thenjiwe's lover, as he struggles with his feelings for Nonceba, the wounded survivor, whose suffering has turned her into stone but who is slowly beginning to rediscover her humanity.

—

That drizzling time of melting anthills; the rain beats the soil till it slides off its mound. Thenjiwe, more beautiful than rain, watches the rain slow the hills, flatten them, leave gaping holes where an anthill, higher than her shoulders and higher than high, used to be; the rain cleaves the air. Ancient mounds, perforated humps of hardened soil that water cannot melt, cling to the side of the sheltering trees, remain imprisoned, the trees high, the bark cracking, the water swelling harmlessly around the firm and fine soil, which clings, dark, to the roof of the mouth, a syrup when you suck on it. *Amavimbandlebe* – a multitude of tiny insects, winged, blind, dashing themselves against each drop of rain, splattering into a white paste on the ground, dizzy and without wings, a multitude of insects rising like glory, ready to die in order to lose their wings, to be buried in rain. The greatest freedom – to shed the possibility of flight.

Suggestions for further reading

The following is an idiosyncratic list of books that readers interested in particular countries may want to investigate – as well as some exceptional books that deal with more than one African country, or the continent as a whole. They include novels, poetry, plays, histories, academic works, and books of photography.

I've restricted myself to no more than twenty-five titles for one country, and no more than two titles for one author (some of whom are already represented earlier in the book). Don't be upset if your favorite writer isn't here: there are still many authors on Africa that I have yet to read.

Algeria
The Plague – Albert Camus
The Star of Algiers – Aziz Chouaki
The Last Summer of Reason – Tahar Djaout
So Vast the Prison – Assia Djebar
Women of Algiers in Their Apartment – Assia Djebar
Amyntas – André Gide
The Process – Brion Gysin
In the Name of God – Yasmina Khadra
Sahara Unveiled – William Langewiesche
"Exterminate All the Brutes" – Sven Lindqvist
My Battle of Algiers – Ted Morgan
An Algerian Childhood – ed. Leila Sebbar
Nedjma – Kateb Yacine

Angola
Jonas Savimbi: A Key to Africa – Fred Bridgland
A Lonely Devil – Sousa Jamba
In Search of Enemies – John Stockwell

Benin
Voodoo – Henning Christoph and Hans Oberlander
A Darkening Stain – Robert Wilson

Botswana
A Question of Power – Bessie Head
Mating – Norman Rush
Mortals – Norman Rush
Nisa – Marjorie Shostak

The No. 1 Ladies' Detective Agency – Alexander McCall Smith
Colour Me Blue – Gaele Sobott-Mogwe

Burkina Faso
Ritual – Malidoma Patrice Somé

Burundi
The Wild Boy of Burundi – Harlan Lane and Richard Pillard
Burundi: Ethnocide as Discourse and Practice – René Lemarchand
Red Sunset – John Stockwell

Cameroon
Cameroon with Egbert – Dervla Murphy
Houseboy – Ferdinand Oyono

Central African Republic
Batouala – René Maran

Comoros
Human Spirits – Michael Lambek

Congo (Democratic Republic of the)
The Magic Drum – W. F. P. Burton
A Burnt-Out Case – Graham Greene
King Leopold's Ghost – Adam Hochschild
The Poisonwood Bible – Barbara Kingsolver
The Fight – Norman Mailer
Before the Birth of the Moon – V. Y. Mudimbe
In Southern Light – Alex Shoumatoff
The Ponds of Kalambayi – Mike Tidwell
The Forest People – Colin M. Turnbull
In the Footsteps of Mr. Kurtz – Michela Wrong

Congo (Republic of the)
Little Boys Come from the Stars – Emmanuel Dongala
African Psycho – Alain Mabanckou
Drums Along the Congo – Rory Nugent
Sweet Smell of Mangoes – Sigfrid Sodergen

Egypt
Flaubert in Egypt – ed. Francis Steegmuller
I Know Many Songs, But I Cannot Sing – Brian Kiteley
Oleander, Jacaranda – Penelope Lively
Arabian Nights and Days – Naguib Mahfouz
Akhenaten – Naguib Mahfouz
Distant View of a Minaret – Alifa Rifaat
Woman at Point Zero – Nawal El Saadawi

Ethiopia
Remote People – Evelyn Waugh

Gabon
One Dry Season – Caroline Alexander
The Rainbird – Jan Brokken
Explorations and Adventures in Equatorial Africa – Paul B. du Chaillu
Days with Albert Schweitzer – Frederick Franck
On the Edge of the Primeval Forest – Albert Schweitzer

Ghana
Changes – Ama Ata Aidoo
Our Sister Killjoy – Ama Ata Aidoo
The Prophet of Zongo Street – Mohammed Naseehu Ali
The Beautyful Ones Are Not Yet Born – Ayi Kwei Armah
Two Thousand Seasons – Ayi Kwei Armah
Beyond the Horizon – Amma Darko
The Clothes of Nakedness – Benjamin Kwakye
The Narrow Path – Francis Selormey
Black Power – Richard Wright

Guinea
In Search of Africa – Manthia Diawara
We Won't Budge – Manthia Diawara

Guinea-Bissau
Armed Struggle in Africa – Gérard Chaliand
Fighting Two Colonialisms – Stephanie Urdang

Ivory Coast
Nine Hills to Nambonkaha – Sarah Erdman
Finding the Center – V. S. Naipaul
As the Crow Flies – Veronique Tadjo

Kenya
Maasai Days – Cheryl Bentsen
The Adventures and Misadventures of Peter Beard in Africa –
 Jon Bowermaster
Out of Africa – Isak Dinesen
The Winds of Mara – Colin Fletcher
Green Hills of Africa – Ernest Hemingway
True at First Light – Ernest Hemingway
Unbowed – Wangari Maathai
West with the Night – Beryl Markham
Kill Me Quick – Meja Mwangi
Petals of Blood – Ngũgĩ wa Thiong'o

The River Between – Ngũgĩ wa Thiong'o
The Lives of Beryl Markham – Errol Trzebinski

Lesotho
Basali! – ed. K. Limakatso Kendall
She Plays with the Darkness – Zakes Mda

Liberia
The Darling – Russell Banks
New Song in a Strange Land – Esther Warner
The Big Killing – Robert Wilson
Beyond the Mango Tree – Amy Bronwen Zemser

Libya
In the Country of Men – Hisham Matar
Libya: The Struggle for Survival – Geoff Simons
Tripoli the Mysterious – Mabel Loomis Todd

Madagascar
Madagascar – Gian Paolo Barbieri
The Aye-Aye and I – Gerald Durrell
Muddling Through in Madagascar – Dervla Murphy
The Great Red Island – Arthur Stratton

Malawi
Napolo and the Python – Steve Chimombo
Sugarcane with Salt – James Ng'ombe
Banda – Philip Short
My Secret History – Paul Theroux
My Other Life – Paul Theroux

Mali
In Griot Time – Banning Eyre
Sundiata – D. T. Niane
Bound to Violence – Yambo Ouologuem
The Cruelest Journey – Kira Salak
The Unveiling of Timbuctoo – Galbraith Welch

Mauritania
Silent Terror – Samuel Cotton

Mauritius
The Rape of Sita – Lindsey Collen
The Overcrowded Barracoon – V. S. Naipaul
The Mauritius Command – Patrick O'Brian

Morocco
A Hundred Camels in the Courtyard – Paul Bowles
Points in Time – Paul Bowles
The Voices of Marrakesh – Elias Canetti
For Bread Alone – Mohamed Choukri
Jean Genet in Tangier – Mohamed Choukri
A Street in Marrakech – Elizabeth Warnock Fernea
The Sacred Night – Tahar ben Jelloun
This Blinding Absence of Light – Tahar ben Jelloun
The Lemon – Mohammed Mrabet
An Invisible Spectator – Christopher Sawyer-Lauçanno
In Morocco – Edith Wharton

Mozambique
Every Man Is a Race – Mia Couto
Under the Frangipani – Mia Couto
A Complicated War – William Finnegan
We Killed Mangy-Dog – Luis Bernardo Honwana
A Shattering of Silence – Farida Karodia
Running to Maputo – Albie Sachs

Namibia
Namibia: The Struggle for Liberation – Alfred Moleah
Never Follow the Wolf – Helao Shityuwete
Morenga – Uwe Timm

Niger
Riding the Demon – Peter Chilson
Still Waters in Niger – Kathleen Hill

Nigeria
Anthills of the Savannah – Chinua Achebe
A Man of the People – Chinua Achebe
Purple Hibiscus – Chimamanda Ngozi Adichie
The Legend of the Rockhills – Funso Aiyejina
Tales of Yoruba Gods and Heroes – Harold Courlander
The Joys of Motherhood – Buchi Emecheta
The Interesting Narrative – Olaudah Equiano
Forest of a Thousand Daemons – D. O. Fagunwa
Beasts of No Nation – Uzodinma Iweala
Abiku – Debo Kotun
The Way of the Orisa – Philip John Neimark
This Is Lagos – Flora Nwapa
The Voice – Gabriel Okara
The Famished Road – Ben Okri

Songs of Enchantment – Ben Okri
The Icarus Girl – Helen Oyeyemi
Sozaboy – Ken Saro-Wiwa
Mandela's Earth – Wole Soyinka
Ibadan – Wole Soyinka
Feather Woman of the Jungle – Amos Tutuola

Rwanda
Machete Season – Jean Hatzfeld
Season of Blood – Fergal Keane

São Tomé and Principe
A History of São Tomé Island 1470–1655 – Robert Garfield
São Tome and Principe: From Plantation Colony to Microstate – Tony Hodges and Malyn Newitt

Senegal
The Beggars' Strike – Aminata Sow Fall
Moustapha's Eclipse – Reginald McKnight
He Sleeps – Reginald McKnight
Senegal – Akihiro Yamamura

Seychelles
The Seychelles Affair – Mike Hoare
Paradise Raped – James R. Mancham

Sierra Leone
In the Land of Magic Soldiers – Daniel Bergner
Blood Diamonds – Greg Campbell
The Heart of the Matter – Graham Greene

Somalia
Black Hawk Down – Mark Bowden
Desert Flower – Waris Dirie
Gifts – Nuruddin Farah
Maps – Nuruddin Farah
The Road to Hell – Michael Maren

South Africa
The True Confessions of an Albino Terrorist – Breyten Breytenbach
A Chain of Voices – André Brink
A Simple Lust – Dennis Brutus
Burger's Daughter – Nadine Gordimer
Waiting for the Barbarians – J. M. Coetzee
Disgrace – J. M. Coetzee
Kafka's Curse – Achmat Dangor
Master Harold ... and the boys – Athol Fugard

The Lava of This Land – ed. Denis Hirson
Heshel's Kingdom – Dan Jacobson
Country of My Skull – Antjie Krog
Time of the Butcherbird – Alex La Guma
Living, Loving and Lying Awake at Night – Sindiwe Magona
My Traitor's Heart – Rian Malan
Ways of Dying – Zakes Mda
Down Second Avenue – Ezekiel Mphahlele
Island in Chains – Indres Naidoo
Fools – Njabulo Ndebele
Cry, the Beloved Country – Alan Paton
And Night Fell – Molefe Pheto
To Every Birth Its Blood – Mongane Serote
Red Dust – Gillian Slovo
You Can't Get Lost in Cape Town – Zoë Wicomb
Biko – Donald Woods

Sudan
The River War – Winston Churchill
What Is the What – Dave Eggers
Wings of Dust – Jamal Mahjoub
Darfur Diaries – Jen Marlowe with Aisha Bain and Adam Shapiro
The Last of the Nuba – Leni Riefenstahl
Behind the Red Line – Jemera Rone

Tanzania
The Lake Regions of Central Africa – Richard F. Burton
The Whales in Lake Tanganyika – Lennart Hagerfors
Sand Rivers – Peter Matthiessen
How I Found Livingstone – H. M. Stanley
Antonia Saw the Oryx First – Maria Thomas
The Book of Secrets – M. G. Vassanji

Tunisia
Salammbô – Gustave Flaubert

Uganda
Elizabeth of Toro – Elizabeth Nyabongo
The Mountain People – Colin M. Turnbull
Kahawa – Donald E. Westlake

Western Sahara
Skeletons on the Zahara – Dean King

Zambia
Zambia Shall Be Free – Kenneth Kaunda
Chirundu – Es'kia Mphahlele

Zimbabwe
The Matabele Campaign – R. S. S. Baden-Powell
The Soul of Mbira – Paul F. Berliner
Harvest of Thorns – Shimmer Chinodya
Nervous Conditions – Tsitsi Dangarembga
Rooms in the House of Stone – Michael Dorris
None But Ourselves – Julie Frederikse
Mukiwa – Peter Godwin
Bones – Chenjerai Hove
Shadows – Chenjerai Hove
Son of the Soil – Wilson Katiyo
Guns and Rain – David Lan
African Stories – Doris Lessing
The Grass Is Singing – Doris Lessing
Of Spirits and Madness – Paul R. Linde
Zenzele – J. Nozipo Maraire
House of Hunger – Dambudzo Marechera
Mindblast – Dambudzo Marechera
The Chitepo Assassination – David Martin and Phyllis Johnson
The Struggle for Zimbabwe – David Martin and Phyllis Johnson
Silent Journey from the East – I. V. Mazorodze
Our Votes, Our Guns – Martin Meredith
The Setting Sun and the Rolling World – Charles Mungoshi
Nkomo: The Story of My Life – Joshua Nkomo
An Ill-Fated People – Lawrence Vambe
From Rhodesia to Zimbabwe – Lawrence Vambe
Butterfly Burning – Yvonne Vera

Various Countries
Fiction
Alphabetical Africa – Walter Abish
The Heinemann Book of Contemporary African Short Stories –
 ed. Chinua Achebe and C. L. Innes
A Good Man in Africa – William Boyd
Brazzaville Beach – William Boyd
Water Music – T. Coraghessan Boyle
The Small Bees' Honey – George Clark
From Africa – ed. Adele King
Under African Skies – ed. Charles R. Larson
Looking for a Rain God – ed. Nadezda Obradovic
African Rhapsody – ed. Nadezda Obradovic
Come to Africa and Save Your Marriage – Maria Thomas
African Visas – Maria Thomas

Sacred Hunger – Barry Unsworth
Jacob's Ladder – John A. Williams

Non-Fiction
In My Father's House – Anthony Appiah
Africa Betrayed – George B. N. Ayittey
Africa in Chaos – George B. N. Ayittey
French Lessons in Africa – Peter Biddlecombe
Blood on the Tracks – Miles Bredin
Wanderings in West Africa – Richard F. Burton
A Slaver's Log Book – Theophilus Conneau
High Noon in Southern Africa – Chester Crocker
The Black Man's Burden – Basil Davidson
The African Slave Trade – Basil Davidson
The Journey Is the Destination: The Journals of Dan Eldon –
 ed. Kathy Eldon
Travels in the Congo – André Gide
The Strong Brown God – Sanche de Gramont
Africa: Dispatches from a Fragile Continent – Blaine Harden
The Fate of Africa – Jeremy Harding
The Exploration of Africa – Anne Hugon
The Electronic Elephant – Dan Jacobson
The Soccer War – Ryszard Kapuscinski
The Race to Fashoda – David Levering Lewis
Missionary Travels and Researches in South Africa –
 David Livingstone
African Silences – Peter Matthiessen
The Tree Where Man Was Born – Peter Matthiessen
The Ukimwi Road – Dervla Murphy
The Scramble for Africa – Thomas Pakenham
Travels in the Interior of Africa – Mungo Park
African Saints – Frederick Quinn
Africa: A Biography of the Continent – John Reader
The Voyage of the Mir-El-Lah – Lorenzo Ricciardi
Out of America – Keith B. Richburg
African Madness – Alex Shoumatoff

Imaginary Countries
Henderson the Rain King – Saul Bellow
Mandoa, Mandoa! – Winifred Holtby
The Coup – John Updike
Black Mischief – Evelyn Waugh

Permissions

Grateful acknowledgement is made to the following for permission to reprint previously published material.
The publishers and author have made every effort to contact the copyright holder of the works extracted in this book.

Should there be any omissions, we shall gladly rectify them in the next impression.

Excerpt from *Things Fall Apart* by Chinua Achebe. Copyright © 1958 by Chinua Achebe. By permission of Harcourt Education.

Excerpt from "The Message" from *No Sweetness Here and Other Stories* by Ama Ata Aidoo. Copyright © 1970 by Ama Ata Aidoo. By permission of The Feminist Press at the City University of New York, www.feministpress.org.

Excerpt from *The Bleeding of the Stone* by Ibrahim Al-Koni. Copyright © by Ibrahim Al-Koni, translation © 2002 by Salma K Jayyusi (PROTA). By permission of Interlink Books.

Excerpt from *The Purple Violet of Oshaantu* by Neshani Andreas. Copyright © 2001 by Neshani Andreas. By permission of Harcourt Education.

Excerpt from *All God's Children Need Traveling Shoes* by Maya Angelou. Copyright © 1986 by Maya Angelou. By permission of Little, Brown Book Group.

Excerpt from *The Catastrophist* by Ronan Bennett, Copyright © 1999 by Ronan Bennett. By permission of David Godwin Associates.

Excerpt from *Journey to Mauritius* by Jacques-Henri Bernardin de St. Pierre. Translation, introduction, and notes copyright © 2003 by Jason Wilson. By permission of Interlink Books.

Excerpt from *Mission to Kala* by Mongo Beti. Translation copyright © 1958 by Frederick Muller Ltd. By permission of Harcourt Education.

Excerpt from *The Book of Color* by Julia Blackburn. Copyright © 1995 by Julia Blackburn. By permission of Random House.

Excerpt from *The Sheltering Sky* by Paul Bowles. Copyright © 1949 by Paul Bowles. By permission of The Wylie Agency.

Excerpt from *First Footsteps in East Africa* by Richard Burton. By permission of Dover Publications.

Excerpt from *The Last Harmattan of Alusine Dunbar* by Syl Cheney-Coker. Copyright © 1990 by Syl Cheney-Coker. By permission of Harcourt Education.